Facsimile Reproduction

The Universal Publishing Association

P.O. Box 24027

Waco, Texas 76702

UniversalPublishing.com

ISBN: 978-1-962573-01-6

Printed in the U.S.A.

PREFACE TO FACSIMILE EDITION

In 1930, Victor Houteff published *The Shepherd's Rod*, Vol. 1 and disseminated it throughout the Seventh-day Adventist denomination to reveal the truth of the 144,000 and to awaken the church from its Laodicean condition. This book is a facsimile of that first work. It is our sincerest prayer the reader finds within its pages a deeper understanding of the Bible and *Spirit of Prophecy.*

The Publishers

ISA. 58:1.

"Cry aloud, spare not, lift up thy voice like a trumpet, and shew my people their transgression, and the house of Jacob their sins."

The Shepherd's Rod

The 144,000 of Revelation 7— Call For Reformation

By

V. T. HOUTEFF

Volume One, Price 75 Cents

Universal Publishing Association
Los Angeles, Calif.

Printed in U. S. A.

Mechanical Drawing Done By
MARTIN S. RAMSTAT

PREFACE

It is the intention of this book to reveal the truth of the 144,000 mentioned in Revelation 7, but the chief object of this publication is to bring about a reformation among God's people. The truth herein contained is divided into seven sections, giving proof from seven different angles, to prevent any doubt or confusion. This subject is made clear by the use of the Bible and the writings given by the Spirit of Prophecy.

The truth revealed here is of great importance to the church just now because of the foretold danger which God's people are soon to meet. It calls for decided action on the part of the believers to separate themselves from all worldlings and worldliness; to anchor themselves on the Solid Rock by obedience to *all* the truth known to this denomination, if we must escape the great ruin. "The Lord's voice crieth unto the city, and the man of wisdom shall see thy name: Hear ye the rod, and who hath appointed it." Micah 6:9.

—AUTHOR.

CONTENTS

TOPICAL INDEX

Introduction of Contents
Preface

SECTION 7.

CHARTS

INTRODUCTION

THIS publication contains only one main subject with a double lesson; namely, the 144,000, and a call for reformation. The object in view is to prepare God's people for the impending doom of Ezekiel's prophecy, chapter 9. There is no new doctrine taught, neither does it condemn the ones we have. The wonderful light between its pages shines upon a large number of scriptures which we have had no understanding of heretofore. The interpretation of these scriptures is supported entirely by the writings of Sr. E. G. White, that is termed the Spirit of Prophecy.

This publication does not advocate a new movement, and it absolutely opposes such moves. It brings out a positive proof which cannot be contradicted that the Seventh-day Adventist church has been used by God to carry on His work since 1844.

The following is a partial list of Bible chapters:

Revelation 7; 13:1-3. Isaiah 4, and chapters 54 to 66 inclusive.

Ezekiel 4 and 9. Micah 4 to 7 inclusive.

The Exodus Movement.

The Patriarchate Types.

The "Loud Cry".

A complete explanation of the 144,000.

Meaning of Esau and Jacob.

Martin Luther's Act in Prophecy.

The Typical and Anti-typical Periods.

The God of the Hebrews hath met with us: Let us go, we pray thee, three days' journey into the desert, and sacrifice unto the Lord our God; lest He fall upon us with pestilence, or with the sword. Ex. 5:3.

SECTION I.

THE ONE HUNDRED AND FORTY-FOUR THOUSAND

This subject of Revelation 7 is doubtless the most frequently discussed Bible subject by Seventh-day Adventists and other Bible students, than any other Biblical truth. Many theories have been advanced by the denomination, but not one has stood the test without contradiction. Great men of both Biblical and secular knowledge have diligently searched the Bible and have proved nothing as to who this company is.

We read in Great Controversy, page 397: "The spirit of error will lead us from the truth; and the Spirit of God will lead us into truth. But, say you, a man may be in an error, and think he has the truth. What then? We answer, The Spirit and word agree. *If a man judges himself by the word of God, and finds a perfect harmony through the whole word, then he must believe he has the truth;* but if he finds the spirit by which he is led does not harmonize with the whole tenor of God's law or book, then let him walk carefully, lest he be caught in the snare of the devil."

Sister E. G. White was doubtless far more acquainted with this subject than any one living at this time, for she wrote much about them and had visions of them. There is no doubt that she, too, spent much time in searching both from the Bible and her own writings, but she has failed to point out the exact company by assembling the references together, and clear the mystery. The question is: Why have all these godly people who earnestly searched for the truth failed to produce any evidence as to who this wonderful company really is? The answer we give is: Because it was not present truth in their time.

Sister White could have given a theory of some kind far more fitting and correct than any other theory ever advanced. She used wisdom and good judgment in leaving out her own opinion. God will make these things known at the appointed time only. Men may be made to believe a thing for a while, but except it be truth, it cannot last. Thus it would be unwise and a waste of time for one to try to tell who the 144,000 are, until the scroll has made a turn and one truth reveals another. If this study would unmask the mystery and harmonize with the Scriptures and the Spirit of Prophecy, then we must conclude that God's appointed time for this subject has come.

Sister White had received inspiration on this subject, but, like Daniel, was not permitted to know who, how, and when made, until God's appointed time. The following is a quotation made by her to Elder E. E. Andross: "I feel confident, Elder Andross, that the brethren in *Southern California* will find blessing in reviewing the teachings of Scripture concerning the 144,000 and bringing to bear upon these teachings whatever of light there may be in the published writings of the Spirit of Prophecy, and as prayerful consideration is given the matter in all its bearings, I believe that God will make the truth sufficiently clear to make possible the avoidance of needless and unprofitable questions not vital to the salvation of precious souls."

Some day this subject must be understood, for Inspiration makes no useless statements, and it cannot be in the Bible for a trinket. It must be understood before the number (144,000) is made or it would be of no value. When understood, it will guide the feet of the 144,000 in the straight path just as the first, second, and third angel's messages have led thousands of souls to Christ.

Matters Not, So Long As One Does Right?

It has been said by some that it matters not whether one understands the subject of the 144,000 or not, so long as he does right. This is certainly true if we DO RIGHT, but how do we *know* whether we do right or not, except we understand Bible doctrines? How can we know whether we keep the right Sabbath, or belong to the right church, unless we understand that doctrine? Why is it important to understand Daniel 7, the beast and his image, and many other Bible prophecies? If we do not understand the subject of the 144,000, we may not be sealed, for it would be worthless to understand it after the sealing, just as it would be of no value to understand the beast and his image after his work on earth is finished.

This angel's message of Revelation 7—the angel ascending from the east—is as important as the first, second, and third angel's messages of Rev. 14:6-11. It must be understood and given to the people at the right time, as also the mighty angel of Rev. 18:1. The loud cry must come at a given time. This angel of Revelation 7, can not be the third angel, for John's explanation of them differ. The three angels of Revelation 14 are flying in the midst of heaven, or where the sun stands at noon, but the one of Revelation 7, is ascending from the east, or the rising of the sun. The message of this angel has never been understood at any time, nor proclaimed by this denomination or any other people, and only theories have been advanced. It is evident that this truth, as other truths, must come at the right time.

MEANING OF SEVEN YEARS OF PLENTY AND SEVEN YEARS OF FAMINE FOUND ONLY ONE WAY

When the perplexing subject is made clear, then we must believe that the time is here, but this as all Bible truth, is found only one way, and in one place; namely, the storehouse (the Bible). Bear in mind that as Joseph of ancient days controlled the storehouse, even so Christ controls the Scriptures and the times. Many godly men in the past went to Christ (Joseph) and got all the present truth (corn) for that particular time that they could assimilate. While He (Christ) is liberal, He is also careful, and therefore has nothing to waste. When Joseph gathered the corn in Egypt and stored it in the storehouses, he did it not for wealth, but to sustain life in the next seven years of famine. The corn was a symbol of Christ's Word as we shall endeavor to prove.

Reasons for believing that the seven years of plenty and the seven years of famine in the days of Joseph in ancient Egypt represent the world's history in two sections of time are as follows:

In Volume 3, page 369, we read, "Isaac was a figure of the Son of God, who was offered a sacrifice for the sins of the world." Again

we read in Desire of Ages, page 112, "And in the ram divinely provided in the place of Isaac, Abraham saw a symbol of Him who was
to die for the sins of men." Thus Isaac and the ram are symbols of
Christ's submission, death, and sacrifice.

Of Jonah, we read in Desire of Ages, page 406, "As Jonah was
three days and three nights in the belly of the whale, Christ was to
be the same time 'in the heart of the earth.' And as the preaching
of Jonah was a sign to the Ninevites, so Christ's preaching was a sign
to His generation." See also Prophets and Kings, page 274.

Elisha was a symbol of Christ. Prophets and Kings, page 240:
"Like the Saviour of mankind, of whom he was a type, Elisha in his
ministry among men combined the work of healing with that of teaching." These are the reasons why Isaac, Jonah, and Elisha are types
of Christ, representing the different phases and imports of the work
of Christ.

Of Joseph we read in Patriarchs and Prophets, page 369:
"Joseph *was a representative of Christ.* In their benefactor, to whom
all Egypt turned with gratitude and praise, that heathen people *were
to behold the love of their Creator and Redeemer."* Egypt was an
idolatrous nation, and is a symbol of the world in sin. Joseph was a
type of Christ, the sovereign of the world. As Joseph was sent into
Egypt to preserve life; just so Christ was sent into the world (Egypt)
to preserve life. Quoting from Patriarchs and Prophets, page 231,
we read: "And God sent me before you to *preserve* you a posterity in
the *earth,* and to save your lives by a great deliverance." Thus it is
written that these deliverances were an object lesson of *spiritual blessing.* But how did Joseph bless the ancient world? Was it not by
the corn he preserved in the seven years of plenty? Had it not been
for the immense storehouses full of life-giving energy, what blessing
could Joseph have been to the ancient world were it not for his God-
given wisdom to gather the corn with which to feed the world in the
time of its great need? The corn which Joseph preserved is the blessing, as it is written, the corn represents spiritual blessing (the Word
of God). God's Word is spiritual bread and men have lived on it.

"Moreover he said unto me, Son of man, eat that thou findest; eat this roll, and go speak unto the house of Israel." Eze. 3:1. "Thy words were found, and I did eat them; and thy word was unto me the joy and rejoicing of mine heart: For I am called by thy name, O Lord God of hosts." Jer. 15:16. "And had rained down manna upon them to eat, and had given them of the corn of heaven." Psalm 78:24. "Our fathers did eat manna in the desert; as it is written, He gave them bread [corn] from heaven to eat. Then Jesus said unto them, Verily, verily, I say unto you, Moses gave you not that bread from heaven; but *My Father giveth you the true bread from heaven.*" John 6:31,32. "To *him that overcometh* will I give to eat of the hidden manna." Rev. 2:17. "And I took the little book out of the angel's hand, and ate it up; and it was in my mouth sweet as honey: And as soon as I had eaten it, my belly was bitter." Rev. 10:10.

The latter prophecy has been applied to William Miller after he had studied the book of Daniel and accepted its teaching. Symbolically speaking, he ate the little book, which became a part of him and his co-workers. Had this not been true, he would not have proclaimed the message with such enthusiasm as he did. As the expected event failed to transpire in 1844, to them it was a bitter experience, thus fulfilling the Scriptures that men *have eaten the Word of God.*

If the corn does not represent the Word as in the Bible, then the question may be asked, Of what is Joseph a type? Isaac, Jonah, and Elisha each represent a certain phase of Christ's work, and if Joseph represents Christ; the food gathered,—the Word; the storehouse,— the Bible, then the seven years of plenty, during which time the food was gathered must be a symbol, otherwise the picture could not be perfect; and if the years of plenty are a type, then the years of famine must be taken into consideration. Each of these two sections of time bear the number "seven", meaning "perfect", fullness of time (entire, or *all* of the time).

The symbol can represent only one thing, and that is the world's history in two great divisions of time; namely B. C. and A. D. with the cross (Christ), the dividing line. "For all the prophets and the law prophesied until John." It is for this reason Jesus made the statement for we have no other thus far. The years of plenty is B. C. in which time God gave plenty to supply the world's need *for* the years of famine (New Testament time, A. D.). As Joseph gathered the corn into storehouses by his servants,—the Egyptians, just so Christ gathered the Word of God (spiritual food) in the Bible (the storehouse) by His servants, the prophets. *"God, who at sundry times and in divers manners spake in time past unto the fathers by the prophets,* Hath in these last days spoken unto us by His Son, whom He hath appointed heir of all things, by whom also He made the worlds." Heb. 1:1, 2. Had it not been for this purpose then we ask, what could it have been for? God, who was responsible for the event did it not to bring hardships to His subjects, or to starve the world, as the famine was not in Egypt only, for we read, "And the famine was over all the face of the earth." Gen. 41:56. Had this not been the symbol, why would God have brought the famine over all the earth? Some people may have difficulty in being convinced, and others can never be convinced, but the harmony of the lesson can hardly be questioned.

If the seven years of plenty and the seven years of famine are not a type of the world's history; Joseph's immense storehouses not a type of the Bible; the corn gathered in the seven years of plenty not a type of the Word in the Bible; the feeding of the world not a type of the New Testament time consuming the Scriptures gathered in the Old Testament time; then we ask, Where are the types for all these events? Has not God given the gospel in types as well as in prophecy? "Christ was the foundation of the Jewish economy. The whole system of types and symbols was compacted prophecy of the gospel, a presentation in which were bound up the promises of redemption." Acts of the Apostles, page 14. If the seven years of plenty and the seven years of famine did not represent the world's history, the coincidents as we shall endeavor to bring forth could hardly have been possible by an accident. Jesus said, "Gather up the crumbs that there be no waste." It was His Word that multiplied the loaves and fishes; these crumbs represent the very words He spoke.

We read the following in Volume 2, page 606: "I am authorized from God to tell you that not another ray of light through the Testimonies will shine upon your pathway, until you make a practical use of the light already given." But now we must have corn or else we shall die. As a people we have much boasted that we have all the truth, but such a statement can not be found between the pages of the Spirit of Prophecy. "Not another ray of light will shine upon your pathway until you make a practical use of the light already given." These words suggest that there is more light to shine, and light is truth. Again, quoting from Testimonies to Ministers, page 107: "No one should claim that he has all the light there is for God's people. The Lord will not tolerate this. He has said, 'I have set before thee an open door, and no man can shut it.' Even if all our leading men should refuse light and truth, that door will still remain open. The Lord *will raise* up men who will give the people the message for this time."

Seven Years of Plenty, and Seven Years of Famine

The seven years of plenty and seven years of famine in the days of Joseph in ancient Egypt represent the world's history in two sections of time as previously explained; namely B. C. and A. D. Each one of these sections bears the Biblical number "seven" (meaning complete). The seven years of plenty is B. C. Though one may doubt the application made here, the lesson we receive from it is true. In the Old Testament time, God gave plenty through His prophets, and Christ (Joseph) stored it in the storehouse (Bible), but as we have no record that there was any of the corn left when the seven years of famine had passed, neither was there any shortage. Therefore, it is plain, that all the Scriptures are to be understood (used up) before the second coming of Christ.

Pharaoh's dream recorded in Gen. 41:17-20, reads as follows: "In my dream, behold, I stood upon the bank of the river: And, behold, there came up out of the river seven kine, fat-fleshed and well favored; and they fed in a meadow: And, behold, seven other kine came up after them, poor and very ill favored and lean-fleshed, such as I never saw in all the land of Egypt for badness: And the lean and the ill favored kine did eat up the first seven fat kine." Note that the seven lean and ill favored kine did eat the fat-fleshed kine. By reading verse 21, we find the seven lean kine did not put on flesh after consuming the seven fat kine, which indicates that there will be no scriptures in reserve, but that all will be brought to light. The thought is that the seven years (A. D.) will consume all the corn (Word) in the seven years (B. C.) as represented also by the ears of corn in verses 22-24. Is this not clear that all the writings in the Old Testament will be fulfilled and understood before the end of A. D. (the second coming of Christ)? But is it not true that the biggest part or portion is not yet understood? How can one say that he has all the truth and does not and cannot explain a large portion of the Bible? Shall we pray to God to open our eyes that we may see and arise from this Laodicean lethargy into which we have fallen?

WHO ARE THE 144,000?

The subject is, "Who are the 144,000?" First mention of this number in the Bible is in Rev. 7:4. "And I heard the number of them which were sealed: And there were sealed an hundred and forty and four thousand of all the tribes of the children of Israel." Verse 2. "And I saw another angel *ascending from the east, having the* seal of the living God: And he cried with a loud voice to the four angels, to whom it was given to hurt the earth and the sea." Note that this angel is *ascending* and not descending. In contrast to this, Rev. 18:1 says, "And after these things I saw another angel *come down* from heaven, having great power; and the earth was lightened with his glory." This mighty angel is not ascending, descending, nor coming, but "come". If the angel made the trip from heaven to earth in less than 15 minutes in answer to prayer (Dan. 9:4-23), while it takes light millions of years to travel part of the distance, we can easily understand why the expression "but come" is used, meaning suddenly appearing without warning. This angel is the Loud Cry angel, an addition to the third angel and the message of the fall of Babylon as given by the second angel is repeated, as foretold in the 18th chapter of Revelation. The people of God are thus prepared to stand in the hour of temptation, which they are soon to meet.

Early Writings, page 277: "Then I saw another mighty angel commissioned to descend to the earth, to unite his voice with the third angel, and give power and force to his message. Great power and glory were imparted to the angel, and as he descended, the earth was lightened with his glory. The light which attended this angel penetrated everywhere, as he cried mightily, with a strong voice, "Babylon is fallen, is fallen, and is become the habitation of devils, and the hold of every foul spirit, and a cage of every unclean and hateful bird." The message of the fall of Babylon, as given by the second angel, is *repeated,* with the additional mention of the corruptions which have been entering the churches since 1844. The work of this angel, comes in at the right time to join in the last great work of the third angel's message, as it swells to a loud cry. And the people of God are thus prepared to stand in the hour of temptation, which they are soon to meet. I saw a great light resting upon them, and they united to fearlessly proclaim the third angel's message . . . This message seemed to be an *addition* to the third message, joining it as the midnight cry joined the second angel's message in 1844."

Of the three angels of Rev. 14:6-11, John writes: "And I saw another angel fly in the midst of heaven, . . . and the third angel followed them." These angels, following each other, were seen flying in the midst of heaven where the sun would be at mid-day, in its full strength. There is a difference between these angels and the ones in Revelation 7 and 18:1. These angels are neither "ascending" nor "come", but continue to "fly in the midst of heaven". The meaning is that these angels' messages are not as powerful as the one of Rev. 18:1, for John says he saw the angel "come", that is, stand upon the earth. The angel mentioned here is near by, but the other three angels are at a distance. This symbol shows that they could not be as powerful as the one that is close by, but these three angels are flying and continue to fly. The meaning is that while they are not as powerful, they continue a long time until this other angel of Rev. 18:1 joins in with them, as it has been with the first, second, and third angel's messages until now.

We go back to the angel of Revelation 7, the one in which we are most interested at the present time. This particular angel is ascending from the east. "Ascending" here could not mean departing or flying away, but simply coming, or advancing. For example, in the morning while the sun is rising or ascending, the temperature gains in heat as it nears mid-day; just so with this angel that is to seal the 144,000. The angel was seen coming, but he is taking time. The sealing cannot begin until after he arrives, for the seal of the living God is in his possession. If we can locate the time when he arrives we may know the beginning of the sealing time of the 144,000. Did we know the time when the first, second, and third angel's messages began? Our answer is: Yes.

There is no reason for not knowing the definite time when this angel of Revelation 7 arrives. If we did not know the time, we would have no message, and if Satan can deceive us from present truth, he has won with his deceptive powers. John's prophecy in Revelation 7, of this ascending angel was only a vision of something to come, and the fulfillment of this prophecy was realized when Sister White was given her first vision in 1844, which was a vision of the 144,000. Read Early Writings, pages 13-20. John prophesied of this movement and the scene of the angel ascending in the east (John's vision) became a reality in 1844, but the angel is in the east, and we must await his arrival, for when he arrives, the sealing begins.

Do The 144,000 Ever Die?

"The living saints, 144,000 in number"; we must not conclude that only a part of the whole can constitute the number and yet be true, for the statement made by Inspiration cannot be contradicted for it reads "144,000 in *number*". When mention is made of this company, it is at the same time when God makes known the day and hour of Jesus' coming. If we can locate at what time of the world's history God speaks the day and hour of Jesus' coming, then we may know more about this company. Quoting Early Writings, page 285: "But there was one clear place of settled glory, whence came the voice of God like many waters, shaking the heavens and the earth. There was a mighty earthquake. The graves were opened, and those who had *died* in faith under the *third angel's message,* keeping the Sabbath, came forth. . . . And as God spoke the day and the hour of Jesus' coming, and delivered the everlasting covenant to His people."

One may here suppose that the risen and the living make the number, but we do not believe the Spirit of Prophecy would call both companies (the living and the resurrected) living saints. The 144,-000 are living saints; the others, resurrected Sabbath keepers. To make it positive, another reference is given, found in Great Controversy, page 637: "*Great hailstones,* every one about the *weight of a talent"* are doing their work of destruction. The proudest cities of the earth are laid low. . . . Graves are opened, and "many of them that sleep in the dust of the earth . . . . awake, some to everlasting life, and some to shame and everlasting contempt". *All who have died in the faith of the third angel's message* come forth from the tomb glorified, to hear God's covenant of peace with those who have kept His law." This makes it positive that the resurrected Sabbath keepers come forth in the special resurrection of Daniel 12. This is the time when the great hailstones are doing their destructive work (7th plague). "And the seventh angel poured out his vial into the air; . . . And there fell upon men a great hail out of heaven, every stone about the weight of a talent: And men blasphemed God because of the plague of the hail; for the plague thereof was exceeding great." Rev. 16.17, 21. The resurrected Sabbath keepers did not live during the time of the plagues, for they were resurrected at the time of the seventh plague, so that they hear the announcement of the day and the hour of Jesus' coming.

If evidence can be brought to view that the 144,000 (in number) lived before the seventh plague, then we have positive proof that the 144,000 never died. Great Controversy, page 649: "And they sing 'a new song' before the throne, a song which no man can learn save the 144,000. It is the song of Moses and the Lamb,— a song of deliverance. None but the 144,000 can learn that song; for it is the song of their experience,—an experience such as no other company have ever had. . . . They have seen the earth wasted with famine and pestilence, *the sun having power to scorch men with great heat,* and they themselves have endured suffering, hunger, and thirst." Here is a positive statement that the 144,000 lived in the time of the fourth plague, the sun having power to scorch men with great heat. "And the fourth angel poured out his vial upon the *sun;* and power was given unto him to scorch men with fire." Rev. 16:8. This is the fourth plague. How could they (144,000) go through the fourth plague if the special resurrection of the Sabbath keepers (those who died under the third angel's message) did not take place until about the end of the seventh plague? If "they have seen the earth wasted with famine and pestilence and they themselves have suffered hunger and thirst", they must have lived through all the plagues.

Again, "They sing a new song" . . . . which no man can learn save the 144,000 . . . . for it is the song of their experience,—an experience such as no other company have ever had." How can it be possible for all to sing the same song if it is a song of their experience except they all have the same experience? Those who had been in the grave would have the experience of death, grave, resurrection, and receiving a new body. But those who never died have seen the fulfillment of Ezekiel 9; Isaiah 63; Isaiah 60; the closing of the third angel's message, (the loud cry, close of probation), all of the seven last plagues, and they sing this song (of their experience and deliverance) "which no man can learn save the 144,000."

WILL SISTER WHITE BE WITH THE 144,000?

Sister White was taken in vision to one of the planets which had seven moons, where she met good old Enoch. This place was so beautiful and her desire for it so keen, she begged the angel to let her stay. "Then the angel said, 'You must go back, and if you are faithful, you, with the 144,000 shall have the privilege of visiting all the worlds and viewing the handiwork of God'." See Early Writings, page 40. There is no contradiction in this statement, for the angel told her that she, *with the* 144,000, meaning she is one *with* them but not one *of* them. She will doubtless be with them for she may be termed as the mother of them (being the messenger and founder of this movement), nor can we suppose they will sing the song of Moses and he (Moses) not be there. Because they are the 144,000, a special company with a special experience, is no reason why others could not travel with them, for undoubtedly Abraham, Isaac, and Jacob will be with them, being the fathers in type. What objection could be made if others would journey with them? We may suppose that Jesus would give to all the redeemed at least one trip to the other worlds.

ONLY 144,000 ENTER TEMPLE

"And as we were about to enter the holy temple, Jesus raised His lovely voice and said, 'Only the 144,000 enter this place', and we shouted, 'Alleluia'. This temple was supported by seven pillars all of transparent gold, set with pearls most glorious. The wonderful things I there saw, I cannot describe. . . . I saw there tables of stone in which the names of the 144,000 were engraved in letters of gold. After we beheld the glory of the temple, we went out." Early Writings, page 19. It is clear that no others were to enter the holy temple except the 144,000, and again it is clear that she went in, for she says, "The wonderful things I there saw, I cannot describe", and "after we beheld the glory of the temple, we went out". She could not see the things inside the temple unless she had gone in, and she could not have come out if she had never entered in.

Some may think that Sister White is *one of* the 144,000 because she entered this temple, and now that she is dead that part of the

144,000 will be resurrected. There is no cause for confusion here. She could have entered the temple before, or after, or she could have gone right along with them, and still it would not change the thought. We must remember this is only a vision and *not the real* 144,000. They were not made up at that time, neither was she bodily there. This vision was given for her to make a report and reveal a certain truth. In other words, she was a reporter. What kind of a report could have been given if she had not entered the temple? The command, "only the 144,000 enter here", had no reference to her whether she should stay out or enter. She is one *with* them, but not one of them.

WHAT KIND OF SEAL IS IT?

Reference is made in Testimonies to Ministers, page 445. The subject is about the sealing of Revelation 7, the 144,000. We quote: "This sealing of the servants of God is the same that was shown to Ezekiel in vision." Now if the sealing of the 144,000 of Revelation 7, is the same as Ezekiel 9, in order to find the kind of sealing it is, and the time of its beginning, we must study Ezekiel 9:1-9: "He cried also in mine ears with a loud voice, saying, Cause them that have charge over the city to draw near, even every man with his destroying weapon in his hand. And, behold, six men came from the way of the higher gate, which lieth toward the north, and every man a slaughter weapon in his hand; and one man among them was clothed with linen, with a writer's inkhorn by his side: and they went in, and stood beside the brazen altar. And the glory of the God of Israel was gone up from the cherub, whereupon he was, to the threshold of the house. And he called to the man clothed with linen, which had the writer's inkhorn by his side; And the Lord said unto him, Go through the midst of the city, through the midst of Jerusalem, and set a mark upon the foreheads of the men that sigh and that cry for all the abominations that be done in the midst thereof. And to the others he said in mine hearing, Go ye after him through the city, and smite: let not your eye spare, neither have ye pity: Slay utterly old and young, both maids, and little children, and women: but come not near any man upon whom is the mark; and begin at my sanctuary. Then they began at the ancient men which were before the house. And he said unto them, Defile the house, and fill the courts with the slain: go ye forth. And they went forth, and slew in the city. And it came to pass, while they were slaying them, and I was left, that I fell upon my face, and cried, and said, Ah Lord God! wilt thou destroy all the residue of Israel in thy pouring out of thy fury upon Jerusalem? Then said he unto me, The iniquity of the house of Israel and Judah is exceeding great." It is positive that the sealing of the 144,000 is Ezekiel 9,—the separation (sifting in the church— the godly from the ungodly). Volume 1, page 181: "I asked the meaning of the *shaking* I had seen, and was shown that it would be *caused* by the straight testimony called forth by the counsel of the True Witness to the Laodiceans." Read the entire page. Note the shaking begins *after* the straight testimony of the "True Witness" is come.

THE TWO SEALS

Is the Sabbath the seal of the 144,000? First of all it will be noticed that the definition of "seal" is: An instrument which is used to seal, fasten up, or enclose securely; to establish or settle beyond question; to point out and *determine; designate*. An effort will be made to bring forth enough Bible evidence to satisfy anyone believing in the Scriptures that all who were saved in the ages past as well as those who are to be saved now must have the seal of God. Paul, in his letter to the Ephesians said that they were to be sealed. "And grieve not the Holy Spirit of God, whereby ye are *sealed* unto the day of redemption." Eph. 4:30. The grace of sanctification wrought in the soul by the Holy Ghost is the seal and assurance of one's redemption to come, of a joyful resurrection. The use and end of this sealing is the sacredness and safety of the thing sealed from the eyes of curosity and hands of violence, which otherwise would be abused by strangers and enemies; thus the children of God are past the censure of the wicked world. They are preserved as precious things for God's own use, to be with Him in heaven. Quoting 2 Tim. 2:19, written to the Corinthians: "Nevertheless the foundation of God standeth sure, having this *seal,* The Lord knoweth them that are His." "Who hath also sealed us, and given the earnest of the Spirit in our hearts." 2 Cor. 1:22.

We read in Revelation 8 and 9, of the seven angels with the seven trumpets. These seven trumpets indicate the principal political and warlike events which were to transpire during the time of the gospel church. The sealing of the 144,000 belongs to the time of the sixth trumpet. Beginning with Rev. 9:1, we read about the angel with the fifth trumpet. Verse 4 of this chapter we quote: "And it was commanded them that they should not hurt the grass of the earth, neither any green thing, neither any tree; but only those men which have not the *seal of God* in their foreheads." Here we see that many years before the third angel's message ever began to be preached, the saints of God were sealed with the seal of God, just the same as the ones under the third angel's message are to be sealed. According to these scriptures which are plainly stated, we must conclude that the saints of God are sealed with present truth in all ages, and whatever that present truth is, that is the seal. Present truth under the third angel's message is Sabbath truth, therefore, the Sabbath is a seal which seals the people who are obedient to it. . Quoting Great Controversy, page 452: "The seal of God's law is found in the fourth commandment. . . . When the Sabbath was changed by the papal power, the seal was taken from the law." Early Writings, page 58: "The sealing time is very short, and will soon be over."

Those who died under the third angel's message, keeping the Sabbath, are sealed with the Sabbath truth, but the 144,000 never die. While they must keep Sabbath and have that seal, they must sigh and cry for the abominations that are in the *church,* for otherwise they can not receive the mark by the angel with the writer's inkhorn of Ezekiel 9, which is the seal according to Testimonies to Ministers, page 445; Volume 5, pages 210-16; Volume 3, pages

266-7. The sealing of the 144,000 is the separation of the faithful from the disloyal ones; the purification of the church. Those who do not keep the truth, and indulge in the sins and abominations, who try to throw a cloak over the existing evils, will fall under the figure of the five men with the slaughter weapons of Ezekiel 9.

The Sabbath has been present truth since 1845, and being the seal of the law of God, has been sealing the law among the people of God ever since that year. Isa. 8:16, "Bind up the testimony, seal the law among my disciples." This has been the work of the third angel, and for this reason the third angel has no seal, for the seal is in the law, but the angel of Revelation 7, has a seal in his hand. Ezekiel calls him the man with the writer's inkhorn who is to set a mark upon the men who sigh and cry for all the abominations that be done in the midst thereof (the church). This is the seal of the 144,000, but all the saved under the third angel are sealed with the Sabbath seal. The 144,000 having this seal are *also* marked (sealed) by the angel of Revelation 7, which is the same as the one of Ezekiel 9. In other words, it may be termed a double seal.

Ezekiel 9 Is Not A Sabbath Seal

This sealing of the 144,000 is not a Sabbath seal. However, those who are sealed must be Sabbath keepers. It is a seal, or mark, that separates the two classes in the church, and those who are sealed, or marked are not marked because they keep Sabbath only, but because they sigh and cry for *all* the abominations that are done in the church. So both the sealing and the slaughter are in God's church, and not in Babylon, or in the world. It is only in Jerusalem, and Judah, the house of Israel (the church). "Judah" in verse 9, refers to those in office, for Judah occupied the office of the Levites after the tribe of Levi was carried away. There is not a thought about the world or the ungodly. When the marking (sealing) is finished, the five men with the slaughter weapons begin with the ancient men which were before the house, meaning the guardians of the spiritual interest of the people. See Volume 3, pages 266, 267, and Volume 5, pages 210-212.

We quote Volume 5, page 211: "The ancient men, those to whom God had given great light, and who had stood as guardians of the spiritual interests of the people, had betrayed their trust. They had taken the position that we need not look for miracles and the marked manifestation of God's power as in former days. Times have changed. These words strengthen their unbelief, and they say, The Lord will not do good, neither will He do evil. He is too merciful to visit His people in judgment." Volume 3, page 265: "But if the sins of the people are passed over by those in responsible positions, His frown will be upon them, and the people of God, *as a body,* will be held responsible for those sins."

Those who are sealed (marked) and escape the ruin are the ones who will constitute the number which prophecy declares to be 144,-000. Our denomination numbers about 300,000. This means the denomination will be divided in half and suggests the ten virgins, five of whom were wise and five were foolish. In other words, half and half. May God help His people, and give us a vision of what sin is that we may put away the existing disastrous iniquity in the church (the house of God). Such a vision would cause us to sigh and cry for the abominations that are done in the midst thereof. He who understands the curse of sin would throw no cloak over the existing evil to obtain the favor of any. May God lift us from the low spiritual level into which we have fallen, and save us from this Laodicean, lukewarm condition. May we, as wise Ninevah of old, defeat the prophecy, that heaven may rejoice.

SEALING BEGINS—CHURCH AT LOW EBB

It is evident that if both the sealing and the slaughter are in the house of God, the church (His people), and if more than one-half of the people must perish for their sins except they repent, and if less than one-half of the present membership would number 144,000, it certainly could not have begun many years ago; and much less with the beginning of the third angel's message, for there was no church then but merely a handful of people. It could not have begun when the church was in a good, spiritual condition. It must have begun when the church is at her lowest level, and polluted with sin. Those who are to receive the seal and escape the slaughter must sigh and cry for all the abomination that is done in the midst thereof. Volume 8, page 250, says, "Unless the church, which is now being leavened with her own backsliding, shall repent and be converted, she will eat of the fruit of her own doing, until she shall abhor herself."

Speaking of the 144,000, Volume 5, pages 210-11, says, "These sighing, crying ones had been holding forth the words of life; [a message] they had reproved, counseled, and entreated. Some who had been dishonoring God, repented and humbled their hearts before Him. But the glory of the Lord had departed from Israel; although many still continued the forms of religion, His power and presence were lacking. In the time when His wrath shall go forth in judgments, these humble, devoted followers of Christ will be distinguished from the rest of the world by their soul-anguish, which is expressed in lamentation and weeping, reproofs and warnings. While others try to throw a cloak over the existing evil, and excuse the great wickedness everywhere prevalent, those who have a real zeal for God's honor and a love for souls, will not hold their peace to obtain favor of any. . . . They lament and afflict their souls because pride, avarice, selfishness, and deception of almost every kind are in the church. . . . The class who do not feel grieved over *their own spiritual declension, nor mourn over the sins of others,* will be left without the seal of God. . . . *Here we see that the church—the Lord's sanctuary—was the first to feel the stroke of the wrath of God.* The ancient men, those to whom God had given great light, and who had stood as guardians of the spiritual interests of the people, *had betrayed their trust."*

Volume 5, page 82: "The call to this great and solemn work was presented to men of learning and position; had these been little in their own eyes, and trusted fully in the Lord, He would have honored them *with bearing His standard in triumph* to the victory. But they separated from God, yielded to the influence of the world, *and the Lord rejected them."*

Volume 5, pages 211-12: "They had taken the position that we need not look for miracles and the marked manifestation of God's power as in former days. Times have changed. These words strengthen their unbelief, and they say, The Lord will not do good, neither will He do evil. He is too merciful to visit His people in judgment. Thus peace and safety is the cry from men who will *never again* lift up their voice like a trumpet to *show God's people their transgressions and the house of Jacob their sins.* These dumb dogs, that would not bark, are the ones who feel the just vengeance of an offended God. Men, maidens, and little children, all perish together. The abominations for which the faithful ones were sighing and crying were all that could be discerned by finite eyes, but by far the worst sins, those which provoked the jealousy of the pure and holy God, were unrevealed. . . . Our own course of action will determine whether we shall receive the *seal of the living God, or be cut down by the destroying weapons."* If we were to mark out the exact time of the beginning of this sealing, we would say it began sometime during 1929. Space will not permit us here to give our reasons for believing thus, but in another study this will be taken up.

To get the proper understanding of the third angel's message we shall divide it into three periods: (1) Beginning of the proclamation of the true Sabbath, Rev. 14:6-11; (2) *Reformation, and sealing of the 144,000,* Rev. 7:1-8; (3) The Loud Cry, Rev. 18:1. The truth of the sealing (144,000) being made known, it is evident that we are in the second period. If we had not known the commencement of the third angel's message in its beginning, we would have had no message. Therefore, we must know the time of the last two periods when they came, being of no lesser importance.

CAUSE OF SIGHING AND CRYING

Volume 5, pages 210, 211: "In the time when his wrath shall go forth in judgments, these humble, devoted followers of Christ will be distinguished from the rest of the world by their soul-anguish, which is expressed in lamentation and weeping, reproofs and warnings. While others try to throw a cloak over the existing evil, and excuse the great wickedness everywhere prevalent, those who have a zeal for God's honor and a love for souls, *will not hold* their peace to obtain favor *of any.* Their righteous souls are vexed day by day with the unholy works and conversation of the unrighteous. They are powerless to stop the rushing torrent of iniquity, and hence they are filled with grief and alarm. They mourn before God to see religion despised in the very homes of those who have had great light. They lament and afflict their souls because pride, avarice, selfishness, and deception of almost every kind are in the church. The Spirit of God, which prompts to reproof, is trampled under foot, while the servants of Satan triumph. God is dishonored, the truth made of none effect. . . . The abominations for which the faithful ones were sighing and crying were all that could be discerned by finite eyes, but by far the worst sins, those which provoked the jealousy of the pure and holy God, were unrevealed."

Volume 1, pages 471, 472: "A great mistake has been made by some who profess present truth, by introducing merchandise in the course of a series of meetings, and by their traffic diverting minds from the object of the meetings. . . . "It is written, My house shall be called the house of prayer, but ye have made it a den of thieves." These traffickers might have pleaded as an excuse that the articles they held for sale were for sacrificial offerings. But their object was to get gain, to obtain means, to accumulate. . . . Ministers have stood in the desk and preached a most solemn discourse, and then by introducing merchandise, and acting the part of a salesman, *even* in the house of God, they have diverted the minds of their hearers from the impressions received, and destroyed the fruit of their labor. . . . Their time and strength should be held in reserve, that their efforts may be thorough in a series of meetings. *Their time and strength should not be drawn upon to sell our books when they can be properly brought before the public by those who have not the burden of preaching the word."*

Volume 8, page 250: "Who can truthfully say, 'Our gold is tried in the fire; our garments are unspotted by the world'? I saw our Instructor pointing to the garments of so-called righteousness. Stripping them off, He laid bare the defilement beneath. Then He said to me: "Can you not see how they have pretentiously covered up their defilement and rottenness of character? 'How is the faithful city become an harlot?' My Father's house is made a house of merchandise, a place whence the divine presence and glory have departed! For this cause there is weakness, and strength is lacking." Thus the time and the condition of the church at the beginning of the sealing of the 144,000 is well portrayed by both the Bible and the Spirit of Prophecy. It is an admitted fact among Seventh-day Adventists that the church has been on the decline for some years, but never has it been in such a low spiritual condition as it is now. There is scarcely any difference now between the church and the world.

PARTIAL LIST OF ABOMINATIONS IN THE CHURCH

1. Lack of reverence in the house of God: Isa. 56:7; Volume 5, pages 492-500.

2. Following the fashions of the world: Isa. 3:16; Volume 1, pages 269, 270; Volume 4, page 632; Volume 3, page 379; Volume 5, page 78; Volume 1, pages 189-191; Volume 1, pages 135, 136; Volume 4, page 631.

3. Spending money for that which is not bread (health reform): Isa. 55:2; Volume 5, page 197; Isa. 56:12. (Many references can be given from the testimonies on this subject, but space will not permit them here.)

4. Use of tithe—school teachers (those who teach the Scriptures)

are not paid by the tithe as they should have been: Volume 6, page 215.

5. The house of God is made into a house of merchandise by buying and selling denominational publications of all sorts: Isa. 58:3; Isa. 56:7; Volume 1, pages 471, 472; Volume 8, page 250.

6. High prices in our institutions while they should be below current expenses: Volume 8, page 142; Isa. 56:12; Isa. 58.

7. Disbelief in the Spirit of Prophecy: If not acknowledged by words, it is admitted by works.

8. Failed to inform church members of Elijah's message: Mal. 4:5; Testimonies to Ministers, page 475; Volume 4, pages 402, 403.

9. Abraham obeyed God in all that He commanded, and was very careful even to the smallest particulars; thus it was counted to him for righteousness, but we have not done so. See Gen. 26:5; Gen. 15:6.

10. The promise of the land (heavenly Canaan) is to Abraham's seed. Jesus said, *"If ye were Abraham's* children, ye would do the works of Abraham. [If ye are not the children of Abraham] Ye are of your father the devil, and the lusts of your father ye will do." See John 8:39-44. (By doing the works of Abraham), "Then are ye Abraham's seed, and heirs according to the promise." Gal. 3:29.

11. Insisting that we have all the truth and have need of nothing.

12. Turning down Scriptural claims without investigation as to its light. Volume 5, page 211: "The abominations for which the faithful ones were sighing and crying were all that could be discerned by finite eyes, but by far the worst sins, those which provoked the jealousy of the pure and holy God, were unrevealed."

WILL THIS SEALING CONTINUE TO THE CLOSE OF PROBATION?

The sealing of the 144,000 can not extend to the close of probation, for they must be sealed long before that time, and it must close before the loud cry of the third angel's message. Early Writings, page 277 says: "I saw angels hurrying to and fro in heaven, descending to the earth, and again ascending to heaven, preparing for the fulfillment of some important event.   Then I saw another mighty angel commissioned to descend to the earth, to unite his voice with the third angel, and give power and force to his message.   Great power and glory were imparted to the angel, and as he descended, the earth was lightened with his glory. . . . This message seemed to be an addition to the third message." It seems in the expression, "the angels hurrying to and fro", the author has reference to the fulfillment of Ezekiel 9; and then follows the mighty angel of the loud cry of Rev. 18:1.

Ezekiel 9, can not meet its fulfillment at the time Christ comes in the clouds, for the slaughter is in the church.   The church of Christ must be pure and clean, free from every stain long before Jesus comes.   If we are not in this pure condition, we can not hope to stand in the time of trouble, nor can we escape the effects of the plagues.   The church could not stand without an intercessor after probation nor before, if there is one unclean thing in the camp of Israel.   "For thus saith the Lord God of Israel, There is an accursed thing in the midst of thee, O Israel: Thou canst not stand before thine enemies, until ye take away the accursed thing from among you." Joshua 7:13.

As an illustration and comparison of the faithfulness and unity of the people at the time of trouble during the plagues, we quote Early Writings, pages 282-3: "I saw the saints leaving the cities and villages, and associating together in companies, and living in the most solitary places. Angels provided them food and water, while the wicked were suffering from hunger and thirst. Then I saw the leading men of the earth consulting together, and Satan and his angels busy around them.   I saw a writing, copies of which were scattered in different parts of the land, giving orders that unless the saints should yield their peculiar faith, give up the Sabbath, and observe the first day of the week, the people were at liberty after a certain time, to put them to death . . . . but angels in the form of men of war fought for them. Satan wished to have the privilege of destroying the saints of the

Most High; but Jesus bade His angels watch over them. . . . Next came the multitude of the angry wicked, and next a mass of evil angels, hurrying on the wicked to slay the saints. But before they could approach God's people, the wicked must *first pass this company of mighty, holy angels.* This was impossible. The angels of God were causing them to recede, and also causing the evil angels who were pressing around them to fall back." It is evident here that God's people are apart by themselves, with no wicked ones among them. Holy angels would not protect unholy people from the wicked multitude. Here we see God's people separated from all wickedness. Therefore this shows they are in perfect unity at the time they leave the villages.

When then was this purification of the church? Ezekiel 8, tells us of the abominations done in the midst of Jerusalem (church); Ezekiel 9, reveals the consequences to those who do not sigh and cry for all the abominations. "One sinner may diffuse darkness that will exclude the light of God from the entire congregation." Volume 3, page 265.

Five Men Follow The One

The men with the slaughter weapons must immediately follow the one with the writer's inkhorn. God must separate His people if the marking is to be of any value, and except the separation takes place, the outpouring of the Holy Spirit can not fall in its fullness upon the people of God. "I asked the meaning of the shaking I had seen, and was shown that it would be caused by the straight testimony called forth by the counsel of the True Witness to the Laodiceans. This will have its effect upon the heart of the receiver, and will lead him to exalt the standard and pour forth the straight truth. Some will not bear this straight testimony. They will rise up against it, and *this is what will cause a shaking among God's people.* . . . I asked what had made this great change. An angel answered, 'It is the latter rain, the refreshing from the presence of the Lord, the loud cry of the third angel'." Early Writings, pages 270-1. It is clear that the shaking must take place before the "Loud Cry". The men with the slaughter weapons were already slaying *before* the man with the writer's inkhorn returned to report the matter that he had done as he was commanded. See Ezekiel 9:8, 11.

DISTINCTION BETWEEN 144,000 AND OTHER SAINTS

Referring to Israel (after the flesh) which is a type of the true Israel; namely, the 144,000, God said, "Israel is My first-born." The priesthood in ancient Israel was supposed to be made up of the first-born of every family, therefore the priesthood is termed the first-born. Had Israel obeyed God in all His precepts, this plan would have been carried out, but when they reached Mt. Sinai they made the golden calf and worshipped it.

When Moses came down from the mountain, he took a record of all who had worshipped the calf. "Standing in the gate of the camp, Moses called to the people, 'Who is on the Lord's side? Let him come unto Me.' Those who had not joined in the apostasy were to take their position at the right of Moses; those who were guilty but repentant, at the left. The command was obeyed. It was found that the tribe of Levi had taken no part in the idolatrous worship." Patriarchs and Prophets, page 324. For this reason God honored the tribe of Levi. We read on page 277: "After the institution of the tabernacle service, the Lord chose unto Himself the tribe of Levi for the work of the sanctuary, instead of the first-born of the people."

But God said, "Israel is My first-born",—the true Israel—the 144,000. That promise, then, would find its fulfillment here. Of them we read "being the first fruits unto God and the Lamb." If such is the case, then the 144,000 would be priests and Levites. Isaiah 61, could have no reference to another class than Israel by the promise, the 144,000, and of the Gentiles who shall come to the Lord by their labors. We read in Isa. 66:19, 20, "And I will set a sign among them, and I will send those that escape of them unto the nations. . . . And they shall bring all your brethren for an offering unto the Lord out of all nations." These (144,000) who escape the ruin of Ezekiel 9, and Isaiah 63, to which Isa. 66:16, 17, refers, will be sent on a great missionary work during the time of the loud cry.

We read in Isa. 61:5, 6, "And strangers [Gentiles, or those who are not of the 144,000] shall stand and feed your flocks, and the sons of the alien shall be your plowmen and your vinedressers. But ye shall be named the Priests of the Lord: Men shall call you the Ministers of our God: Ye shall eat the riches of the Gentiles, and in their glory shall ye boast yourselves." Others than themselves (144,000) shall feed their flocks and dress their vines (do their farming) in the same manner as it was with the tribe of Levi, for they had no land. Though the Levites had no inheritance of the land, they received about 25% of the increase in tithes and offerings, thus others than themselves did their work. So with the 144,000, who will be priests in the new earth. The idea here is not that tithe and offerings from the people would be their support in the earth made new. These scriptures are merely given to illustrate the position which they occupy.

Isa. 61:7 says: "For your shame ye shall have *double;* and for confusion they shall rejoice in their *portion:* Therefore in their land they shall possess the double: Everlasting joy shall be unto them." Having two pronouns, "ye" and "they", the pronoun "ye" receives double for their shame, but the pronoun "they" shall possess the land. "Ye" is the pronoun of the second person to whom God is speaking, and in this case refers to Israel (which is the 144,000), but the pronoun "they" refers to the Gentiles who were not numbered among the twelve tribes and therefore are not included in the 144,000, but are saved for "they" rejoice in their portion.

In Volume 5, pages 475-6, speaking of the 144,000, we read: "They are to be as kings and priests unto God. . . . 'These are they which follow the Lamb whithersoever He goeth'." Therefore the 144,000 are priests, and Christ the High Priest, (and King). It may be said that when probation closes Christ takes off His priestly garments, and is Priest no longer, but there need be no confusion in this, for we read in Isa. 66:22, 23: "For as the new heavens and the new earth, which I will make, shall remain before Me, saith the Lord, so shall your seed and your name remain.   And it shall come to pass, that from one new moon to another, and from one Sabbath to another, shall all flesh come to worship before Me, saith the Lord." Thus we see that there is to be a system of worship in the new heaven and earth which will require Priests and Levites.

SECTION II.

THE FOUR CLASSES OF THE REDEEMED

The ensuing study is given to prove that the great multitude of Rev. 7:9, are living saints, who, with the 144,000, are to be translated at the second coming of Christ. All the saved in the history of the world, from righteous Abel to the close of probation, are divided into four great, separate, and distinct classes, as follows:

CLASS 1: The 144,000 of Rev. 7; namely, the twelve tribes of Israel of the promise; a special company with a special experience.

CLASS 2: The translated at the coming of Christ in the clouds (the great multitude of Rev. 7:9).

CLASS 3: The millions of all ages who were martyred for their faith.

CLASS 4: "Those who were once zealous in the cause of Satan, but who, plucked as brands from the burning, have followed their Saviour with deep, intense devotion." Great Controversy, page 665.

Earthly nations and governments glory in the splendid order of their armies, and their uniforms are made according to ranks, so that by the uniform, one can recognize the rank of a soldier, and to which division or regiment he belongs. We must not suppose the great God has less order for His redeemed than earthly nations for their armies. We know God has far better order than any earthly government can ever devise. An endeavor shall be made to prove that each one of the four classes mentioned above have their uniforms by which they can be discerned and classified.

CLASS 1

In Early Writings, pages 16, 17, we read: "Here on the sea of glass the 144,000 stood in a perfect square. Some of them had very bright crowns, others not so bright. Some crowns appeared heavy with stars, while others had but few. All were perfectly satisfied with their crowns. And they were all clothed with a glorious white mantle from their shoulders to their feet." The 144,000 are described as having this *"glorious white mantle"* as part of their garments.

CLASS 2

Class 2, are the translated (besides the 144,000). Rev. 7:9, says, "After this [the 144,000] I beheld, and, lo, a great multitude, which no man could number, of all nations, and kindreds, and people, and tongues, stood before the throne, and before the Lamb, clothed with white robes, and palms in their hands." It will be noticed this company have *palms* in their hands.

CLASS 3

Early Writings, pages 18, 19: "As we were traveling along, we met a company who also were gazing at the glories of the place. I noticed *red as a border* on *their garments;* their crowns were brilliant; their robes were pure white. As we greeted them, I asked Jesus who they were. He said they were martyrs that had been slain for Him. With them was an innumerable company of little ones; they also had a hem of red on their garments." Thus class 3, (the martyrs) are described as having *"red on their garments"*.

CLASS 4

Great sinners plucked as brands from the burning, but who died a natural death.

These have neither a mantle over their shoulders, palms in their hands, nor red as a border around their garments, but they do have crowns of gold. Their crowns differ from the crowns of the 144,-000, the latter having "stars" in their crowns, as stated under heading "CLASS 1". Thus we have the description of these four classes, and the symbols of their garments, and can be summarized as follows:

Class 1—The 144,000 have the *glorious white mantle,* and *stars in their crowns.*

Class 2—The great multitude of Rev. 7:9, have *palms in their hands.*

Class 3—The millions of all ages who were martyred, have *red* around *their garments* as a border.

Class 4—Great sinners plucked as brands from the burning, but who died a natural death, who have *white robes,* and *golden crowns,* but *no stars* on their crowns. Same as those of Rev. 4:4.

There must have been a definite reason for describing the special uniforms which must have been for the purpose of disclosing this truth.

Types and Anti-Types

The Spirit of Prophecy says Elijah represents those who will be living when Christ comes, and be changed in the twinkling of an eye, and be translated. Desire of Ages, page 421: "Elijah, who had been translated to heaven without seeing death, represented those who will be living upon the earth at Christ's second coming, and who will be 'changed in a moment, in the twinkling of an eye, at the last trump'."

Reference is made of Enoch in Patriarchs and Prophets, pages 88, 89: "The godly character of this prophet represents the state of holiness which must be attained by those who shall be *'redeemed from the earth'* at the time of Christ's second advent. . . . But like Enoch, God's people will seek for purity of heart, and conformity to His will, until they shall reflect the likeness of Christ. Like Enoch they will warn the world of the Lord's second coming, and of the judgments to be visited upon transgression, and by their holy conversation and example they will condemn the sins of the ungodly. As Enoch was translated to heaven before the destruction of the world by water, so the living righteous will be translated from the earth before its destruction by fire."

Though Elijah represents those who shall be translated at the second coming of Christ, Enoch does, too. Both men were translated without seeing death. The question is, Why *two* types? Because there are two companies of people to be translated; the 144,000, and the great multitude of Rev. 7:9. The 144,000, are Israelites; the great multitude are not. Enoch is not an Israelite, therefore he can not represent Israel, the 144,000. (The name "Israel" did not come into existence until the time of Jacob, which was many centuries after Enoch was translated. A clearer explanation on the subject will be given in another section.) We shall determine which class Enoch represents by the uniform he wears. Early Writings, page 40, says: "There I saw good old Enoch, who had been translated. On his right arm he bore a glorious palm, and on each leaf was written 'Victory'." Here we see Enoch, too, has the "palm" in his hand, the same as the great multitude, class number 2.

Enoch is said to be the seventh from Adam. "Seven" means complete, finished; thus perfectly typifying the class represented by him in Rev. 7:9 (the great multitude). We shall endeavor to bring another proof that the great multitude with the "palms in their hands" are translated with the 144,000. In Great Controversy, page 665, we read about classes 2, 3, and 4. The part referring to class 4, reads as follows: "Nearest the throne are those who were once zealous in the cause of Satan, but who, plucked as brands from the burning, have followed their Saviour with deep, intense devotion. Next are those who perfected Christian characters in the midst of falsehood and infidelity, those who honored the law of God when the Christian world declared it void." Here is included every possible sin to a sinner in all ages (who have taken their stand for God).

But of class 2 (the great multitude), there is no reference given as to what kind of sinners they are. Class 1 (the 144,000), are called Israel, a special company with a special experience.

After including every possible sin to a sinner in Class 4 (those who shall be resurrected), and the martyrs in class 3, Inspiration says, "And beyond is the 'great multitude' . . . . with white robes, and palms in their hands." Therefore, this company could not be classed with the other two, or with the 144,000. *If* Class 2 (the great multitude), were the saved and resurrected from all ages, then *all* of the saved must have palms in their hands, but as it is plain that *not* all have the palms, then these are not *all* the saved in *all* ages, but are the translated ones only, besides the 144,000. The palm is a symbol of victory over *death* and the *grave;* that is, they never died.

Again, speaking of the same company, we read in Rev. 7:14, last part: "And he said unto me, 'These are they which came out of great tribulation, and have washed their robes, and made them white in the blood of the Lamb'." Thus this company went through the tribulation of Daniel 12, which is in the time of the seven last plagues. Rev. 7:16, last part: "neither shall the sun light on them, nor any heat." They go through the fourth plague, so it is clear that this company lives in the time of the end, at the second advent of Christ,—to be translated.

An Explanation of Early Writings, Page 15

Speaking of the announcement made of the coming of Christ (the day and the hour), which is *before* the general resurrection, and *at* the time of the special resurrection, we read: "Soon we heard the voice of God like many waters, which gave us the day and hour of Jesus' coming. The living saints, 144,000 in number, knew and understood the voice, while the wicked thought it was thunder and an earthquake. When God spoke the time, He poured upon us the Holy Ghost, and our faces began to light up and shine with the glory of God, as Moses' did when he came down from Mount Sinai. The 144,000 were all sealed and perfectly united. On their foreheads was written, God, New Jerusalem, and a glorious star containing Jesus' new name. At our happy, holy state the wicked were enraged, and would rush violently up to lay hands on us to thrust us into prison, when we would stretch forth the hand in the name of the Lord, and they would fall helpless to the ground."

We are not to understand that all who were present at this time and heard the announcement made of the "day and the hour" were the 144,000 only. The language used makes it clear that there were more, for the pronouns "we", "us", "they", and "our" are used. In pointing to the 144,000, the definite article "the" is used. She does not put herself as one of the 144,000, but, instead, the pronoun "us" is used; therefore, there must be another company living besides the 144,000.

ELIJAH REPRESENTS THE 144,000

If Enoch represents the great multitude of Rev. 7:9, then Elijah represents the 144,000, for only two in the world's history have been translated without seeing death. Further proof is not necessary; however, other reasons shall be given why Elijah typified the 144,-000. Elijah saw the drought and the famine in Israel; so will the 144,000, for we read in Great Controversy, page 649: "They have seen the earth wasted with famine and pestilence, the sun having power to scorch men with great heat." Elijah had a mantle over his shoulders (2 Kings 2:8); likewise the 144,000 have a mantle. "And they were all clothed with a glorious white mantle from their shoulders to their feet." Early Writings, page 17.

Quoting from Testimonies to Ministers, page 475: "Prophecy must be fulfilled. The Lord says: 'Behold, I will send you Elijah the prophet before the coming of the great and dreadful day of the Lord'. Somebody *is to come* in the spirit and power of Elijah, and when he appears, men may say: "You are too earnest, you do not interpret the Scriptures in the proper way. Let me tell you how to teach your message." Sister White does not mean to say that she is that prophet Elijah, but plainly says a prophet must come, and it is said to be a prophet with the "same spirit and power of Elijah". This prophet must come before Ezekiel 9 is fulfilled, for the prophecy of Ezekiel is similar to Elijah's experience with Israel in the days of Ahab. Elijah's work in the days of Ahab, king of Israel, was to prove to Israel that they had apostatized, and after doing so, he took the priests, or prophets, and cut their heads off, and threw them in the brook. Such was the spirit and power of Elijah.

We read in Testimonies to Ministers, page 445: "This sealing of the servants of God [the 144,000: Rev. 7] is the same that was shown to Ezekiel in vision." Then the sealing of the 144,000, is the same as Ezekiel 9, and the marking by the man with the writer's inkhorn is the seal. As soon as the marking is done, "the five men with the slaughter weapons go after him and slay both old and young, both maids and little children, and women. And they began at the ancient men which were before the house."

It is at this time the 144,000 are marked, or sealed. Ezekiel 9, fits Elijah's experience for this reason: The prophet, or the message is called, Elijah, "with the spirit and the power of Elijah." The prophet Elijah thought all Israel had apostatized, and that he alone was left, but the Lord said He had 7,000 men that had not bowed a knee to Baal. "Seven" signifies a complete or perfect number, which stands as a symbol, in this instance meaning a complete number of thousands. The complete number of the very elect is 144,000. So we, too, like Elijah, think the whole church is drifted into the world (bowed a knee to Baal). Thus Elijah stands as a type of the 144,000 living, translated saints.

MOSES—TYPE OF RESURRECTION OF JUST

"Moses upon the mount of transfiguration was a witness to Christ's victory over sin and death. He represented those who shall come forth from the grave at the resurrection of the just." Desire of Ages, page 421. Moses represents the first, or general resurrection of Rev. 20:6.

TYPE OF SPECIAL RESURRECTION

If Moses represents the general resurrection, who, then, would represent the mixed, or special resurrcetion of Dan. 12:2? We have the one of Matt. 27:52, 53. "And the graves were opened; And many bodies of the saints which slept arose, and came out of the graves after His resurrection, and went into the holy city, and appeared unto many." The saints who had part in this resurrection were gathered from all ages. Some who, perhaps, had lived at the very time Christ was preaching, and were acquainted with Him and

His work, were witnesses to His resurrection.   Read Early Writings, page 184; Great Controversy, page 786.

There is still another reason why Matt. 27:52, is a type of this mixed resurrection.   Those who were resurrected with Christ witnessed of the deity of Christ to the very ones who crucified Him. Speaking of this mixed resurrection, Daniel says: "And many of them that sleep in the dust of the earth shall awake, some to everlasting life, and some to shame and everlasting contempt."   Then there will be some righteous included who lived and witnessed the crucifixion; also those who crucified Him, and pierced Him, for, (Rev. 1:7) "Behold, He cometh with clouds: And every eye shall see Him, and they also which pierced Him."   Therefore, the resurrection which witnessed of the power of God to these murderers of His Son, typified the just who are raised in the mixed (special) resurrection.

The Type of The Second Resurrection

The wicked who come up in the mixed resurrection of Dan. 12:2, and who must die the second death at the coming of Christ, typify the ones who come up at the end of the millennium, called the resurrection of the wicked.   Read Great Controversy, pages 661, 662; Early Writings, pages 52, 53.

Type of The Second Death

It has been a perplexing question whether the wicked ones who arise in the special resurrection of Dan. 12:2, continue to live, or die with the *living* wicked at the second coming of Christ, and be resurrected at the end of the 1,000 years.   As God leaves nothing undone, He has foretold everything in prophecy, and types as well.   If we have a type for every other event, we must have a type of this.   The wicked ones who are resurrected, must die with the rest of the wicked at the coming of Christ in the clouds to typify the second death at the end of the millennium.

Now the question is, Will they arise again in the second resurrection with the wicked?   In answer to this question, Early Writings, page 292 says: "At the first resurrection all come forth in immortal bloom; but at the second the marks of the curse are visible on all. The kings and noblemen of the earth, the mean and low, the learned and unlearned, come forth together. All behold the Son of man; and those very men who despised and mocked Him, who put the crown of thorns upon His sacred brow, and smote Him with the reed, behold Him in all His kingly majesty. *Those who spit* upon Him in the hour of His trial now turn from His piercing gaze, and from the glory of His countenance. *Those who drove the nails* through His hands and feet now look upon the marks of His crucifixion. Those who *thrust* the *spear* into His side behold the marks of their cruelty on His body." By this we understand that these very men are there again in the second resurrection. Therefore they were resurrected the second time at the end of the 1,000 years, to die in the second death, which they themselves typified, (by dying the second death with the living wicked at the second coming of Christ in the clouds). Thus we have a prophecy and a type for every event that has, or will take place in this wicked world of ours.

A THOUGHT OF PERFECTION:

1. The resurrection of Moses.
2. The resurrection at the time when Jesus arose.
3. The special resurrection of Daniel 12:2.
4. The first resurrection of Rev. 20:6.
5. The translation of Enoch.
6. The translation of Elijah.
7. The general translation at the coming of Christ.

Thus, we again have the number "seven", the sign of perfection, all, or finished. The four resurrections and three translations comprise all the saints resurrected and translated, all of which make a total of seven, or the end.

PROCESSION OF THE REDEEMED

What a wonderful parade it will be when the redeemed of all

ages shall march through the golden streets in heavenly places amidst the pure and the blessed.

1.   Escorting the great procession we see the millions of angels who ministered to the redeemed in all ages.

2.   Moses, the type of the resurrected, and the first man to write in the Bible, we see marching ahead as a leader of the resurrected ones, clothed in white and a glittering golden crown on his head.   The resurrected ones whom he represents are Class 4, clad in white robes and having golden crowns.

3.   Next we see good, innocent Abel, representing the martyrs with the glorious white robe and red around his garment as a border, leading millions of martyrs of all ages (Class 2), whose robes are just like the one worn by their leader, Abel.

4.   We now behold good old Enoch, having around his head a dazzling white wreath: Above it a lovely crown brighter than the sun and on his right arm a glorious palm.   It is by him the great translated multitude are both lead and represented, all in pure white robes, palms in their hands, and golden crowns on their heads.

5.   Last of all the redeemed, the brave Elijah, with a glorious white mantle from his shoulders to his feet: A type and leader of the most wonderful company, though small in number.   Being a special company, with a special experience, a royal priesthood, the 144,000, in pure white, and a glorious mantle from their shoulders to their feet, with stars in their crowns.   Rev. 14:5, "And in their mouth was found no guile: For they are without fault before the throne of God."

6.   If the sons of God (Adams) from other worlds presented themselves before the Lord according to Job 1:6, in a council meeting, then surely the sons of God (Adams) from all the worlds would not be excluded from the most wonderful, and the only procession in Eternity's endless expanse.

7.   Last of all, Jesus and the majestic, heavenly throng with ten thousand times ten thousand, and thousands of thousands of angels.   What a wonderful gathering that will be!   Can we find anything more harmonious than this in all the Bible?   It will be no-

ticed we again have the complete Biblical number "seven", and it cannot be made more or less, and yet include all. Ought this not to wake up our interest and zeal when we see what a glorious event is in store for God's faithful people?

AN EXPLANATION OF THE WRITER'S INKHORN OF EARLY WRITINGS, P. 279

The man with the writer's inkhorn of Ezekiel 9, is the one who performs the sealing of the 144,000 long before the close of probation. Some may misunderstand the statement made in Early Writings, and thereby be confused. For the benefit of such a one we make this explanation. Quoting the statement found in Early Writings, page 279, we read: "I saw angels hurrying to and fro in heaven. An angel with a writer's inkhorn by his side returned from the earth, and reported to Jesus that his work was done, and the saints were numbered and sealed. Then I saw Jesus, who had been ministering before the ark containing the ten commandments, throw down the censer. He raised His hands, and with a loud voice said, 'IT IS DONE'."

It is unmistakably plain that it was an angel with a writer's inkhorn, and that his work was *done;* also that Jesus' work was finished in the heavenly Sanctuary (probation closed). Because this angel has a writer's inkhorn by his side same as the man in Ezekiel 9, is no proof that it is the same angel, for it may be supposed that there would be more than one angel with such an instrument. However, it may be the same sealing angel in both instances, but the thought is, when the man of Ezekiel 9, seals the 144,000, his work continues on through the harvest time.

The saints must be numbered and sealed in this generation the same as those who have been sealed in the ages past. Evidently his work has been continuing ever since sin entered into the human family, perhaps beginning with Abel, and would continue to the close of probation, at which time his work would be done.

SECTION III.
ESAU AND JACOB

"And Isaac entreated the Lord for his wife, because she was barren: And the Lord was entreated of him, and Rebekah his wife conceived. And the children struggled together within her; and she said, "If it be so why am I thus?" "And she went to enquire of the Lord. And the Lord said unto her, Two nations are in thy womb, and two manner of people shall be separated from thy bowels; and the one people shall be stronger than the other people; and the elder shall serve the younger. When her days to be delivered were fulfilled, behold, there were twins in her womb. And the first came out red, all over like an hairy garment; and they called his name Esau. And after that came his brother out, and his hand took hold on Esau's heel; and his name was called Jacob." Gen. 25:21-26.

Inspiration says that Rebekah had no children and Isaac entreated the Lord and the Lord was entreated of him and the Lord gave her twins. If this be the case certainly it was not an accident. The Lord was in it. But if she only asked for *a child,* why did He give her *twins?* We do not suppose the Lord gave her twins to cause a lot of trouble in the family as it did. Why did they struggle within the mother? Why one red and hairy, and the other white and smooth? And why one take hold of the heel of the other? All these questions come to our minds. Whatever the reason, it was divinely designed, for *He gave* her the children. Certainly no one would think God did this without a purpose in view. God Himself told the mother it is an object lesson, for He said to her, "Two manner of people shall be separated from thy bowels and the one people shall be stronger than the other people." It is true that the result was two nations on the stage of action; Edom and Israel, but where is the lesson?

Whatever the lesson, it must be to God's people. It cannot be for the Old Testament time, for they never profited by it in any way.

We read in Gal. 4:22-25, that Isaac typified the New Testament church, and Ishmael the Old. "For it is written, that Abraham had two sons, the one by a bondmaid, the other by a freewoman. But he who was of the bondwoman was born after the flesh; but he of the freewoman was by promise. Which things are an allegory: For these are the two covenants; the one from the Mount Sinai, which gendereth to bondage, which is Agar. For this Agar is Mount Sinai in Arabia, and answereth to Jerusalem which now is, and is in bondage with her children."

Paul writes here that Ishmael represents Israel after the flesh. Agar represents the church that was organized at Mount Sinai at the time when Moses selected the seventy elders. See Patriarchs and Prophets, page 382. The Sanhedrin was composed of seventy men, therefore, the number "70" represents a church organization. Thus Paul says, "For this Agar is Mount Sinai [woman—symbol of the church] which is in Arabia." This same organization, after they wandered forty years in the wilderness, crossed the Jordan and established themselves in Jerusalem. "For this Agar is Mount Sinai in Arabia, and answereth to Jerusalem which now is, and is in bondage with her children." Agar, then, symbolized the church before the cross; Jerusalem, of old.

Again we read beginning with the 26th verse: "But Jerusalem which is above [New Jerusalem in heaven now. Rev. 21.] is free, which is the mother of us all. For it is written, Rejoice, thou barren that bearest not [Sarah]; break forth and cry, thou that travailest not: For the desolate hath many more children [desolate—for Sarah stepped aside and gave her husband to Agar] than she which hath an husband [Agar]. Now we, brethren, as Isaac was, are the children of promise. But as then he that was born after the flesh [Ishmael] persecuted him that was born after the Spirit [Isaac], even so it is now." Gal. 4:26-29. (For ancient Israel in the days of the apostles persecuted the Christians.) Here Inspiration says Sarah represents Jerusalem which is above, in heaven now (Rev. 21), and she is the mother of us all. Paul, in writing to the New Testament church

(Gentiles) says, "Now we, brethren, as Isaac was, are the children of promise." Paul means that Isaac represents the children of the New Testament, and Sarah is the symbol of the church.

Coming back to our subject, "Esau and Jacob", whatever the lesson of these twins, it cannot apply to the Old Testament church, for if Isaac is the father of them, and represents the New Testament church, then the lesson must apply to the church represented by him. If the father was sixty years of age at the time Esau and Jacob were born, the lesson can not be for the early part of the church. The symbol must be for a later period.

SYMBOL OF STRUGGLE

The children struggled before they were *delivered*. In this, too, must be a lesson. It is intended to point out the time when the application is made. It has been defined by the father's age that the lesson is for a later period. The children's struggle was before they were delivered; the lesson, then, is for God's people just before *they* are delivered.

THE TIME AND CHURCH

The lesson can not be in two churches. Why? Because they are born from one mother. They must come under the same message. Why? Because they are begotten by the same father. If this is the generation that will witness the end, and the church that shall be delivered and be translated without tasting death, then this must be the time to which this lesson applies. Now the question is, In which church shall it find its fulfillment? It can only find its fulfillment in *God's true church*. If the Protestant churches have fallen and are termed Babylon, then they have neither part nor lot in this lesson. If the Seventh-day Adventist church is the true Israel, and has a message which no other organization teaches; and if the message we bear is, the advent of Christ and the end of the world in this generation, *then this is the church.*

Two Classes of People

The Bible says the twins represent two classes of people. If this is true, then we have two classes of people in the church. One class is represented by Esau, the other by Jacob. Referring to Testimonies to Ministers, page 46, we read: "There are two opposing influences continually exerted on the members of the church. One influence is working for the purification of the church, and the other for the corrupting of the people of God." One of the twins was red and hairy, and the other smooth and white. Both people are sinful. Why? Because Esau was red, which is scarlet, the sign of sin. Jacob was white, but the name betrays the man, for the name "Jacob" means "deceiver".

Symbol of Birthright

Esau was the one born first. Whatever was to be inherited by the birthright was to be Esau's. The law of the Bbile is that the first-born had the right to the priesthood. For this reason, Jacob coveted Esau's birthright. Esau, then, represents a class of priesthood.

Symbol of Hair

As he was born hairy, his body must have been covered with a heavy coat of hair, for when Jacob wished to deceive his father in order to obtain the blessing, Rebekah, his mother, covered his neck and hands with the skins of the kids. Isaac's suspicion of whether it was Esau or Jacob speaking, compelled him to examine the body of his son. Gen. 27:22, 23, "And Jacob went near unto Isaac his father; and he felt him, and said, The voice is Jacob's voice, but the hands are the hands of Esau. And he discerned him not, because his hands were hairy, as his brother Esau's hands: So he blessed him." The heavy coat of hair, over Esau's body was unnatural, and the only reason why God should have made him thus was to symbolize the character of the class he represents.

The hair was a symbol of power, honor, glory, and talent (God-given gifts), to enable him to execute the duties of his office as family priest. The following reasons are given for believing thus: God, in the beginning created man and the woman. He made the man to be king and ruler over all His creation, and He crowned him with honor, glory, and power—talents necessary to execute his office. To the man he gave the beard, and not to the woman. Samson's hair was a symbol of his power. In I Cor. 11:15, we read: "But if the woman have long hair it is a glory to her."

SYMBOL OF ESAU'S HEEL

At birth of the twins, Esau came first, and Jacob took hold of Esau's heel, thus the younger was lead out by the older. This could not have just "happened", for it seems to be a miracle. This is the only time our attention is called to an occurrence of this kind, there-fore, God must have intended it so, and if He did, there must be a lesson in it. It would not be hard for one to see the lesson taught here by the miracle. Jacob was lead out by the heel of Esau, there-fore, Esau must represent a class of leaders.

SYMBOL OF BEING RED

Esau was born red, but Jacob white and smooth. As a rule, twins are born alike, but in this instance it was reversed. There is no similarity between Esau and Jacob as twin brothers, in character, appearance, color, or covering. Therefore, we have another miracle. This symbol is simple to understand. Red is the same as scarlet. The Bible uses scarlet as a symbol of sin, as in Isa. 1:18; Rev. 17:3; Rev. 12:3. Esau represents a sinful class of people, as well as Jacob. But the class whom Esau represents are given great privi-leges and opportunities to make good.

SYMBOL OF ESAU'S CHARACTER

The character of Esau's manhood reveals the character of the priesthood whom he represents. Esau was a mighty hunter, a man of the field. All his interest was in game and his stomach, but very much disinterested in his position as priest of the family. The class represented by him is far more interested in pleasure, gain, and the affairs of the world than they are in the God-given privileges. Esau could not control his appetite. He thought more of his stomach than he did of his position (office of priest). He represents a class of people whose god is their stomach. They would rather satisfy their lustful appetite than to execute their duty and keep God's truth.

Esau's Blessing

Esau had a valuable blessing within his reach: The immortal inheritance of life. It was his privilege to bring forth (inherit) the 12 sons (tribes) of Israel. From Esau were to come prophets, kings, and princes. Through the line of Esau the king of Kings, the blessed Christ was to come. All of these wonderful blessings were to be his.

There are many who are like Esau. He represents a class who have a special blessing within their reach. What is the blessing? It is an inheritance—the 12 tribes of the true Israel, the 144,000, who are to be as priests and kings. Read Volume 5, pages 475, 476. This class have the privilege of bringing about the second coming of Christ, and to lead the church over the borders of the heavenly Canaan, and into the glories of God. Just as the line of Esau had the privilege to bring about the first advent of Christ, and as Esau failed on his part, just so, this class represented by Esau is in danger of failing on their part. Think of the loss of inheritance immortal, life that is as enduring as the life of God, the Creator of the universe; happiness immeasurable, and an eternal weight of glory.

But Esau lusted for a favorite dish and sacrificed his birthright to gratify appetite, and received but little for it,—a bowl of red pottage. He represents this class who have been given great light and privileges to make good, but fail to do so. This class is to sacrifice an eternal weight of glory which no human lips can tell. Esau flattered himself that he could dispose of his birthright at will, and buy it back at pleasure, but when he sought to buy it back, even at a great sacrifice on his part, he was not able to do so. He sought for repentance carefully and with tears, but it was all in vain. How fearful the thought to sacrifice truth for worldly gain at the expense of life everlasting. Read Volume 2, pages 38, 39. The following quotation is taken from Patriarchs and Prophets, page 182: "As Esau awoke to see the folly of his rash exchange when it was too late to recover his loss, so it will be in the day of God with those who have *bartered* their *heirship* to heaven for selfish gratification."

Because of his indifference to the divine blessings and requirements, Esau is called in Scripture, "a profane person". He represents those who lightly value the redemption purchased for them by Christ, and are ready to sacrifice their heirship to heaven for the perishable things of earth. Multitudes live for the present with no thought or care for the future. Like Esau, they cry, "Let us eat and drink, for tomorrow we die." Patriarchs and Prophets, page 181.

SYMBOL OF POTTAGE

Jacob was a plain man dwelling in tents, while Esau hunted in the field. "Jacob sod pottage", made of lentils, and colored red. We do not know the kind of coloring Jacob used to obtain the tempting shade of that fancy dish; evidently he alone knew the secret.

"And Jacob sod pottage: And Esau came from the field, and he was faint: And Esau said to Jacob, Feed me, I pray thee, with that same red pottage; for I am faint: Therefore, was his name called "Edom". And Jacob said, Sell me this day thy birthright. And Esau said, Behold, I am at the point to die: And what profit shall this birthright do to me? And Jacob said, Swear to me this day; and he sware unto him: And he sold his birthright unto Jacob. Then Jacob gave Esau bread and pottage of lentils; and he did eat and drink, and rose up, and went his way: Thus, Esau despised his birthright." Gen. 25:29-34.

Esau came from the field that day without any game. As he entered the house, he saw Jacob garnishing the fancy article of food.

Immediately Esau exclaimed: "Feed me I pray thee with that same red pottage; for I am faint." Esau was not faint because of great hunger, but, seeing the new article of food, could not control his appetite. Jacob's answer was, "Sell me this day thy birthright", if you must have any of this pottage. And Esau said, "Behold, I am on the point to die: And what profit shall this birthright do to me?" Esau was not on the point to die because of hunger or physical ailment, for a sick man cannot eat as he did. Neither was it because of lack of food, for he was in his father's house, and Isaac was a rich man. It was because of his lust for the pottage, for "He did eat and drink and *rose up* and *went his way*". The symbol of the pottage is health reform. "Because of his indifference to the divine blessings and requirements, Esau is called in Scripture, 'a profane person'. *He represents those who lightly value the redemption purchased for them by Christ,* and are ready to *sacrifice* their heirship to heaven *for the perishable things of earth.* Multitudes live for the present, with no thought or care for the future. Like Esau, they cry, "Let us eat and drink, for tomorrow we die." Patriarchs and Prophets, page 181.

"As Esau awoke to see the folly of his rash exchange when it was too late to recover his loss, so it will be in the day of God with those who have bartered their heirship to heaven for selfish gratifications." Id. page 182. We must make our choice while we are given the freedom to select either the pottage or the birthright.

Edom—A Type

The transaction was made. "And he sold his birthright unto Jacob." Just then his name was changed, therefore, was his name called "Edom". Thus, "Esau despised his birthright". The name "Edom" means "red", or scarlet, the symbol of sin. Esau was born red but was not called by that name (Edom) at first. The class which Esau represents are in danger of losing out because of lustful appetite (disregard of health reform), thus they are called "Edom".

This is the class of whom the prophet Isaiah has reference to in Isa. 63:1.

CHANGE OF NAMES

Both Esau and Jacob represent two sinful classes: Esau, by the color of his skin, and Jacob, by his name. The names of both were changed: Jacob, because he coveted something worthwhile; Esau, because of lust. Jacob's name meant "deceiver"; the name "Esau" (in Hebrew: Hairy, which symbolically would be "honored", as previously explained) means "he that finishes". Note the remarkable meaning of the name, signifying the class given the privilege to finish the work. In Rev. 3:14-16, we read: "And unto the angel of the church of the Laodiceans write; . . . . I know thy works, that thou art neither cold nor hot: I would thou wert cold or hot. So then because thou art lukewarm, and neither cold nor hot, I will spue thee out of my mouth." Volume 5, page 82: "The call to this great and solemn work was presented to men of learning and position; had these been little in their own eyes, and trusted fully in the Lord, he would have honored them with bearing his standard in triumph to the victory. But they separated from God, yielded to the influence of the world, and the Lord rejected them."

LOSS AND GAIN

Jacob, the younger twin, or the one who came last, by holding to Esau's heel, represents a class which came into the third angel's message by the leadership of the class represented by Esau. Jacob had an earnest desire and great zeal for the position which his brother occupied. Though he was destitute of the qualifications which Esau possessed for performing the duties of this office, which he coveted and bought, yet, by his great zeal and determination, he made good. The price he paid was food—worth nothing; but that which he received was of great value. Regardless of how much training or talent one has in a certain occupation, he can never be successful unless he has a great zeal and interest in that particular line.

Esau had a great deal to lose, but his loss was Jacob's gain. That which Jacob offered as payment for Esau's valuable possession was of little worth, therefore, what Esau gained was little more than nothing. It was not long after Jacob secured the blessing from his father, Isaac, that Esau, filled with remorse, threatened Jacob's life. Both classes represented by Esau and Jacob may be in trouble: One, because of realization of their loss; the other, because of hatred manifested toward them.

JACOB'S DREAM

Jacob, at the advice of his parents, left home and went to Padan-Aram, and on his way, the very first night, God appeared unto him in a dream, "And behold a ladder set up on the earth, and the top of it reached to heaven: And behold the angels of God ascending and descending on it." Gen. 28:12. The ladder represents Christ; God, the Father stood above it; Jacob at the foot of it. (Verse 13). This dream gave Jacob great courage, and he made a vow to God.

Jacob was now to become the father of Israel (12 tribes) through whom many nations shall be blessed; a type of Israel by the promise, the 12 tribes, the 144,000. The dream which he had in the night was only a vision and representation of some future event. The meaning of the dream can be only one thing. If the ladder represents Christ, the angels as messengers, God the Father at the head, and Jacob at the foot, it means a complete connection with heaven and the true Israel,—the latter rain, the loud cry of the third angel's message. See Rev. 18:1.

MOTHERS OF ISRAEL

But note that Jacob went to Padan-Aram, to the house of Bethuel, his mother's father, there he married Leah and Rachel, the daughters of Laban. Zilpah and Bilhah, the maids of Leah and Rachel, also became his wives. These are the mothers whence the twelve tribes came, but they are only the mothers in type of the true tribes—the 144,000. Leah was the only legal wife to Jacob; Rachel was her sister.   Zilpah and Bilhah were bondwomen.

Let Leah represent the true church of Christ (Seventh-day Adventists) ; Rachel, a sister church, but not the true (Protestant) ; Zilpah and Bilhah, the world (religious and irreligious).   These are the mothers of the 144,000, and the way they (144,000) are gathered.   But while the twelve tribes came from many mothers, they were begotten by the same father.   So with the true—the 144,000. While they are gathered from all churches and the world, they must be brought into one church, at the same period of church history, by the same message (the third angel's message).

Jacob Homeward Bound: Time of Trouble

At the end of the twenty years Jacob was homeward-bound to the promised land and his father's house with great possessions.   By the time he arrived at his father's house, he had his twelve sons (the heads of the twelve tribes).   Before Jacob entered his father's house he went through that terrible struggle and wrestled with the angel till the breaking of the day.   Gen. 33:24-29.

Jacob's wrestling with the angel typifies the time of "Jacob's trouble" (for the church).   We read in Early Writings, pages 36, 37: "A decree went forth to slay the saints, which caused them to cry day and night for deliverance.   This was the time of Jacob's trouble."   See also Patriarchs and Prophets, pages 202-3.

Type of Promised Land—Israel in Father's House

If the promised land of Canaan is the type of the promised heavenly Canaan, then Jacob's father's house is the type of our Father's house.   Just so, when Israel (the true) enters our Father's house in the heavenly Canaan, there will be the twelve tribes, the 144,000.   The question arises, Are these all that will be saved in the third angel's message?   Remember that when Jacob entered his father's house with his twelve sons he had many servants, male and female, that outnumbered his tribes (sons) many times.   Just so with Israel (the true), who will have with them "a great multitude which no man could number". Rev. 7:9. (The great multitude came by the effort of the tribes after the fulfillment of Ezekiel 9).

This study can not fit another case nor any other church in all the history on the earth. Seventh-day Adventists are the only people and church that has ever been called Israel, who have the truth of health reform, and that would be in danger of selling their birthright for a bowl of pottage. By this fact alone, while there are many others, we may know that the Seventh-day Adventist church is God's church.

SECTION IV.

WHO IS ISRAEL BY THE PROMISE?

"This experience of the Israelites [in departing from Egypt] was written for the instruction of those who should live in the last days. Before the overflowing scourge shall come upon the dwellers of the earth, the Lord calls upon all who are Israelites indeed to prepare for that event." Volume 6, page 195. The twelve tribes of Israel after the flesh are but a type of Israel by the promise (the 144,000). As there were Gentiles among Israel (the type), there would be Gentiles in Israel the true.

The early part of the Christian church (apostolic time) could not be called Israel, for the history of the church then was typified by Isaac, according to Gal. 4:22-31, and as explained on pages 53, 54. Isaac was not called Israel, for he was the father of Jacob, and it was Jacob who was called Israel, therefore, Israel, whatever part of the church it is, must come sometime later in the history of the church. Jacob was the father of the twelve tribes of Israel, and if Israel after the flesh is a type of Israel by promise (the true), then let us study the beginning of Israel after the flesh, if we are to locate, or to know of Israel by the promise,—the 144,000.

The journey of Israel down into Egypt could not have been an accident. Whatever the reason for it, God was in it. Joseph said to his brothers (Gen. 45:5): "Now therefore be not grieved, nor angry with yourselves, that ye sold me hither: For God did send me before you to preserve life." Joseph declares that God was the cause for him going into Egypt. God had also told Abraham that he, and his seed would sojourn and be afflicted in a strange land 430 years. But why did God send them into Egypt? Why was Joseph sold at the age of 17, merely a lad, into the hands of cruel Ishmaelites, and lead to a strange land to be re-sold as a slave? We certainly would not make a mistake by thinking that Joseph became faint-hearted on the way. There surely must have been a reason for all this ill treatment.

In Egypt, Joseph was sold to serve as a slave, and later was thrown into the dungeon for a number of years. Why did God lead Israel into that strange land where idolatry prevailed everywhere? God certainly knew that in that land they would become slaves in just a short while. Why would heaven allow God's chosen people to become servants to a nation whose idols were their gods? Why did God permit the lashes of the Egyption taskmasters to be applied upon the backs of His people? Why would divine love permit the children of Abraham (God's friend) while yet in infancy, to be drowned in the river Nile? Who can say our great God was ignorant of all these things which took place, or that He made a mistake? The only answer that can be offered is, that it was all heavenly designed. But what was it all about? God must have had some special reason and specific purpose for an object lesson to be taught at a certain time. One may say, God did it all to show His power, but, would the all-wise and great God, full of love and mercy, destroy His children to show His power? Not even an earthly, mortal, human father would dare destroy his children to show his power. Who would dare say human beings have greater love or better judgment than the great God, whose mercy is immeasurable, whose love fills the universe, whose wisdom is unsearchable, whose judgment is justice?

Not only His chosen suffered of bondage and cruelty, but the Egyptians as well. At the time of the Exodus movement, at the departure of Israel, the plagues came upon all Egypt, and the nation was nearly ruined. On the night of the Passover, there was death in every dwelling where there was no blood on the door post, and in every stall of beasts.

"And all the first-born in the land of Egypt shall die, from the first-born of Pharaoh that sitteth upon his throne, even unto the first-born of the maidservant that is behind the mill; and all the first-born of beasts." Ex. 11:5.

Israel journeyed to the Red Sea, and Moses stretched out his hand over the sea, and the waters were divided. Israel went into the sea, and walked across over dry ground. The Egyptians pursued after them to the midst of the sea, and Moses stretched his hand over the sea, the waters returned, and covered the chariots, horsemen, and all the host of Pharaoh which came into the sea after them; "there remained not so much as one of them".

Israel came into the wilderness where they wandered about for 40 years. Thousands of them perished because of unbelief. At the end of the wilderness journey, the people crossed the Jordan. During the time Israel was away from Canaan, the land was thickly inhabited by heathen nations. Israel was compelled to destroy them by the sword in order to possess the land. Think of the loss of life, grief, and suffering: All because God took Israel into Egypt, and brought them back again. God certainly would not destroy His subjects "just to show His power".

In I Cor. 10:11, 12, speaking of the experience of the children of Israel, we read: "Now all these things happened unto them for ensamples: And they are written for our admonition, upon whom the ends of the world are come. Wherefore let him that thinketh he standeth take heed lest he fall." If we are the people upon whom the end of the world is about to come, then their ensamples are written for our admonition. This is the reason why God lead the children of Israel into Egypt and back again. Think how great the price to work out the picture. The lessons to be derived from these great examples are far greater than we have ever realized. Many thousands lost their lives to produce the picture, with the intention that many more thousands would be saved than those who perished. Let us therefore carefully study into the lessons that were intended for our learning and admonition.

"Pharaoh dreamed: And, behold, he stood by the river. And behold, there came up out of the river seven well favored kine and fatfleshed: And they fed in a meadow. And, behold, seven other kine came up after them out of the river, ill favored and leanfleshed;

and stood by the other kine upon the brink of the river, And the ill favored and leanfleshed kine did eat up the seven well favored and fat kine. So Pharaoh awoke. . . . And it came to pass in the morning that his spirit was troubled; and he sent and called for all the magicians of Egypt, and all the wise men thereof: And Pharaoh told them his dream; but there was none that could interpret them unto Pharaoh. . . . Then Pharaoh sent and called Joseph, and they brought him hastily out of the dungeon. . . . And Pharaoh said unto Joseph, I have dreamed a dream, and there is none that can interpret it: And I have heard say of thee, that thou canst understand a dream to interpret it. . . . And Pharaoh" told the dream to Joseph. "And Joseph said unto Pharaoh. . . . God hath shewed Pharaoh what He is about to do. The seven good kine are seven years; . . . And the seven thin and ill favored kine that came up after them are seven years. . . . Behold, there come seven years of great plenty throughout all the land of Egypt. And there shall arise after them seven years of famine; and all the plenty shall be forgotten in the land of Egypt. . . . And the plenty shall not be known in the land by reason of that famine following; for it shall be very grievous. . . . And in the seven plenteous years the earth brought forth by handfuls. And he gathered up all the food of the seven years, which were in the land of Egypt, and laid up the food in the cities: The food of the field, which was round about every city, laid he up in the same. And Joseph gathered corn as the sand of the sea, very much, until he left numbering; for it was without number." Gen. 41:1-49.

We shall endeavor to bring enough evidence in this study to show that Israel's experience in Egypt is a photograph of Israel the true (the 144,000) in the Seventh-day Adventist church. "While the exodus movement was a great movement, the second advent movement will be still greater. God will take out a people, not from one nation only, but from every nation under heaven, and He will lead them into the heavenly Canaan. This advent movement, of which the exodus movement was *a type*, we believe was foretold in prophecy in the following stirring language: 'It shall come to pass in that day, that the Lord shall set His hand again the second time to recover the remnant of His people, which shall be left.' There shall be a highway for the remnant of His people; . . . like as it was to Israel in the day that he came up out of the land of Egypt." Review and Herald, Oct. 10, 1929, pages 4, 5. "The Exodus Movement is in a way a type [photograph] of the closing work of God under the Advent Movement." "Each movement rises in fulfillment of time prophecy." Certainties of the Advent Movement, by W. A. Spicer. The fact that Israel after the flesh is a type (photograph), their experience must be duplicated by the true, otherwise there can be no type.

YEARS OF PLENTY, AND FAMINE

God permitted the plenty, as well as the famine. Each one bears the number "seven", meaning "perfect", or "complete". These two sections of time can only mean one thing, which is none other than this world in history, in two great divisions; namely B. C. and A. D., with the cross as the dividing line. The seven years of plenty represent the Old Testament period in which time God gave plenty, for by His holy prophets He stored it in the great storehouse, what we today call the Bible. In Matt. 11:13, we read: "For all the prophets and the law prophesied *until John.*" It is for this reason that Jesus made the above statement, for we have no other thus far.

In the seven years of plenty (B. C.) God stored His word in the Bible to feed the world (Egypt) in the next seven years of famine (A. D.). "God, who at sundry times and in divers manners spakes in *times past unto the fathers by the prophets,* Hath in these last days spoken unto us by his Son, whom he hath appointed heir of all things, by whom also he made the worlds." Heb. 1:1, 2. The New Testament is the fulfillment of the Old.

JOSEPH TYPE OF CHRIST

Joseph typified Christ. See Patriarchs and Prophets, pages 239, 240. Our God in the Old Testament time (seven years of plenty) spoke to His people in divers manners by His prophets, and commanded these things to be written, with the intention to speak to His people in these last days (New Testament time, or seven years of famine) to each one of us individually by the voice of His Word as found (stored) in the Bible.

"Thou shalt be over my house, and according unto thy word shall all my people be ruled: Only in the throne will I be greater than thou. And Pharaoh said unto Joseph, See, I have set thee over all the land of Egypt. And Pharaoh took off his ring from his hand, and put it upon Joseph's hand, and arrayed him in vestures of fine linen, and put a gold chain about his neck; and he made him to ride in the second chariot which he had; and they cried before him, bow the knee: And he made him ruler over all the land of Egypt. And Pharaoh said unto Joseph, I am Pharaoh, and without thee shall no man lift up his hand or foot in all the land of Egypt." Gen. 41:40-44. No greater favor or honor could Pharaoh have shown to Joseph; and all the Egyptians bowed down to him. As we proceed in this study we shall prove beyond a doubt that Joseph is a perfect type of Christ.

PHARAOH, TYPE OF—

If Joseph typified Christ, and Pharaoh honored Joseph above any man ever honored by any king, and Joseph—and Pharaoh work hand in hand, then Pharaoh must stand for some figure, or type. It would not be hard to determine what Pharaoh represents. That which honored Christ above everything that can be honored upon earth, is what Pharaoh represents.

The church of the apostles honored Christ above everything that can be honored, so much so, that all sacrificed their lives. No greater homage has Christ received upon earth by any other part in the history of His church. By this we understand that Pharaoh represents the apostles' church, or organization. The application made here will prove correct as we advance in this study. (Further explanation upon this subject is given on the last page of this section.)

THE BEGINNING OF FAMINE

The dividing line between the seven years of plenty and seven years of famine is the cross. "For all the prophets and the law prophesied until John." Matt. 11:13. Where the seven years of plenty end, the seven years of famine begin. The first year of famine is the beginning of the church of Christ at the time of the apostles. One may ask, Why a famine in the beginning of the Christian church? Did they not get sufficient corn (truth)? Yes, but they got it from the great storehouse (the Bible) in the same way as the Egyptians received their corn in the years of famine,—from the immense storehouse at the hand of Joseph. See pages 15-18.

EGYPTIANS, TYPE OF GENTILES

The seven years of famine began when the Egyptians came to Pharaoh for bread, and Pharaoh told all the Egyptians, "Go unto Joseph; what he saith to you, do . . . . and Joseph opened all the storehouses, and sold unto the Egyptians." Gen. 41:55, 56. "And Joseph gathered up all the money that was found in the land of Egypt, and in the land of Canaan, for the corn which they bought: And Joseph brought the money into Pharaoh's house. And when money failed in the land of Egypt, and in the land of Canaan, all the Egyptians came unto Joseph, and said, Give us bread: For why should we die in thy presence? For the money faileth. . . . And they brought their cattle unto Joseph: And Joseph gave them bread in exchange for horses, and for the flocks, and for the cattle of the herds, and for the asses: And he fed them with bread for all their cattle for that year. When that year was ended, they came unto him the second year, and said unto him, We will not hide it from my Lord, how that our money is spent; my lord also hath our herds of cattle; there is not ought left in the sight of my lord, but our bodies, and our lands: Wherefore shall we die before thine eyes, both we and our land? Buy us and our land for bread, and we and our land will be servants unto Pharaoh: . . . And Joseph bought all the land of Egypt for Pharaoh; for the Egyptians sold every man his field. . . . And they said, Thou hast saved our lives: Let us find grace in the sight of my lord, and we will be Pharaoh's servants." Gen. 47:14-25.

In the beginning of famine, the Egyptians went to Pharaoh for corn, instead of to Joseph. They were well acquainted with Joseph, for he had been a governor of Egypt for eight years or more. Joseph rode over all the land of Egypt, and every Egyptian bowed down to him. During the years of plenty, it was *Joseph* who bought the corn from the Egyptians, and it seems strange that they should go to Pharaoh. It must have been by divine providence that they came to him.

It has been explained that Pharaoh represented the church organization, or leadership. The Egyptians can not represent anything else but the Gentiles in the days of the apostles. The Gentiles came to the church (Pharaoh) where they were told to go to Joseph (Christ). "What he saith to you, do." That is, the church, in her purity, without one strange thing in their midst, directed the Gentiles to Christ as their life giver, as Pharaoh directed the Egyptians to Joseph.

EGYPTIANS SOLD THEMSELVES TO PHARAOH

"And Joseph bought all the land of Egypt for Pharaoh; for the Egyptians sold every man his field, because the famine prevailed over them: So the land became Pharaoh's." Gen. 47:20. In the preceding verses of the chapter we red the Egyptians spent all their money for corn; and when the money was gone, they gave the cattle in exchange; and when the cattle were gone, they gave the land; and when the land was gone, they sold themselves and became servants to Pharaoh. This is the type, but of the fulfillment of this type, we read in the following texts: "And the multitude of them that believed were of one heart and of one soul: Neither said any of them that ought of the things which he possessed was his own; but they had all things common. And with great power gave the apostles witness of the resurrection of the Lord Jesus: And great grace was upon them all. Neither was there any among them that *lacked:* for as many as were *possessors* of *lands* or *houses sold* them, and *brought* the *prices* of the things that were sold. And *laid* them down at the apostles' feet: . . . And Joses, who by the apostles was surnamed Barnabas, . . . a Levite, . . . Having land, sold it, and brought the money, and laid it at the apostles' feet." Acts 4:32-37. Thus Jew and Gentile sold all houses and lands and brought the prices and laid them at the apostles' feet, and became servants to the church (Pharaoh).

Again, we read Acts 5:1-10, "But a certain man named Ananias, with Sapphira his wife, sold a possession, And kept back part of the price, his wife also being privy to it, and brought a certain part, and laid it at the apostles' feet. But Peter said, Ananias, why hath Satan filled thine heart to lie to the Holy Ghost, and to *keep back part of the price* of the land? . . And Ananias hearing these words fell down, and gave up the ghost." Thus any who pretended to sell, and held back part of the price received, in the days of the apostles, died just as those who would not sell all to Pharaoh in Egypt. Jesus said, "Sell all and follow Me." Therefore type met anti-type.

JOSEPH REMOVES PEOPLE THROUGHOUT EGYPT

"And Joseph bought all the land of Egypt for Pharaoh; . . . And as for the people, he removed them to cities from one end of the borders of Egypt even to the other end thereof." Gen. 47, part of verses 20, 21. This is the type; following is the fulfillment of the type: Acts 8:1, "And Saul was consenting unto his [Stephen's] death. And at that time there was a great persecution against the church which was at Jerusalem; and they were all scattered abroad throughout the regions of Judaea and Samaria, *except the apostles."*

It will be noticed that the apostles were at home (Jerusalem), and there is no record where the apostles sold their land. Now we quote the type of the latter: Gen. 47:22, "Only the land of the priests bought he not; for the priests had a portion assigned them of Pharaoh, and did eat their portion which Pharaoh gave them: Wherefore *they sold not their lands."* It is remarkable to note how this coincides to the smallest of details.

70 SOULS, TYPE OF ORGANIZATION

Israel arrived in Egypt in the second year of famine. Gen. 45:10, 11, "And thou shalt dwell in the land of Goshen, and thou shalt be near unto me, thou, and thy children, and thy children's children, and thy flocks, and thy herds, and all that thou hast: And there will I nourish thee; for *yet there are five years of* famine; lest thou, and thy household, and all that thou hast, come to poverty." The arrival of Israel in Egypt stands for some symbol in which there must be a lesson. Note that this lesson can not be for the early part of the Christian church, for Israel came in the *second year of famine.* The lesson, then, intended here, is for a later period in the history of the church. If we are to know the truth of the incident, and the lesson intended to be derived from it, reference must here be made to the number of souls which entered into Egypt. "And the sons of Joseph, which were born him in Egypt, were two souls: All the souls of the house of Jacob, which came into Egypt, were threescore and ten." Gen. 46:27.

The Bible says *all* the souls who came into Egypt were *seventy* in number. If we can, in some way, find the meaning of the number, then we shall understand the lesson. When Moses, with the children of Israel, came to Sinai, he organized the church there, and in organizing, selected *seventy* elders. This same organization, years later, crossed the Jordan and went into the promised land. There they had the Sanhedrin which was composed of seventy men. Thus, the number "seventy" is a symbol of church organization. The meaning, then, is that there will be a church organization, sometime in the history of A. D. If this is true, then that church which Christ, with the apostles organized must disband, and of necessity be re-organized. This is true, for the Christian church was disorganized in the dark ages during the time of the beginning of papal rule. When again organized, it would partially fulfill Joel 2:32, "And in the remnant whom the Lord shall call." The 2300 days, or years, of Daniel's prophecy in the eighth chapter gives us the entire truth of church history to 1844, until which time there was no call for re-organization. If there had been, or if this call for re-organization had met its fulfillment before 1844, then Daniel's prophecy would have made mention of it. As the prophecy is silent, and there has no *prophet* of God risen since the church fell into papal power about A. D. 538 to 1844, then the truth of the symbol was yet in the future.

As the prophetic period ended in 1844, the "Most Holy" place in the heavenly Sanctuary was opened, into which Christ entered. If this incident marked the beginning of the atonement, there would have been no better, or more opportune time for a call from heaven than at the end of the great prophetic period; the day of atonement being the most solemn time for the church. Seventh-day Adventists were called out by a prophet, and are practically the only people who believe in the 2300 days. We are the only people who have pro-claimed it since 1844, and are now in the atonement, or the time of the judgment. The text for this is here quoted: "And I saw another angel fly in the midst of heaven, having the everlasting gospel to preach unto them that dwell on the earth, and to every nation, and kindred, and tongue, and people, Saying with a loud voice, Fear God, and give glory to him; for the hour of his judgment *is come:* and worship him that made heaven, and earth, and the sea, and the fountains of waters." Rev. 14:6, 7. Seventh-day Adventists *only* can fulfill the type, for just at this time they were called by a prophet of God, to organize as a denomination, and to proclaim the glad news: "This gospel in all the world in this generation." Thus the symbol "seventy" met its fulfillment at that time.

Still another thought on the experience of Israel:—When Joseph's brethren came into Egypt, they went directly to him for corn. "And Joseph's brethren came, and bowed down themselves before him with their faces to the earth." Gen. 42:6. The sons of Jacob were strangers in the land and knew not their brother who was a governor. They providentially came not to Pharaoh, as the Egyptians did, for corn, but directly to the right person,—Joseph. In contrast to this, the Egyptians who should have known better, being acquainted with the rule of their country, went to Pharaoh for corn, but their king told them to "go to Joseph. What he saith to you, do." The Egyptians must have known Joseph, being their governor for more than eight years by that time. In the seven years of plenty, it was Joseph to whom they sold the food which he preserved for the time of famine. Joseph rode in Pharaoh's chariot over all the land of Egypt, and all the Egyptians bowed down to him, thus it would have been impossible for them to be ignorant of him. This being a symbol, it can only find its fulfillment in the following narrative:

The Egyptians (Gentiles) went to Pharaoh (leadership of the apostolic church) for corn. The apostles directed the Gentiles (converts) to Christ as Pharaoh directed the Egyptians to Joseph, saying, "Go to Joseph. What he saith to you, do." If this is the meaning we get from the Egyptians' going to Pharaoh, then the significance of the sons of Jacob going directly to Joseph means that when that church is re-organized, the people would have to go directly to Christ (Joseph). The lesson intended is, that in the beginning of the church in 1845, which had no true leadership (Pharaoh) to go to, they of necessity went directly to Christ (as the sons of Jacob came to Joseph).

JACOB TYPE OF JAMES

The Seventh-day Adventist Church which came into existence in 1845 became Israel (the movement from which the true Israel, the 144,000 are made). It will be noticed that the names of the fathers after the flesh, and by the promise coincide. The father's name of Israel after the flesh was "Jacob". So is the name of the father of Israel by the promise (Seventh-day Adventist movement). But one may say, It was Jacob in the former, and James White in the latter. True it is, but the names "Jacob" and "James" are the same. Again, the very first vision Sister White had was about the 144,000, and the aim of this denomination has been to make that number.

The Land of Goshen

The beginning of this denomination was typified by Israel's entrance into Egypt as previously explained. We shall now consider the truth of the land of Goshen. Joseph brought Israel into Egypt and gave them the part of the land to dwell in which was the best land in the country of Egypt, and there Joseph nourished them, their flocks, herds and cattle, and all they had. See Gen. 45:10.

The land of Goshen stands as a symbol of the United States of America in which the church came into existence. While our country is productive like the land of Goshen, the richest in the world, and a Protestant nation, it is the best for missionary work, for it is made up of all nations, and therefore like the land of Goshen, the most productive in Egypt (the world).

Joseph Nourished Israel

In the beginning of the seven years of famine the Egyptians sold all and became servants to Pharaoh, which has reference to the apostles' church, and of the Gentiles then, who sold their houses, and lands, and had all things in common, as previously explained. But Israel did not sell any of their possessions, nor did they pay for the food with which Joseph nourished them. Israel, then, represents the church now. In the beginning of the church in 1845, Christ (Joseph) opened the storehouse and gave us all the truth (corn) we could possibly assimilate. Is it not a fact that no other people at any time in the history of the church have received as much truth as God has given us in our time? Line upon line, precept upon precept, instruction upon instruction, have been given us, so that we, as a people, may know and understand the ways of the Lord, obey His voice, keep His charge, commandments, statutes, and laws; thus becoming the "children of Abraham, and heirs according to the promise". When this is realized in the hearts of men then they will fulfill the charge given to Peter. Peter said, "Thou knowest I love Thee." Jesus saith unto him, *"Feed My sheep."*

SHEPHERDS

"And Pharaoh said unto his brethren [Joseph's], What is your occupation? And they said unto Pharaoh, Thy servants are shepherds, both we, and also our *fathers.*" Gen. 47:3. Israel were shepherds which is a symbol of missionaries such as feed the lambs of God. In the early part of the church, the by-word was, "Every Seventh-day Adventist a missionary, and every missionary a preacher." It ought to be so now. "The great struggle has not been between religion and no religion; it is between *God's* religion and *man's* religion." Review and Herald, Jan. 23, 1930.

ANOTHER PHARAOH AROSE

"Now there arose up a new king over Egypt, which knew not Joseph". Ex. 1:8. If the first Pharaoh, who exalted Joseph (Christ), represented the leadership in the days of the apostles, then this new Pharaoh must represent the leadership of this present movement at the time this subject became known. Note, this new Pharaoh knew not Joseph (Christ). The meaning is that the leadership of this organization has left following their Master,—"Christ". Volume 5, page 217: "Grievous and presumptuous sins have dwelt among us. And yet the general opinion is that the church is *flourishing,* and that peace and spiritual *prosperity* are in all her borders. The church has *turned back* from following Christ her Leader, and is steadily retreating toward *Egypt.* Yet few are alarmed or astonished at their want of spiritual power. Doubt and even disbelief of the testimonies of the Spirit of God, is leavening our churches everywhere. Satan would have it thus. Ministers who preach self, instead of Christ would have it thus. The testimonies are unread and unappreciated." Further explanation of the Pharaohs being types, is given on the last page of this section.

TASKMASTERS

"Now there arose up a new king over Egypt, which knew not

Joseph. And he said unto his people, Behold, the people of the children of Israel are more and mightier than we: . . . Therefore, they
did set over them taskmasters to afflict them with their burdens. And
they built for Pharaoh treasure cities, Pithom and Raamses. But the
more they afflicted them, the more they multiplied and grew. . . .
And the Egyptians made the children of Israel to serve with rigor:
And they made their lives bitter with hard bondage, in morter, and
in brick, and in all manner of service in the field." Ex. 1:8-13.

"The children of Israel," said Pharaoh, "are too strong and
mightier than we. Let us deal wisely and reduce their strength."
So they (Israelites) were drafted from the sheepfolds to the brick
yards, and the field, but this did not reduce their strength. Said
Pharaoh, "Let us set taskmasters over them to wear them out." Note
the application. Pharaoh is the king, the one who rules. The taskmasters in this case could be none other than a class of ministers referred to in Volume 5, page 217: "Doubt and even disbelief of the
testimonies of the Spirit of God, is leavening our churches everywhere. Satan would have it thus. Ministers who preach self instead of Christ would have it thus. The *testimonies* are *unread* and
unappreciated."

No longer is the by-word of Seventh-day Adventists, "every
Seventh-day Adventist a missionary; every missionary a preacher," as
what it used to be. But, how much per capita? or, have you made
your budget? instead of, Have you brought any souls to Christ? Are
your church members nearer to Him? It is not meant here that
Christians ought not to give for the support of the cause. We ought
to give, and give more liberally than we have given in the past, but
our gifts ought to come from a *willing heart,* and not from the result
of *lashes.* The people should be fed with spiritual food so that they
would feel the need of giving without overbearing on the subject.

When Moses was about to build the sanctuary in the wilderness,
God commanded him, saying: "Speak unto the children of Israel, that
they bring Me an offering: Of every man that giveth it *willingly
with his heart* ye shall *take* My offering." Moses was commanded

to take offerings only from those who willingly gave from their heart. We are told by the Spirit of Prophecy that ministers should not put all their efforts and time with the church. Members are not to expect a sermon every Sabbath. Ministers should rather engage themselves in working for outsiders. Read Volume 9, page 140. Have we taken heed to this instruction? For example, we have scores of ministers in Los Angeles and immediate vicinity, but how many public efforts have we? It was announced just a short time ago that there were only two. Thus it has been for some years. What are these ministers doing day after day, and week after week? It seems they are doing nothing but preparing a sermon during six days of the week to preach on Sabbath, and then it is either something to sell, or some particular budget to raise.

How many sermons preached do we read of in the Bible urging people to give money, or to buy something to support the cause? Not one. We have polluted the house of God with merchandise even on Sabbath morning, which hour is dedicated as a day of rest to worship God. Volume 1, pages 471, 472: "A great mistake has been made by some who profess present truth, by introducing merchandise in the course of a series of meetings, and by their traffic diverting minds from the object of the meetings. If Christ were now upon earth, He would *drive out* these peddlers and traffickers, whether they be ministers or people, with a scourge of small cords, as when He entered the temple anciently. . . . Ministers have stood in the desk and preached a most solemn discourse, and then by introducing merchandise, and acting the part of a salesman, *even* in the house of God, they have diverted the minds of their hearers from the impressions received, and destroyed the fruit of their labor. . . . Their time and strength should be held in reserve, that their efforts may be thorough in a series of meetings. Their time and strength should not be drawn upon to sell our books when they can be properly brought before the public by those who have not the burden of preaching the word [colporteurs].

" 'It is written, My house shall be called the house of prayer, but

ye have *made* it a den of thieves.' These traffickers might have
pleaded as an excuse that the articles they held for sale were for
sacrificial offerings. But their object was to get gain, to obtain
means, to accumulate."—Id. p. 472.

Our conference is not ignorant of the instruction here given, and
the evil which is practised in the churches. At the Autumn Council
held in Milwaukee, Wisconsin, in 1923, the question of book sales on
the Sabbath day was brought forth in connection with other matters,
and the following resolution was passed and published: "That *all*
campaigns for the promotion of periodicals or book sales on the Sabbath day be eliminated, and that those responsible for the promotion
of these campaigns be directed to the method of *house to house* solici-
tation by visiting committees in connection with campaigns for literature sales:

"That we invite our publishing houses to exercise caution circu-
larizing our people on behalf of publishing house projects, and to
refrain from sending to church officers matters to be presented on the
Sabbath, with previous arrangements with the Local, Union, and
General conferences."—Milwaukee Autumn Council, Oct. 9-17,
1923. Review and Herald of Nov. 22, 1923. Read Volume 9,
page 260.

We read in Testimonies to Ministers, page 477: "A strange
thing has come into our churches. Men who are placed in positions
of responsibility that they may be wise helpers to their fellow workers, have come to suppose that they were set as kings and rulers in
the churches, to say to one brother, Do this; to another, Do that; and
to another, Be sure to labor in such and such a way." Thus Pharaoh has drafted the people from the sheepfold to the brickyards, or
the field. The taskmasters, being commanded to oversee the work,
urge the bricks (budgets), and wear out the people. The existing
sins in the church are passed over and no one cares. Those who do
reprove wrongs incur their displeasure. In Volume 3, page 266,
speaking of the condition in the church at the time of the sealing
(marking) of the 144,000, and the slaughter in the church, we read:

"Those who have excused these wrongs have been thought by the people to be very amiable and lovely in disposition, simply because they shunned to discharge a plain Scriptural duty. The task was not agreeable to their feelings; therefore, they avoided it."

FURNISH STRAW NO MORE

"And Pharaoh commanded the same day the taskmasters of the people, and their officers, saying, Ye shall no more give the people straw to make brick, as heretofore: Let them go and gather straw for themselves. And the taskmasters of the people went out, and their officers, and they spake to the people, saying, Thus saith Pharaoh, I will not give you straw. Go ye, get you straw where ye can find it: Yet not ought of your work shall be diminished." Ex. 5:6, 7, 10, 11.

Pharaoh will not furnish straw: That is, he will not render any help, but the people must produce the same amount of bricks. In the beginning of this organization (Seventh-day Adventists), the denominational institutions, sanitariums, and hospitals were built for the purpose of caring for our own people (members of the church). After the case of the patient had been diagnosed, the cause being made known, with instruction, some aid or treatments were to be given. This help was to be rendered whether they were able to pay much, little, or nothing. Such is the work of the good Samaritan.

"In former numbers of Testimonies for the Church, I have spoken of the importance of the Seventh-day Adventists establishing an institution for the benefit of the sick, especially for the suffering and sick *among us.* I have spoken of the ability of *our own people,* in point of means, to do this; and have urged that, in view of the importance of this branch of the great work of preparation to meet the Lord. . . .

"When I saw those who managed and directed, running into the dangers shown me, of which I had warned them in public, and also in private conversation and letters, a terrible burden came upon me. That which had been shown me as a place where the suffering sick *among us* could be helped, was one where sacrifice, hospitality, faith, and piety should be the ruling principles. But when unqualified calls were made for large sums of money, with the statement that stock taken would pay large per cent; when the brethren who occupied positions in the institution seemed more than willing to take larger wages than those were satisfied with who filled other and equally important stations in the great cause of truth and reform; when I learned, with pain, that, in order to make the institution popular with those *not of our faith,* and to secure their patronage, a spirit of compromise was rapidly gaining ground at the Institute, manifested in the use of *Mr.; Miss,* and *Mrs.,* instead of Bro. and Sister, and in popular amusements, in which all could engage in a sort of comparatively innocent frolic;—when I saw these things, I said, This is not that which was shown me as an institution for the sick, which would share the signal blessing of God. This is another thing. And yet calculations for more extensive buildings were made, and calls for large sums of money were urged. As it was then managed, I could but regard the Institute, on the whole, as a *curse.* . . .

"Several who came to Battle Creek humble, devoted, confiding Christians, went away almost infidels. The general influence of these things was creating prejudice against the health reform in very many of the most humble, the most devoted, and the best of our brethren, and was destroying faith in my Testimonies and in the present truth. .

"The brethren who have stood at the head of this work have appealed to our people for means, on the ground that the health reform is a part of the great work connected with the third angel's message. In this they have been right. It is a branch of the great, *charitable, liberal, sacrificing, benevolent* work of God. Then why should these brethren say, 'Stock in the Health Institute will pay a large per cent,' 'it is a good investment,' 'a paying thing'? Why not as well talk of stock in the Publishing Association paying a large per cent? If these are two branches of the same great closing work of preparation for the coming of the Son of man, why not? Or why not make them both matters of liberality? The pen and the voice that appealed to the friends of the cause in behalf of the publishing fund, held out no such inducements." Vol. 1, pages 633-36.

How do our institutions now measure with this straight testimony? Can we say they are *charitable, liberal, sacrificing, benevolent* institutions? Listen to the enormous profits they make. Presentment is here made of the annual report of St. Helena Sanitarium, as it appeared in the Pacific Union Recorder of April 25, 1929. "The notes payable at the end of 1925, were $60,044 (the cents are not here given). In 1926, they had been reduced to $49,031; in 1927, to $36,321; and at the close of 1928, they were down to $26,-415. In three years they were reduced from $60,000 to $33,629. Resources, fixed and current, at the close of 1928, $371,105. The liabilities $45,809. There is a decrease in the liabilities of nearly $5,000. Cash on hand at the close of 1928, $10,749. Present worth, $325,296. . . . The gross income, $456,258. The *net income, $437,284.* The average daily attendance of patients was 85 plus, and the income from patients direct, $261,363. The net gain $10,-439.39."

How could it be possible for an institution to do any charitable work at all, and yet earn $111,988 above its present worth in one single year? Note: Present worth, $325,296. *Net income,* $437,-284 in 1928. But this is not the worst. Our brethren have gone so blind that they think these enormous profits give them a wonderful credit for their wise management, and boast over it, and say that the sanitarium is facing sunshine. Truly our God knew what He was saying when He said the Laodiceans are blind, wretched, and miserable, and poor, and naked, though they think they are rich and increased with goods, and have need of nothing. See the contrast of boasting between the Laodiceans, and other institutions of whom some often think the devil is their leader. Following is the annual report of a mission in Los Angeles for the corresponding year, 1928: These items being given free of charge to the needy. "The annual report for the year ending Dec. 31, 1928, shows 527,481 meals served; 137,-287 lodgings furnished; laundry service, 53,334 pieces; barber service,

20,394; baths, 12,339; garments distributed, 32,541; 1791 shoes repaired; employment secured for 9,204 individuals; medical aid given to 3,117; while the chapel report shows that during the year 15,340 persons professed salvation in the daily meetings which are continuous from 11 A. M. to 11 P. M., and are conducted by groups from the churches of all denominations." (Copied from a Los Angeles newspaper.)

Is the devil become more charitable than Christ? Why have we gone to sleep? Is it dollars and cents that the Lord wants? Are these things not destroying the confidence of the public in the people of God? Are these things adding or detracting from the fruit of our labor? Are we representing God and carrying the third angel's message to a dying world? Is Christ our pattern and example? Why have we allowed the devil to deceive us? Is not this a call to arouse the people of God to a Christlike service? How long shall we stay asleep? It is bad enough for God's people to turn down one who is not in the faith from receiving the benefits of God at the hand of His people, but it is a thousand times worse to turn down one of Israel, he who would sacrifice and cast his lot with the people of God, faithful in tithe-paying and offerings as the Lord has prospered. If God should permit poverty to overtake such a one with sickness or old age, what do we do with them? Do we send them away and tell them, God bless thee? Is the county hospital for God's people, and God's hospitals for money-making? Is the county farm for God's people, there with the ungodly, and with the unclean on their table as we believe from a religious standpoint, amidst profanity, swine, and tobacco? Is this the kind of place for the child of God, and the temple of the Holy Ghost according to our faith? What kind of answer will we give Him when He comes? Will we hear the words, "Well done, good and faithful servant," as we read in Matt. 25:35, 36? "For I was an hungered, and ye gave me meat: I was thirsty, and ye gave me drink: I was a stranger, and ye took me in: Naked, and ye clothed me: I was sick, and ye visited me: I was in prison, and ye came unto me." Shall this saying be ours, or will we find ourselves at the left hand with the terrible curse as in verses 41-43, 46: "Depart from me, ye cursed, into everlasting fire, prepared for the devil and his angels: For I was an hungered, and ye gave me no meat: I was thirsty, and ye gave me no drink: I was a stranger, and ye took me not in: naked, and ye clothed me not: sick, and in prison, and ye visited me not. And these shall go away into everlasting punishment but the righteous into life eternal."

Quoting Volume 1, page 639: "As early as 1850 this brother became a Sabbath-keeper, and from that date he contributed liberally to the several enterprises that have been undertaken to advance the cause, till he became reduced in property. Yet when the urgent, unqualified call came for the Institute, he took stock to the amount of one hundred dollars. At the meeting at ——— he introduced the case of his wife, who is very feeble, and who can be helped, but must be helped soon, if ever. He also stated his circumstances, and said that if he could command the one hundred dollars then in the Institute, he could send his wife there to be treated; but as it was, he could not. We replied that he should never have invested a dollar in the Institute, that there was a wrong in the matter which we could not help; and there the matter dropped. I do not hesitate to say that this sister should be treated, a few weeks at least, at the Institute *free* of charge. Her husband is able to do but little more than to pay her fare to and from Battle Creek." Do we have such cases as these at the present time? Do we deal with these people like some farmer deals with his horse? He takes good care of the horse while it is young and doing his work, but when the animal gets old and feeble, he then drives it out in the open field in the winter weather, just at the time the poor horse needs the best of care. Are we not like this hard-hearted farmer who starves his horse in the winter weather, with the frost on the back of the worn-out animal, to save a few bundles of straw? Cruel, is it not? It is left to the reader to answer the question.

MIDWIVES

"But the more they afflicted them, the more they multiplied and grew. And they were grieved because of the children of Israel. And the king of Egypt spake to the Hebrew midwives, . . . And he said, When ye do the office of a midwife to the Hebrew women, . . . if it be a son, then ye shall kill him: But if it be a daughter, then she shall live." Ex. 1:12, 15, 16. The "midwives" symbolize the church school teachers, who nurse the children in the system of education. You may ask, Is it possible that the devil would attempt to deceive the teachers, and poison the children's minds? The devil is not leaving one string loose. Reference is here made to the Home and School Journal of Christian Education, of Dec., 1929, published by the General Conference of Seventh-day Adventists, Washington, D. C., and every teacher in the denomination is supposed to be a subscriber of this magazine. The above-mentioned issue is full of Christmas stories, Christmas-keeping, and Christmas programs and gifts, which the teachers are supposed to pass on to the children. As it would be too lengthy to quote it all, only the very last sentence, and the closing words under the paragraph "What Christmas May Always Mean" is quoted here: "And, in general, a baptism of reality, simplicity, and sincerity in the observance of the world's *supreme birthday."* Think of these words, dear reader. A Seventh-day Adventist paper, published by the General Conference, to exalt the world's supreme idolatrous day to a birthday of Christ, and hand it to the teachers of the denomination.

"But the midwives feared God, and did not as the king of Egypt commanded them, but saved the men children alive." Ex. 1:17. Here we have one good symbol, and let us say, Amen for the teachers. "They feared God." We urge you to send your children to the school of the denomination, for it is the best place for them. "The name of the one was Shiphrah, and the name of the other Puah." Verse 15. The meaning of these names are: "Beauty" and "splendor". Indeed it is. It would have been impossible for two midwives to wait on the great multitude of women, but the fact is, that there were only two. The reason for this is to make the symbol perfect, meaning both classes of teachers, male and female, "beauty" and "splendor".

MALE CHILDREN IN THE NILE

"Therefore God dealt well with the midwives: And the people multiplied, and waxed very mighty. Pharaoh charged all his people, saying, Every son that is born ye shall cast into the river, and every daughter ye shall save alive." Ex. 1:20, 22. The chief object of Pharaoh's scheme was not to reduce the people in number. Had this been his aim, he should have killed the female, for in those days they practiced polygamy. Had he given an order to cast the female children in the river, and save the males, he could have accomplished his purpose, and also added to his slaves for it was the men who produced the bricks. We read in Patriarchs and Prophets, page 242: "Satan was the mover in this matter. He knew that *a deliverer* was to be raised up among the Israelites; and by leading the king to destroy their children he hoped to defeat the divine purpose." This was the object of the whole affair. As this is a symbol, the application will now be made.

Testimonies to Ministers, page 475, under the chapter entitled "Let Heaven Guide", we read: "Prophecy must be fulfilled. The Lord says: 'Behold, I will send you Elijah the prophet before the coming of the great and dreadful day of the Lord.' Somebody *is to come* in the spirit and power of Elijah, *and when he appears, men may say:* "You are too earnest, you do not interpret the Scriptures in the proper way. Let me tell you how to teach your message." No plainer statement could have been made than this, that we must look for a prophet, or a message in the near future. If this is an inspired statement, then it seems it would be the duty of the watchmen on the walls of Zion to educate and instruct the people that there is a prophet, or a message, to look for. But what have we? On the contrary, the general opinion of the entire denomination is, "no prophet cometh, neither is there any message to be expected. We have all the truth, and we need none," is the cry from the camp of Israel. Thus we see how the old enemy has duplicated his underhand deception with the church at the present time. Just as Pharaoh was unconcious of the main purpose of his command, just so by the unconsciousness of the leaders, the shrewd deceiver has attempted to drown the prophet, or the message of reform for the present time. Thus it proves in every instance that the experience of Israel in Egypt is a photograph of Israel, the true. If a prophet, or even a message should come, the church is not ready to accept either. The result may be the same as it was with the Jewish nation and the coming of Christ. How terrible the thought. "While it seemed to the Egyptians in the interests of the empire to hold these people in bondage, the real purpose behind it all was the determination of Satan, the dragon power (Isa. 51 :9), to hold the people of Israel in the *bondage of sin,* and to *prevent the work of reform* to which God had set His hand as the time of the prophecy came." Review and Herald, January 23, 1930.

MALE CHILDREN OF DENOMINATION; HOW DROWNED

Has the devil drowned any of the male children in the river Nile at this time? Where are the men in this denomination? They must be in the river Nile, for it is a symbol of the sins in the world, and that is where we generally find the men; and the women in the church. The question may be asked, What sifted out the men? The Spirit of Prophecy teaches that we should see to it that employment is furnished to new comers in the truth, to make it possible for them to keep the Sabbath. Also to take care of the poor and sick among us. This instruction has been altogether disregarded, with the result that the men are sifted out of the church. Men love the truth as much as women do, but as soon as they hear the truth, they begin to inquire about things. Immediately the difficulty arises, and the question is asked, How can I keep the Sabbath, and yet hold my position? If I should let my position go, can I secure another? Would the church help me find something to do? Would the church render some assistance in case of great need, such as lack of food, clothing, or in case of sickness? All these questions are answered at once with, NO. The result is, the decision is made and the truth is turned down.

If the church had furnished some encouragement along these lines, this position would not have been taken by these newly interested parties, and the result would have been that the men as well as the women would have been in the church. Men being the wage earners, the increase of tithes and offerings cannot be estimated, and the little expenditure in helps would be but a fragment in comparison. Employment agency would be a great help to the denomination. Not only employment would have been secured from people outside of the organization, but the work among Adventists would be secured by Adventists. Thus the men are "cast" into the world ("Nile"), but the women left ("alive") in the church.

MOSES FOUND BY PRINCESS

Quoting Ex. 2:2, 3: "And the woman conceived, and bare a son: And when she saw him that he was a goodly child, she hid him three months. And when she could not longer hide him, she took for him an ark of bulrushes, and daubed it with slime and with pitch, and put the child therein; and she laid it in the flags by the river's brink." Providence lead the Egyptian princess to the river to wash herself, and after seeing the ark, she sent her maid to fetch it. She saw that the babe wept, and she had compassion on him. The sister of the babe stepped to Pharaoh's daughter, and said, "Shall I go and call to thee a nurse of the Hebrew women, that she may nurse the child for thee?" On the arrival of the child's mother, Pharaoh's daughter said, "Take this child away, and nurse it for me." And the child grew, and she brought him unto Pharaoh's daughter at the age of 12, and the princess named him "Moses". The lesson here is, with all the Satanic schemes, it would be impossible to defeat the divine purpose.

MOSES' CHOICE

As Moses (the type) received the highest education the courts
of Pharaoh could produce, after becoming of age he was compelled to
choose one of two things: either the throne of Egypt, or to suffer
affliction with the children of Israel. Just so, modern Moses (the
anti-type) receives the highest education the denomination can produce; (when of age) finished education, "professor".

Modern Moses as well being compelled to choose one of two
things: Either professor in the world (Egypt) with a large income,
fame, and the pleasures of sin for a season; or to work for the denomination with a small salary, and suffer affliction with the church
(the children of Israel). As Moses (the type) chose the latter, just
so Moses the anti-type prefers to stay with the denomination, "Es-
teeming the reproach of Christ greater riches than the treasures of
Egypt". The statistics of the movement so we are told, show that
90% of the children who go to schools of the denomination remain
true to the message. This proves the *lesson* taught here is correct.

MOSES' MISCONCEPTION

"And it came to pass in those days, when Moses was grown, that
he went out unto his brethren, . . . and he spied an Egyptian smiting
an Hebrew . . . . he slew the Egyptian, and hid him in the sand. And
when he went out the second day, behold, two men of the Hebrews
strove together: And he said to him that did the wrong, Wherefore
smitest thou thy fellow? And he said, Who made thee a prince and
a judge over us? intendest thou to kill me, as thou killest the Egyptian? And Moses feared. . . . But Moses fled from the face of
Pharaoh, and dwelt in the land of Midian." Ex. 2:11-15.

Moses supposed he was to deliver the children of Israel by force
of arms, therefore he rolled up his sleeves, and went about his duty.
Moses' misconception of the method to be used in the deliverance of
Israel was not the only thing wrong with the man. If that was the
way he understood Israel was to obtain their freedom, he failed to
carry out the plan. His trouble was not because of lack of education, or training as a general of armies, that he failed to carry out his

project, but because he was too cowardly and feared Pharaoh. If this was not the cause of his failure, why then kill only one Egyptian, bury him in the sand, and after it was made known, run away and leave Israel to perish in slavery? If his intention, or understanding, was to lead Israel against the armies of Egypt, he should not have hidden the Egyptian in the sand, but left him upon the ground for an example, and then go after others. Failing to carry out his proposed scheme, Moses made a double mistake.

This ancient Moses is a symbol of modern Moses (present leadership). As Moses' failure was not because of lack of training, but because of a misconceived idea of the method to be carried out, just so with the leadership now. As Moses failed to accomplish his own mistaken plan (what he supposed was wise judgment), just so the leadership have now failed on their part. The aim has been to finish the work in this generation which is practically past, and at the rate of speed the work is going now, it could not be finished in another 100 years. "We are in danger of trusting to methods, organization, and high-pressure service, which if taken alone, can, in the end, result only in confusion, dissatisfaction, and defeat." Review and Herald, Feb. 20, 1930.

THE APPLICATION OF THE TYPE

If Pharaoh is the king, the one (the leadership) who rules over the people, then the church is the "queen". If the church is the queen, then the "princess" is the church school. Egypt is a symbol of the world, and the Nile a symbol of the sins of the world. By the aid of the God-fearing mother, Moses (the type) was not cast into the river Nile. Just so with modern Moses, who, by the help of his Christian mother is saved from the river Nile (the sin in the world), but when she can not keep him any longer, and must send him to the schools of the land where sin reigns, the church school (the "princess") finds him. As Moses (the type) received his education by the aid of the princess, just so modern Moses receives *his* education by the aid of the church school.

We, like Moses, have thought that *we* are to deliver Israel by force of arms (the aid of men). Like Moses, we are too cowardly to accomplish anything. It has been said by a good minister of God, "This is wrong in the church, and that is not right, and should be corrected, but we can not do it." Why? Because he is afraid he will lose his job. But what shall we do? Work for God and trust in Him, or work for Pharaoh and trust in the job?

Quoting Volume 5, pages 80-82: "But the days of purification of the church are hastening on apace. God will have a people pure and true. In the mighty sifting soon to take place, we shall be better able to measure the strength of Israel. The signs reveal that the time is near when the Lord will manifest that His fan is in His hand, and He will thoroughly purge His floor. . . . Those who have trusted to intellect, genius, or talent, *will not* then stand at the head of rank and file. They did not keep pace with the *light.* Those who have proved themselves unfaithful will not then be entrusted with the flock. In the last solemn work *few* great men will be engaged. They are *self-sufficient,* independent of God, and He cannot use them. The Lord *has* faithful servants, who in the shaking, testing time *will* be disclosed to view. There *are* precious ones now hidden who have not bowed the knee to Baal. They have not had the light which has been shining in a concentrated blaze upon you. But, it may be under a rough and uninviting exterior the pure brightness of a genuine Christian character will be revealed. . . . *In this time,* the gold will be *separated* from the dross in the church. . . . Many a star that we have admired for its brilliancy, *will then go out in darkness. . . . The most weak* and hesitating in the church *will* be as David—willing to do and dare. . . . *Then* will the church of Christ appear 'fair as the moon, clear as the sun, and terrible as an army with banners' . . . . God will work a work in our day that but few anticipate. He will raise up and exalt among us those who are taught rather by the unction of His Spirit, *than* by the outward *training* of *scientific institutions.* These facilities are not to be despised or condemned; they are ordained of God, but they can furnish *only* the exterior qualifications. God *will* manifest that He is not dependent on *learned, self-important* mortals."

"But Moses fled from the face of Pharaoh, and dwelt in the land of Midian. . . . And the priest of Midian . . . . gave Moses Zipporah his daughter to wife. . . . Now Moses kept the flock of Jethro his father-in-law, the priest of Midian: And he led the flock to the backside of the desert, and came to the mountain of God [Horeb], . . . and, behold, the bush burned with fire and the bush was not consumed. And Moses said, I will now turn aside, and see this great sight, why the bush is not burned. . . . God called unto him out of the midst of the bush, and said, Moses, Moses. And he said, Here am I. . . . And the Lord said, I have surely seen the affliction of my people which are in Egypt, ... And I am come down to deliver them out of the hand of the Egyptians, . . . Come now therefore, and I will send thee unto Pharaoh, that thou mayest bring forth my people the children of Israel out of Egypt. And Moses said unto God, Who am I, that I should go unto Pharaoh, . . . And Moses said unto the Lord, O my Lord, I am not eloquent, neither heretofore, nor since thou hast spoken unto thy servant: But I am slow of speech, and of a slow tongue. 'I am of uncircumcised lips, and how shall Pharaoh hearken unto me?' And the Lord said unto him, Who hath made man's mouth? or who maketh the dumb, or deaf, or the seeing, or the blind? Have not I the Lord? Now therefore go, and I will be with thy mouth, and teach thee what thou shalt say. . . . And the Lord said unto him, What is that in thine hand? And he said, A rod. And he said, Cast it on the ground. And he cast it on the ground, and it became a serpent; and Moses fled from before it. And the Lord said unto Moses, Put forth thine hand and take it by the tail. And he put forth his hand, and caught it, and it became a rod in his hand. . . . And he said, O my Lord, send, I pray thee, by the hand of him whom thou wilt send. And the anger of the Lord was kindled against Moses." Read Ex. 2:15 to 4:13.

APPLICATION OF THE LESSON

This last Moses is *the unlearned* Moses. Note, he is *slow of speech,* has *no eloquence,* is of *a slow tongue,* and *"uncircumcised lips"* (untrained). He knows not how to approach Pharaoh. He shrinks with the thought of standing before the great monarch, like the mercury shrinks from the north wind, but though this Moses is handicapped, he has *nerve;* he is not a coward. He risks his life, for he was asked only once to take that fabulous serpent by the tail, and he did so. This Moses is not a crown prince, but a common shepherd only. The shepherd Moses is a type of men who are to bring about reformation and be used in the time of the "Loud Cry", brought to view in the following quotations. Quoting Life Sketches, page 245: "God *is* putting burdens upon more inexperienced shoulders. He is fitting them to be caretaking, to venture, to run risks also." Volume 5, page 82: "He *will* raise up and exalt among us those who are taught rather by the unction of His Spirit, than by the outward training of scientific institutions."

Testimonies to Ministers, page 300: *"Unless* those who can help in—are aroused to a sense of their duty, they *will not* recognize the work of God when the loud cry of the third angel shall be heard. When light goes forth to lighten the earth, instead of coming up to the help of the Lord, they will want to bind about His work to meet their narrow ideas. Let me tell you that the Lord *will* work in this last work in a manner very much out of the common order of things, and in a way that will be *contrary* to *any* human planning. *There will be* those among us who will always *want* to control the work of God, to *dictate* even what movements shall be made when the work goes forward under the direction of the angel who joins the third angel in the message to be given to the world. God will use ways and means by which it *will* be seen that *He is taking* the reins in His *own* hands. The workers will be *surprised* by the *simple* means that *He will* use to bring about and *perfect* His work of righteousness. Those who are accounted good workers *will need* to draw nigh to God, they will need the divine touch." Also read Isaiah 3. "It is *not* men of great *talents* and *titles* that are needed so much as it is men who are *great* in *faith, holiness, consecration,* and *love.* Men who are great for God and great in simplicity, fidelity, and self-denial,—*upon such transmitting* God's message, life, and blessings to humanity, and for advancing His kingdom in *all* the earth." Review and Herald, Feb. 20, 1930.

The Shepherd's Rod

The Spirit of Prophecy says in Patriarchs and Prophets, page 251, that the *rod* of Moses was a *symbol of God's power.* The shepherd's rod: Power of God; the sheep: God's people; the shepherd's rod is an instrument which is used to catch sheep. The rod in this instance is an instrument which is used to catch people. What could it be? It can not be anything else but some wonderful, plain, clear-cutting Bible truth which could not be contradicted. When it is revealed, it will produce serpents (people), or converts, by reformation. But the Egyptians did the same also, for they cast down every man his rod, and they became serpents, and perhaps more in number, for every man cast his rod, but they were counterfeit. Symbols of hypocrisy (untrue Christians); but Moses' rod swallowed the rods of the Egyptians. Symbol of victory for true Israel. The result is opposition, but true Israel wins at last.

In Volume 5, page 696 we read: "They did not really cause their rods to become serpents, but by magic, aided by the great deceiver, made them appear like serpents, to counterfeit the work of God." Symbol of an outward appearance of Christianity by Seventh-day Adventists. But one may say, What? God's people symbolized by a serpent? Why not by sheep? If the meek and lowly Christ was symbolized by the brazen serpent in the wilderness which Moses raised up for the children of Israel to look upon, and be healed from bites of the fiery serpents, then God's people could be symbolized by a serpent as well. If the rod would have turned into a sheep it would have spoiled the symbol, for the 144,000 are not to be sheep in the sheep-fold and cared for by an earthly shepherd, but the opposite. For this reason the serpent is used as a symbol, meaning wise; cannot be frightened (would not run away from anything: The opposite of sheep). They are to be filled with the Holy Spirit, proclaim the message and triumph with victory. "And the remnant of Jacob shall be in the midst of *many people* as a dew from the Lord, as the showers upon the grass, that tarrieth not for man, nor waiteth for the sons of men. And the remnant of Jacob shall be among the Gentiles in the midst of many people *as a lion* among the beasts of the forest, as a young lion among the flocks of sheep: Who, if he go through, both treadeth down, and teareth in pieces, and none can deliver." Micah 5:7, 8.

Death of Firstborn

"And Moses said, Thus saith the Lord, About midnight will I go out into the midst of Egypt: And all the firstborn in the land of Egypt shall die, from the firstborn of Pharaoh that sitteth upon his throne, even unto the firstborn of the maidservant that is behind the mill; and all the firstborn of beasts." Ex. 11:4, 5. "And it came to pass, that at midnight the Lord smote all the firstborn in the land of Egypt, from the firstborn of Pharaoh that sat on his throne unto the firstborn of the captive that was in the dungeon; and all the firstborn of cattle . . . . and there was a great cry in Egypt: For there was not a house where there was not one dead." Ex. 12:29, 30.

The firstborn, a symbol of a class of priesthood, a representation of Ezekiel 9:6, last part, "the ancient men that were before the house." "From the firstborn that sitteth upon the throne to the firstborn in the dungeon," symbol of Eze. 9:6: "Slay utterly old and young, both maids, and little children, and women: . . . Then they began at the ancient men which were before the house." "The firstborn of cattle" symbol of Isa. 63:18 and 64:1; Num. 26:10.

"In the case of Achan's sin, God said to Joshua, 'Neither will I be with you any more, except ye destroy the accursed from among you.' How does this instance compare with the course pursued by those *who will not* raise their voice *against sin and wrong,* but whose sympathies are ever found with those who *trouble* the camp of Israel with their sins? Said God to Joshua, 'Thou *canst not* stand before thine enemies, *until* ye take away the *accursed* thing from among you.' He pronounced the punishment which would follow the transgression of his covenant. . . . And Joshua, and all Israel with him, took Achan the son of Zerah, and the silver, and the garment, and the wedge of gold, and *his sons,* and his *daughters,* and his *oxen,* and his *asses,* and his *sheep,* and his *tent,* and *all* that he had; and they brought them unto the valley of Achor. And Joshua said, Why hast thou troubled us? The Lord shall trouble thee this day. And all Israel stoned him with stones, and burned them with fire after they had stoned them with stones." Volume 3, pages 267-8.

"And the Lord spake unto Moses, saying, Sanctify unto me all the firstborn, whatsoever openeth the womb among the children of Israel, both of man and of beast; *it is mine."* Ex. 13:1, 2. A symbol of a new priesthood, and the firstborn of cattle representing a system of support, or maintenance. "Should a case like Achan's be among us, there are many who would accuse those who might act the part of Joshua in searching out the wrong, of having a wicked, faultfinding spirit. God is not to be troubled with, and His warnings disregarded with impunity by a perverse people." Volume 3, page 270.

THE PASSOVER LAMB

"Speak ye unto all the congregation of Israel, saying, In the tenth day of this month they shall take to them every man a lamb, according to the house of their fathers, a lamb for an house: . . . And ye shall keep it up until the fourteenth day of the same month: And the whole assembly of the congregation of Israel shall kill it in the evening. And they shall take of the blood, and strike it on the two side posts and on the upper door post of the houses, wherein they shall eat it. . . . And thus shall ye eat it; with your loins girded, your shoes on your feet, and your staff in your hand; and ye shall eat it in haste: It is the Lord's passover. . . . And the blood shall be to you for a token upon the houses where ye are: And when I see the blood,

I will pass over you, and the plague shall not be upon you to destroy you, when I smite the land of Egypt." Ex. 12:3-13.

"All the ceremonies of the feast were types of the work of Christ. The deliverance of Israel from Egypt was an object-lesson of redemption, which the Passover was intended to keep in memory. The slain lamb, the unleavened bread, the sheaf of firstfruits, represented the Saviour." Desire of Ages, page 77.

The lamb represents Christ. Isa. 53:7.

The lamb roasted by *fire,* the Spirit of God. Gen. 15:17; Acts 2:3; Lev. 9:24.

The eating of the flesh: Christ is our life, for "in Him we live, and move, and have our being." John 6:53.

The loins girded: The truth of God, the Word. Eph. 6:14.

The shoes on the feet: The preparation of the gospel. Eph. 6:15.

The staff in the hand: The sword of the Spirit. Eph. 6:17.

Ye shall eat it in haste: Do not hestitate; get ready; quick delivery. Ex. 12:11.

Ex. 12:34, "And the people took their dough before it was leavened, their kneading-troughs being *bound up in their clothes* upon their shoulders."

The kneading-trough is the Bible. Eph. 6:13.

The dough is the word of God it contains. Eze. 44:30 (the type).

Unleavened: The unadulterated word of God, and it must be kept as such. Rev. 22:18.

The kneading-troughs on their shoulders: Means make sure you have the whole Word of God continually with you. Thus shall you depart from Egypt. Eph. 6:13. "The bondage in Egypt represents the *bondage* of *sin.* The promises of deliverance are the promises of the gospel. The power revealed in the judgments upon the gods of Egypt indicates the measure of power provided for the deliverance from the hard service of *'the god of this world'.''* Review and Herald. Jan. 23, 1930.

The *blood* on the door post is the symbol of the "seal", Revelation 7; "mark," Ezekiel 9 (Rev. 7 and Eze. 9, is the same mark or seal). See Testimonies to Ministers, page 445.

The blood being applied on the *door post* is to signify that the seal, or mark by which the 144,000 are to be sealed, is to be visible.

The "door post" and the "forehead" both have the same significance. We do not mean to say that it is a certain visible brand, or mark on their foreheads, but a "seal" of character, principal, or rule; the standard being the pure Word of God. Thus they apply the blood on the door post, and their brethren in the church could be conscious of a change.

The only ones who can have the seal are those who sigh and cry for all the abominations (sins) that are done *in the church.* But if any take part and try to throw a cloak over the existing evil in the church, then they are left without the seal. Read Volume 5, pages 207-12; Volume 3, page 266.

THE RED SEA

The Red Sea symbolizes Isaiah 63. Edom means "red". "Edom" is Esau, the twin brother of Jacob. His name was changed to Edom because he sold his birthright for a bowl of *"red pottage"*, and Esau himself was *red*, therefore, we have *Red Sea, red man, red pottage.* Read Esau and Jacob, Section 3.

"Sea", a symbol of "people". Rev. 17:15.

Pharaoh and his host: The chief instigators against reformation. "Egypt had developed an intricate ecclesiastical organization. It was *proud* of its religious institutions; it *despised* this people Israel who did not worship according to the *popular* religion, and who *now*, under the message of *reform* preached by Moses, were taking their stand yet *more fully* to represent the truth and the law of Jehovah." Review and Herald, Jan. 23, 1930.

Bozrah: sheep-fold (the church). Micah 2:12; Isa. 34:6.

Edomites: Those who sold their birthright to gratify appetite. They make their stomachs their god; violators of health reform. For further explanation see page 156, under heading "Afflicted for His

People's Sake". "The bondage in Egypt represents the bondage of *sin.* The promises of deliverance are the promises of the gospel. The power revealed in the judgments upon the gods of Egypt indicates the measure of power provided for the deliverance from the hard service of "the god of this world." The glorious triumph at the Red Sea *foreshadows* the victory which is assured to every trusting child of God." Review and Herald, Jan. 23, 1930.

Mount Sinai

"In the third month, when the children of Israel were gone forth out of the land of Egypt, the same day came they into the wilderness of Sinai." . . . "And God spake all these words, saying, I am the Lord thy God, which have brought thee out of the land of Egypt, out of the house of bondage. Thou shalt have no other gods before Me." Ex. 19:1; 20:1-3. Here is where the 430 years ended, beginning with Abraham going out of Ur. Patriarchs and Prophets, page 760. Here is where Moses organized a church, when he appointed seventy elders, and where God spoke to the people Himself. The experience at Sinai is a symbol of re-organization of the church,—God Himself takes charge of the flock. We read in Volume 5, page 80: "We have been inclined to think that where there are no faithful ministers, there can be no true Christians; but this is not the case. God has promised that where the shepherds are not true he *will take charge of the flock himself.* God has never made the flock wholly dependent upon human instrumentalities. But the days of purification of the church are hastening on apace. God will have a people pure and true. In the mighty sifting soon to take place, we shall be better able to measure the strength of Israel."

New Name Given To Church

"And unto the angel of the church of the Laodiceans writes; . . . I know thy works, that thou art neither cold nor hot: I would thou wert cold or hot. So then because thou art lukewarm, and neither cold nor hot, *I will spue* thee out of my mouth." Rev. 3:14-

16. Note that the existence of the present name—"Seventh-day Adventist" is conditional, otherwise the name will be spued out of His mouth. "And the Gentiles shall see thy righteousness, and all kings thy glory: And thou shalt be *called* by a *new name,* which the *mouth of the Lord shall name."* Isa. 62:2. "And ye shall leave your name for a curse unto my chosen [the 144,000]: For the Lord God *shall slay thee,* and call his servants by *another* name." Isa. 65:15. Read Testimonies to Ministers, page 300.

This is where Isaiah's prophecy in chapter 52:1, will be fulfilled: "Awake, awake; put on thy strength, O Zion; put on thy beautiful garments, O Jerusalem, the holy city: For henceforth there shall *no more* come unto thee the uncircumcised and the unclean." Also read Isaiah 4. Zeph. 3:13, "The remnant of Israel *shall not* do iniquity, nor speak lies; *neither* shall a deceitful tongue be found in their mouth: For they shall feed and lie down, and none shall make them afraid."

"The remnant of Israel will not do iniquity." This prophecy has never yet met its fulfillment in the history of the church, for there have always been the unclean in the midst of her; but let us thank God for this generous promise. The scroll is making a turn. Shall we pray to God that we fall not out by the way in making the bend? "Clad in the armor of Christ's righteousness, the church is to enter upon her final conflict. 'Fair as the moon, clear as the sun, and terrible as an army with banners,' she is to go forth into all the world, conquering and to conquer." Prophets and Kings, page 725.

WHAT IS THE NUMBER OF ISRAEL?

It has been made clear that Israel after the flesh is a photograph of Israel by the promise. In the exodus movement, all the tribes went out of Egypt. If this is a photograph of Israel by the promise, then all the twelve tribes must come out now as well. Twelve tribes must escape the ruin of Ezekiel 9 (death of the firstborn), and Isaiah 63 (The Red Sea). The number of them is said to be 12,000 from each tribe, making a total of 144,000. For the reason that they have passed through a similar experience as ancient Israel, they (the 144,000) sing a new song of Moses and the Lamb. "Then he remembered the days of old, Moses, and his people, saying, Where is he that brought them up out of the sea with the shepherd of his flock? Where is he that put his holy Spirit within him? That led them by the right hand of Moses with his glorious arm, dividing the water before them, to make himself an everlasting name? That led them through the deep, as an horse in the wilderness, that they should not stumble? As a beast goeth down into the valley, the Spirit of the Lord caused him to rest: So didst thou lead thy people, to make thyself a glorious name." Isa. 63:11-14. This Scripture can not refer to another company than the one we speak of.

WHAT CONSTITUTES THE REMNANT?

The definition of "remnant" is: That which is left after the separation, removal, or destruction of a part. (Standard Dictionary). The beginning of the church of Christ in the days of the apostles was *not* a large "bolt" just starting to unroll, getting smaller and smaller down through the ages, and now, being at the end of the history of the church be the smallest portion, or that which is left. But, on the contrary, the church just began then to roll on, and had but a very small beginning. It has been rolling and rolling, and putting on all through the ages, and the *very end* of the *history* of the *church* is by no means a remnant. "Remnant" signifies a very small portion, a fragment, or a small bit. The Master said the harvest is at the end of the world; the angels are the reapers. Then there is reaping to be done. "Harvest" means a collection of crops; to gather, store up, or garner in. According to this the harvest is by no means a remnant, but just the opposite, for at harvest we gather in the most.

The remnant of Israel must be something else than what we have thought it to be, for "remnant" is a small portion, or part which is left after a destruction. The destruction is the mighty shaking, sifting time which is the separation of the two classes in the church (the sealing of the 144,000) as prophesied in Ezekiel 9, and Isaiah 63. Those who escape are the "remnant". The Bible gives no other definition of "remnant" than the one given here. See Lev. 5:13; 2 Kings 19:4; Isa. 37:4; Ezra 9:8; Isa. 1:9; 11:11; 16:14; Jer. 44:28; Eze. 6:8; Joel 2:32; Rom. 11:5; Rev. 11:13.

In the eleventh chapter of Isaiah, is recorded the same incident we have tried to explain here. In the eleventh verse we read of the remnant which we speak of: "And it shall come to pass in that day, that the Lord shall set his hand again the *second time* to recover the remnant of His people, which shall be *left."* Isa. 11:11. Early Writings, page 270: "I asked the meaning of the shaking I had seen, and was shown that it would be caused by the *sraight* testimony called forth by the counsel of the True Witness to the Laodiceans. This will have its effect upon the heart of the receiver, and will lead him to exalt the standard and pour forth the straight truth. Some *will not* bear this straight testimony. They *will rise* up against it, and *this is* what will cause a shaking among God's people."

Isa. 11:12, first part: "And he shall set up an *ensign* for the nations." Again we read in Isa. 66:19, "And I will set a sign among them, and I will send *those that escape* of them unto the nations." The 63rd chapter has the same reference as Isaiah 59, part of verse 19, is here quoted: *"So* shall they fear the name of the Lord from the west, and his glory from the rising of the sun." The "sign" is extensive from the east to the west, and has a meaning for the entire world. The "destruction" is the "sign" and example to the nations, and the "remnant" are those who are left (the 144,000). Following this we have the "Loud Cry" (the harvest): "Those who come up to every point, and stand every test, and overcome, *be the price what it may,* have heeded the counsel of the True Witness, and *they* will receive the latter rain, and *thus* be fitted for translation." Vol. 1, page 187. "But he said, Nay; lest while ye gather up the tares, ye root up also the wheat with them. Let both grow together *until* the harvest: And *in* the time of harvest I will say to the reapers, Gather ye together *first* the *tares,* and bind them in bundles to burn them: But gather the wheat into my barn." Matt. 13:29, 30.

The same thought is also supported in Patriarchs and Prophets, page 541: "The feast of Tabernacles was not only commemorative, but typical. It not only pointed back to the wilderness sojourn, but, as the feast of harvest, it celebrated the ingathering of the fruits of the earth, and pointed forward to the great day of final ingathering, when the Lord of the harvest shall send forth his reapers to gather the tares together in bundles for the fire, and to gather the wheat into his garner. At that time the wicked will all be destroyed." (Those outside the church.)

Note that the separation takes place just at the beginning of harvest; also that the tares are gathered in *first*. The separation marks the beginning of harvest. The harvest is the loud cry of the third angel's message. (Rev. 18:1). In this time of harvest the great multitude (of Rev. 7:9) with the palms in their hands is gathered. While this great multitude is being made up and gathered into His barn, the reapers are binding the wicked in bundles (separated, or kept apart from the church) for the wrath of God. See Rev. 14:19.

Cloud By Day—Fire By Night

"And the Lord went before them by day in a pillar of a cloud, to lead them the way; and by night in a pillar of fire, to give them light; to go by day and night: He took not away the pillar of the cloud by day, nor the pillar of fire by night, from before the people." [It was not Moses that lead Israel out of Egypt, but the pillar of cloud that went before the people.] "And the Lord went before them . . . . to lead them in the way . . . to go by day and by night. He took not away the pillar . . . . from before the people." Ex. 13:21, 22. According to 1 Cor. 10:4, in this pillar of cloud by day and pillar of fire by night was Christ Himself: "And did all drink the same spiritual drink: for they drank of that spiritual Rock that followed them: And that Rock was Christ." Thus, we see that the Lord lead out Israel Himself, and not Moses. The people as well as Moses followed the cloud. All Moses did was to convey to the people the words and instructions received from the Lord.

This is the experience of Israel after the flesh, which we call a photograph of Israel by promise. If this is true, then the 144,000 must experience the same in departing out from worldlings (Egypt). Volume 5, page 80: "God has promised that where the shepherds are not true he will take *charge of the flock Himself."* Patriarchs and Prophets, page 283: "In one of the most beautiful and comforting passages of Isaiah's prophecy, reference is made to the pillar of cloud and of fire to represent God's care for His people in the great final struggle with the powers of evil: 'The Lord will create upon every dwelling place of Mount Zion, and upon her assemblies, a cloud and smoke by day, and the shining of a flaming fire by night; for above all the glory shall be a covering. And there shall be a tabernacle for a shadow in the daytime from the heat, and for a place of refuge, and for a covert from storm and from rain'." Thus, the idea of Israel being a photograph is supported by both the Bible and the Spirit of Prophecy.

JOSEPH, TYPE OF CHRIST

Joseph stands as a perfect type of Christ. First of all, the name "Joseph" means "he shall add". So Christ added the human family to the heavenly. Had any sin been recorded against Joseph, it would have spoiled the type, for Christ is not a sinner. Joseph was loved by his father *above all his brethren.* Of Christ we read in Heb. 1:9, "Thou hast loved righteousness, and hated iniquity; therefore God, even thy God, hath annointed thee with the oil of gladness *above* thy *fellows."*

Joseph was sent down into Egypt to preserve the lives of his brethren in the seven years of famine. Just so, Christ descended to preserve the lives of His brethren in this world of sin, in A. D.

Joseph was *sold* to Ishmaelites who were the descendants of *Ishmael, Abraham's seed* after the flesh. Just so, Christ was *sold* to priests, the *descendants* of *Abraham,* (Israel after the flesh).

Joseph was a *governor,* and no man could lift hand or foot, in all the land of Egypt, without the knowledge of Joseph. Just so,

Christ is a *governor* over the world (Egypt), and no man can lift hand or foot without the knowledge of Christ.

As there was only *one above* Joseph, namely Pharaoh, just so, there is only *one above* Christ: God, the Father.

Joseph was *30 years* old when he became governor; Christ was *30 years* of age when annointed.

As Joseph married the daughter of an *idolatrous* priest, just so, Christ marries His church which is made up of *idolatrous* nations.

As Joseph gathered the corn in the seven years of *plenty* into the storehouses to feed the world in the seven years of *famine,* just so, Christ gathered the Word of God in the *Old Testament* time into the great storehouse (the Bible) to feed the world in the *New Testament* time. One may say, The New Testament came in A. D. True, but the New Testament is only the fulfillment of the Old.

Had not Joseph become a governor of Egypt *before* the beginning of the seven years of plenty, it would have spoiled the significance, and the type would not then have indicated that Christ ruled *before* the world's history began. Thus we see Joseph is a perfect type of Christ.

Pharaoh, Type of Leaders

The Pharaoh who honored Joseph is a perfect type of the earthly head of the church of the apostles. Had Pharaoh not been an *Egyptian* it would have spoiled the type. Egypt, a symbol of the world, signifies an earthly leadership taken out of the world. Had not Pharaoh honored Joseph *above every man* in Egypt, or had he not commanded the Egyptians to go *to Joseph* for corn, it would have spoiled the symbol of the church leadership in the days of the apostles, for they *exalted* and *honored Christ above every man* in the entire world, also *commended* the Gentiles *to Christ as their life giver.*

If the *first* Pharaoh makes a perfect type of the church leadership in the days of the apostles, then we must accept the *last* Pharaoh who knows not Joseph, as a perfect type of the church leadership who have turned from following Christ, their Leader. Volume 5, page

217: "The church has turned back *from following Christ,* her Leader, and is steadily retreating *toward Egypt."* Thus Israel the true (the 144,000) became slaves under Egyptian bondage (the sins in the world). "The bondage in Egypt represents the bondage of *sin."* Review and Herald, Jan. 23, 1930. "And the *harp,* and the *viol,* the *tabret,* and *pipe,* and *wine,* are in their *feasts:* But they regard *not* the work of the Lord, *neither* consider the operation of his hands. Therefore my people are gone into *captivity,* because they have *no* knowledge: and their *honorable* men are famished, and their multitude *dried* up with thirst." Isa. 5:12, 13.

Israel being a type of this Advent movement is *not* a *new* idea just thought of in this lesson. The whole denomination believes so, for we read in the Review and Herald of Oct. 10, 1929, the following statements: "While the *exodus* movement was a great movement, the second *advent* movement will be still greater. God will take out a people, not from one nation only, but from every nation under heaven, and He will lead them into the heavenly Canaan. *This advent movement,* of which the exodus movement *was a type, we believe* was foretold in prophecy in the following stirring language: 'It shall come to pass in *that day,* that the Lord shall set His hand *again the second time* to recover the *remnant* of His people, which shall be *left,'* 'There shall be a *highway* for the remnant of His people; . . . *like* as it was to Israel in the day that he came up out of the land of *Egypt.'* Isa. 11:16."

The word "type" means the same as the word "photograph". The very first photo invented was called "tin *type".* Thus we have the approval of the denomination that "Israel after the flesh" is a *photograph* of Israel by the promise (the 144,000). As God called out Israel from Egypt anciently, just so now, God is calling His church out from worldlings and worldliness, to be a *separate, peculiar* people to His honor and glory. This does not mean another movement, but it does mean that God is to deal with the entire body, and those who escape are Israel, the 144,000.

Quoting Review and Herald, May 1, 1930: "Every evil thing

must be shaken from the movement. So it was in the exodus movement. When there was sin among the people, the Lord *did not* give
up that movement which He had brought out of Egypt and start
another one. He *did not* call the believers *out,* but He shook *unbelief out* of the movement [by destruction causing their death]. He
purified it by setting aside from it every element that *did not belong*
with the movement that *He* was leading according to His promise.
On one pretext or another, unbelief and disorder *moved out,* while
the movement itself *marched on."*

    If the exodus movement is a photograph of the true, then the
430 year period connected with ancient Israel must be considered with
the one now.

THE 430 YEARS OF SOJOURNING AND AFFLICTION

    The 430 year period of sojourning and affliction with Abraham,
Isaac, and Israel, which dates with Abraham going out of Ur, coincides with our time from the Reformation by Luther, to the sealing of
Israel by the promise (the 144,000). Quoting Patriarchs and
Prophets, page 760: "The actual time spent in Egypt could have
been only about 215 years. The Bible says that *'the sojourning of*
the children of Israel' was 430 years. Abraham, Isaac, and Jacob,
the ancestors of the Israelites, were sojourners *in Canaan.* The
period of 430 years dates from the promise given to Abraham when
he was commanded to *leave Ur* of the Chaldees. The 400 years of
Gen. 15:13 dates from a *later* period. Notice that the period of 400
years is not only a time of *sojourning,* but of *affliction.* This, according to the Scriptures, must be reckoned from *thirty years later,* about
the time when Ishmael, 'he that was born after the flesh, *persecuted*
him [Isaac] that was born after the Spirit.' Gal. 4:29."

    Paul, in Gal. 3:15-17, says that from the making of the cove-
nant with Abraham to the giving of the law at Sinai was 430 years.
From these Scriptures then, we are not to understand that the Israelites were in Egypt 400 years. See Ex. 12:40. According to this,
the 430 years began with Abraham going out of Ur, and ended with

Mount Sinai. Consequently we have to take the entire period into consideration, beginning with Abraham, which has a definite time of certain existing conditions. At the beginning of the 430 years, idolatry prevailed everywhere: Abraham alone was called out. Such is the spiritual condition that marked the beginning of the prophetic period in its type. Just so the beginning of the time of the duplicate or antitype must be marked with a time of low spiritual condition. In the time of Martin Luther we have the exact reproduction of Abraham's experience, for in Luther's time spiritual darkness and idolatry prevailed everywhere. Abraham is a fitting figure of Luther.

Abraham was called of God by the *spoken* word, Luther by the *written*. Abraham is the father of *faith;* so is Luther. The doctrine taught by Luther was "the just shall live by *faith*". If this is true, then the 430 years in our time began with Luther. About 1500 A. D. Luther discovered in the library of the University of Urfurt, a *Latin Bible,* and found to his no small delight that it contained more than the excerpts in common use. Thus God, by His word, called Luther out of Papal Rome.

We have first, a period of 400 years, and then it was extended to 430 years. We therefore, have a 30 year period to deal with first. It has been stated that the 30 years ended about the time Ishmael persecuted Isaac. According to this, about the year 1530 A. D., something must have been brought forth. What took place in 1530? The Augsburg Confession: A document compiled by Luther which was presented by the Protestants at the Diet of Augsburg to the Emperor Charles V, and the Diet, and being signed by the protestant states was adopted as their creed, and who *protested* against the pope. This coincides with Sarah *protesting* against Agar and Ishmael when they departed from the house of Abraham, and the assurance of the covenant of promise that was made with Isaac. As Sarah protested against *Agar* and Ishmael, so Protestants protested against *papal rule.* This is just exactly what should have taken place in 1530 A. D. to fit the occurrence of the prophecy.

At the time Isaac was persecuted by Ishmael, he (Isaac) was

five years old, and at the time Jacob was born, Isaac was *60;* therefore, we add 55 years to 1530 which brings us to 1585 A. D. Explanation of this period will be given later. From the birth of Jacob to the time Israel went into Egypt was 130 years. Adding this number to 1585 gives us 1715 A. D. The explanation of this period also will be given later. From the time Israel went into Egypt to the *birth of Moses* was 135 years. Adding this to 1715 brings the total to 1850 A. D. This period is marked by the birth of Moses, which was a hope, a deliverer, for Israel.

What took place in 1850? The *first testimony* was written to the church and addressed "To Those Who Are Receiving the *Seal* of the Living God". Signed, E. G. White. Thus the *birth of Moses,* the hope of Israel after the flesh, coincides with the *birth of the first testimony* for the church, the *hope* of Israel by the promise, the 144,000. Thus we see a perfect harmony in the type with antitype. See Origin and Progress of Seventh-day Adventists, page 749.

Moses at the age of 40 years attempted to deliver Israel, and *failed.* Adding 40 years to 1850, we have 1890 A. D. What happened at this time? The following statement was made by Sister White in 1892: *"If* the people of God had gone to work as they should have gone to work right after the Minneapolis meeting in 1888, the world could have been warned *in two years* and the *Lord would have come."* General Conference Bulletin, 1892. (This reference was given us by a Seventh-day Adventist minister of Los Angeles, Calif.) About the same time (1890) National *Religious Liberty* was organized by the denomination. Thus the attempt and failure of Moses' experience to set freedom to Israel from Egyptian bondage coincides with organizing religious liberty, and God's people failed to do their duty. "National Religious Liberty Association organized July 21, 1889." Origin and Progress of S. D. A., page 752.

Forty years later Moses was called and sent back to Egypt and did set Israel *free* from the Egyptian *bondage.* Adding 40 to 1890 brings the total to 1930. This period should be marked by a reformation and purification of the church, fulfilling Malachi 3, and

Ezekiel 9. "And it *shall* come to pass in *that day,* that the Lord shall set his hand *again* the *second time* to *recover* the *remnant* of his people, which shall be *left.*" Isa. 11:11.

The two periods, 1585 and 1715, will now be explained. 1585 corresponds with the birth of Jacob, and 1715 corresponds with Israel going down into Egypt. The entering into Egypt with seventy souls typified the birth of Seventh-day Adventists, as explained on pages 73-4, but Seventh-day Adventism was not born until 1845. To get the truth of these two periods we must count back to the birth of Jacob, for it is a birth that we are dealing with. We have 130 years from the entrance into Egypt to the birth of Jacob, and 85 years from the birth of Jacob to Abraham's departure out of Ur. Therefore, we must go backwards and subtract the first 85 year period (from the going out of Ur to the birth of Jacob) from 1930 and we have 1845. Thus, we get the year of the birth of Seventh-day Adventists. Miss Ellen Harmon then had her *first* vision and it was about the *144,000* (Israel by the promise), and the *first* paper published then on the *Sabbath truth* was called "The *Hope* of Israel". See Origin and Progress of Seventh-day Adventists, page 749.

Now subtract the 130 year period (from the birth of Jacob to the entering into Egypt) from 1845 and we have 1715 A. D., the year which was marked by Israel going into Egypt. Thus, 1715, becomes the dividing line between Canaan and Egypt, just as Christ became the dividing line between B. C. and A. D. Note how it coincides on the chart. If these coincidents were divinely designed, then the beginning and ending of the prophecy as on the following chart, would be correct.

COINCIDENT CHART

TYPE   ANTI-TYPE

KING JAMES' CHRONOLOGY

Years B. C.	Years A. D.
The calling of Abraham. Beginning of the 430 year period. PP. 760, No. 6.................... 2126	The calling of Luther. Beginning of the 430 year period 1500
From departure out of Ur to persecution of Isaac was........ -30 and —— Sarah protested against him that was born after the flesh. Departure of Agar and Ishmael in 2096	From 1500 (call of Luther) was .... 30 to —— Adoption of Protestant creed a n d protesting to papal church in ·................................. 1530
From persecution of Isaac to the birth of Jacob was .... -55 —— Birth of Jacob in 2041	From adoption of Protestant creed to 1585 we have .... 55 1585 coincides with 1845 as —— explained below, by subtracting the number of years from the departure from Ur to the birth of Jacob—becoming the birth of S.D.A. See p. 111. E.W. pp. 13, 14 1585
Birth of Jacob to the entrance into Egypt was .... 130 —— Jacob enters into Egypt in 1911	Add to 1585 the typical .... 130 and we have the —— Dividing line between Canaan and Egypt. See last panel, also p. 111. Note there are 6 lines of numbers on either side of 1715
— — 1 — 7 — 1 — 5 — —	— — 1 — 7 — 1 — 5 — —
From the entrance into Egypt to the birth of Moses (hope of Israel) was .... 135 —— Date of Moses' birth (hope of Israel) was in 1776	From 1715 to the birth of the first testimony we have .... 135 The birth of the first testimony to the church addressed "To Those Who Are Receiving the Seal of the Living God," signed "E. G. White" 1850

KING JAMES' CHRONOLOGY

Years B. C.		Years A. D.	
From Moses' birth to the time he attempted to liberate Israel was	40	From the birth of the first testimony to the time National Religious Liberty was organized is	40
and	—	God's people failed to do their duty (Vol. 5, pp. 80-2) (See p. 110.) in	
Moses failed and fled away in	1736		1890
Moses spent in the wilderness	40	From the time National Religious Liberty was organized to 1930 is	40
	—	Time due for reformation; a call to depart from worldliness; purification of the	—
Deliverance of Israel by Moses in	1696	church (Mal. 3; Vol. 5, 80-2; Isa. 11:11)	1930
From the call of Abraham to the birth of Jacob	85	From 1930 we subtract the typical	85
	—	Birth of S.D.A.; Ellen Harmon has her first vision. First paper published on Sab. truth, titled "The Hope of Israel"	—
			1845
From the birth of Jacob to the entering into Egypt	130	From 1845 we subtract the typical	130
	—	and we have the Dividing line (something like the cross; B. C. and A. D.) between Canaan and Egypt..	—
			1715

This is the reason why we have 1500 A. D. as the starting point of this prophecy, and if these coincidents were divinely designed, then the beginning and ending of the prophecy as on this chart, would be correct. See chart on Ezekiel's prophecy on page 133.

SECTION V.

THE PROPHECY OF EZEKIEL FOUR

(What Transpires Within the 390 Days)

"For I have laid upon thee the years of their iniquity, according to the number of the days, three hundred and ninety days: So shalt thou bear the iniquity of the house of Israel. And when thou hast accomplished them, lie again on thy right side, and thou shalt bear the iniquity of the house of Judah forty days: I have appointed thee each day for a year." Eze. 4:5, 6. The prophecy of the fourth chapter of Ezekiel finds its fulfillment in our day. This prophecy could not possibly refer to Israel after the flesh, though it deals with a period of 430 years in about the same manner as the prophecy made to Abraham. "And he said unto Abraham, Know of a surety that thy seed shall be a stranger in a land that is not their's, and shall serve them; and they shall afflict them four hundred years." Gen. 15:13. But Ex. 12:40 says, "Now the sojourning of the children of Israel, who dwelt in Egypt, was four hundred and thirty years." So the prophecy to Abraham was made in two sections, first being 400 years, and then to 430 years. Ezekiel's prophecy is made exactly the same way, in two sections, but not the same number of years in each section. Instead of 400 years, we have 390, and instead of 30 years, we have 40, making the same total of 430 years in each case. If this prophecy had a reference to the prophecy made to Abraham, there should have been the same number of years in each section, but since it is not the same, it must be another period of time.

Again, the prophecy of Israel after the flesh is that they should sojourn and be afflicted 430 years, but this prophecy of Ezekiel says in verse 13, "And the Lord said, Even thus shall the children of Israel eat their defiled bread among the Gentiles, whither I will drive them." Therefore it is evident that this prophecy refers to another period of time, and experience, than that of the experience of Israel in Egypt. The prophecy made to Abraham of 430 years ended at the time the children of Israel went out of Egypt, which is according to Bible chronology (King James' Version) 1491 B. C. According to the same chronology, the 430-year period of the children of Israel had ended 896 years before Ezekiel was even given the vision of his prophecy, and he put the prophecy in the future, for he uses future tense. "Even thus *shall* the children of Israel eat their defiled bread." So it is altogether impossible for one to form a conclusion that these two prophecies deal with the same period and experience of Israel down in Egypt.

This period (by Ezekiel) had no reference to Israel after the flesh in Ezekiel's time, for the Lord said (Eze. 4:5), "For I have laid upon thee the years of their iniquity, according to the number of the days, three hundred and ninety days: So shalt thou bear the iniquity of the house of *Israel*." In this verse the Lord said the 390 days (or years) are for the iniquity of the house of Israel, but in the next verse the 40 year period has reference to Judah. "And when thou hast accomplished them, lie again on thy right side, and thou shalt bear the iniquity of the house of *Judah* forty days." Therefore, Israel and Judah are referred to.

The kingdom of the twelve tribes of Israel was divided into two divisions in their early years; namely, Israel and Judah. But at the time Ezekiel had this vision there was only one division, for the ten tribes had been conquered and carried away in 721 B. C., 126 years before this prophecy was made, according to the same chronology. Being in the future, the prophecy, then, could have no reference to Israel after the flesh. This 430 year period has never yet been applied to any time, or people, in the past, and therefore, has never been explained, just the same as many other prophecies that were never understood until they met their fulfillment. If the time of its fulfillment has come, *then only* shall we understand this prediction.

We begin with the fourth verse and onward (we shall later take the first three, and last two verses). Israel after the flesh was a *type* of Israel by the promise (144,000), as explained on pages 64-113. The experience of the children of Israel in Egypt was a photograph of our denomination, thus their experience is being reproduced in every particular with this people, and if there are 430 years connected with Israel after the flesh, then the same period of time must be connected with the true. The 430 year period (by Abraham) did not have to do only with ancient Israel, but with Abraham, Isaac, and Jacob as well. The prophecy to Abraham of the 430 years began with the call to come out of Ur, and ended at Mt. Sinai; but this 430 years which ended at Mt. Sinai was a type as explained on pages 108-9.

The typical 430 years prophesied to Abraham began in the true (our time) with Martin Luther, as explained on pages 108-11, therefore both prophecies—the one to Abraham and the one to Ezekiel—refer to the same period in our time. The one to Abraham stands as a type, but the other is a direct prophecy, and both run parallel in our time. We may suppose the 390 year period began in about 1500 A. D., (when Luther found the Bible), and ended in 1890 A. D., where the 40 year period began, which would end in 1930. However, we cannot point out the exact day or month, or even the year, because (1) we do not know the exact day of the call of Luther; (2) prophecy deals with the Jewish, or perhaps the Hebrew year, therefore, it is a matter of months that we cannot determine. It may run until 1931, or even after, if the coincidences as explained on chart, pages 112-13, were not divinely designed to point out this fact. The question may be asked, Why would God make a double prophecy for the same thing?—because the old prophecy (the type) only gives the details from the beginning of the third angel's message to the fulfillment of Ezekiel 9. The prophecy by Ezekiel gives the information in detail from the beginning of Luther's reformation to Ezekiel 9, marking of the 144,000, and unrolling of the scroll. ("Not all in regard to this matter is yet understood, nor will it be understood *until* the unrolling of the scroll." Volume 6, page 17.)

It makes it clear that there is a 430 year period from the reformation by Luther to the purification of the church, as we shall endeavor to prove by Ezekiel's prophecy which we quote here. "Lie thou also upon thy left side, and lay the iniquity of the house of Israel upon it: According to the number of the days that thou shalt lie upon it thou shalt bear their iniquity. For I have laid upon thee the years of their iniquity, according to the number of the days, three hundred and ninety days: So shalt thou bear the iniquity of the house of Israel. And when thou hast accomplished them, lie again on thy right side, and thou shalt bear the iniquity of the house of Judah forty days: I have appointed thee each day for a year. Take thou also unto thee wheat, and barley, and beans, and lentils, and millet, and fitches [margin, spelt], and put them in one vessel and make thee bread thereof, according to the number of the days that thou shalt lie upon thy side, three hundred and ninety days shalt thou eat thereof, And thy meat which thou shalt eat shall be by weight, twenty shekels a day: From time to time shalt thou eat it. Thou shalt drink also water by measure, the sixth part of an hin: From time to time shalt thou drink." Eze. 4:4-6, 9-11.

Ezekiel was commanded to lie on his left side for 390 days during which time he was to eat and drink. After the 390 days were ended, he must turn to his right side and lie for forty days, but during this time he must *not* eat. The 390 days are 390 *literal years* according to the last part of verse 6. As we have made the application, the 390 years began with Luther and ended in 1890. During this period of time Ezekiel was told to eat and drink while he lay on his left side. What is he told to eat?—six varieties of food; namely, wheat, barley, beans, lentils, millet, and spelt (margin). We are not to understand these six varieties to be material food to sustain physical life, but as symbols of spiritual food (doctrines) of six varieties to sustain spiritual life. Had these not been symbols of truth, the Lord would not have asked Ezekiel to get a specified number of cereals, and that he should put them in one vessel, and bake them into a certain cake, and eat them at a specified time, in a particular way, with a fixed measure of water. These six doctrines may be represented by six steps upward (Reformation); an effort to bring the church to her state of purity.

WHEAT, SYMBOL OF FAITH

The first portion of spiritual food or truth which we were to receive, represented by the wheat, was "faith", as taught by Luther, as his doctrine was "The just shall live by faith". The wheat, which symbolized the doctrine Luther gave us must be perfect in itself to make a perfect symbol of that doctrine. Note the truth of the wheat: It has always been used by all generations, and everybody uses it and it is hard to get along without. Just so, all must have the doctrine of "faith". "Without faith it is impossible to please Him" so the Bible says. Not only Christians, but other religions must have faith as well as they must have wheat. Even the infidel, and the atheist must exercise faith in whatever he may believe. We can see that inspiration used the right kind of symbol to represent the doctrine of "faith".

BARLEY, SYMBOL OF SPIRIT

The second portion of food, or truth which we were to get was represented by barley. John Knox was the next man who made the second step by teaching the doctrine represented by the barley which was the truth of the "Holy Spirit". Barley is not so commonly or widely used as wheat. In fact, few people would use it, and at that, very seldom. Many people do not know what barley is; so with the doctrine of the "Holy Spirit". While the doctrine of the Holy Spirit is believed by some Christians, it is not believed by others. Some do not understand what the truth of the Spirit is, even as some do not know what barley is; so the symbol representing the second doctrine is perfect, even as the first. Gideon's experience with the Midianite's dream of the barley cake overturning the tent proves the same. Read Judges 7:13, 14.

BEANS, SYMBOL OF GRACE

Beans are just as widely and commonly used by all the people and all generations the same as wheat. John Wesley, the third man on the stage of action as a great reformer, made the third step upward by teaching the doctrine of "Grace", which was represented by the beans. All believe in grace. So much so, that men no longer fear God, and have declared His law void. He is too gracious, and too merciful, they say, and as we are under grace, God will do neither good nor evil. Thus, Christians these days have perverted its true meaning, even as they all love beans, and have perverted the proper name by calling them "pork and beans". What more fitting symbol could have been chosen to represent the doctrine of grace than the one God has selected?

LENTILS, TYPE OF DOCTRINE OF BAPTISM BY IMMERSION

Lentils are used to represent the fourth portion of truth. Alexander Campbell is credited with making the fourth step upward by teaching the doctrine of baptism by immersion, symbolized by the lentils. The variety (lentils) representing the fourth doctrine (baptism by immersion) is not known or used even as much as barley: so with the truth of immersion. Baptism by immersion in the old-fashioned way is not generally practiced, even as lentils are not generally used. Again God has used the right kind of symbol to represent this portion of truth.

MILLET, SYMBOL OF 2300 DAYS

The fifth portion of truth is represented by millet, and the fifth reformer was William Miller. He taught the prophecy of Daniel 8:14, which was the doctrine of the 2300 days. Millet is scarcely known, and those who do know what it is say it is of little worth, merely a wild grass with scarcely any farming value, and not desired by anybody. Nevertheless it is a good cereal. Just so with the doctrine taught by Miller. No one has any use for it and Seventh-day Adventists are practically the only people who teach it. Those who do not accept this doctrine say it is good for nothing, and charge Miller as being a false prophet. Though it is a wonderful prophecy and reveals a great truth, yet people will not accept it. "It is good for nothing, with no spiritual value, and we have no need of it", is the cry. Again the question is asked, Could a better symbol than millet be found to represent the doctrine of the 2300 days?

SPELT, SYMBOL OF THE SABBATH IN CONNECTION WITH THE SANCTUARY

The last cereal mentioned in Ezekiel's prophecy is spelt, which represents the sixth truth or doctrine which is the Sabbath truth in the light as given by Sister E. G. White, in connection with the heavenly Sanctuary. The definition of "spelt" (as in the margin) according to the Standard Dictionary is as follows: "A cereal intermediate between wheat and barley. . . . It was the chief cereal of ancient Egypt, being probably the rye of the time of Moses, but cultivated now mainly in Switzerland, southern Germany, and northern Spain."

Spelt is an ancient cereal, used in ancient Egypt in the days of Moses, and it was the rye in the days of Joseph. So is the Sabbath an ancient truth which originated in the Garden of Eden, and was the last recorded act of Creation. It was the truth in the days of Moses, the first man in the Bible who instituted Sabbath keeping. Spelt is a little better known than millet, and has some farming value, but only in certain portions of the globe, even as the Sabbath is better known than the 2300 days. Would any dare say these are not all perfect symbols, or that it is only a certain man's interpretation, and only an accident, or just happened, and yet fit so perfectly? But thus far only one phase has been explained.

ALL IN ONE VESSEL

The Lord said to the prophet Ezekiel, "Put them in one vessel" (verse 9). It will now be considered as to whether he really did put all these doctrines in one vessel. Luther believed in the doctrine he taught, but the great enemy flooded the church with deception. Not with arguing the truth. No, no. But suggesting to the people that they now have all the truth, and that they surely were right, thus hardening their hearts against more light. Soon additional truth came, but Satan had already flooded the church with his agents, and prejudice was aroused against the new light. The result was that the majority turned down the truth. A few saw the light, and as the case generally is, they were voted out by the church. Necessity gave birth to a new movement, or denomination. Such has been the experience with the church in each advancing truth up the line to our own time.

In like manner, the truth represented by the barley (Spirit) was turned down by those who had accepted the doctrine symbolized by the wheat (faith). Knox believed in all the truth he had and also all the truth Luther taught. Thus the wheat and the barley were in one vessel and carried to the second step.

We next have the truth symbolized by the beans (grace) and presented by Wesley, who believed also in the truths previously taught by Luther and Knox, which were represented by the wheat and barley. The third step was made, and the wheat, barley, and beans were in one vessel. The fourth truth was represented by lentils (baptism by immersion) and taught by Campbell, who believed in the doctrines of Luther, Knox, and Wesley. Thus the wheat, barley, beans and lentils were carried to the fourth step, and in one vessel. The fifth truth (2300 days) was represented by millet, and this step upward was made by William Miller who believed in all the truths symbolized by wheat, barley, beans, and lentils. The fifth step was made and the five varieties of food or truth were carried in one vessel.

We now come to the last variety of the cereals: "spelt" (Sabbath), in connection with the judgment. Is it not a fact that the Seventh-day Adventist denomination believes in all these truths: The wheat (faith); barley (Holy Spirit); beans (grace); lentils (immersion); millet (2300 days); spelt (Sabbath, with the sanctuary truth)? It will be noticed the Lord said, "Put them in one vessel". He did not say in two, or more, but in *one*. There are no other people besides Seventh-day Adventists who believe in the 2300 days (cleansing of the Sanctuary), and it is this denomination (vessel) which teaches all the six doctrines as represented by the six varieties of food. Thus the prophecy meets its fulfillment in our day, and we are amazed with the difficulty to comprehend the great wisdom of the Lord our God.

BARLEY CAKE

The Lord told Ezekiel, "Thou shalt eat it as barley cakes." Verse 12. Why the wheat, beans, lentils, millet, and spelt made as barley cake? Why not as wheat cake, or cake of some of the other cereals? The truth of the Holy Spirit was represented by the barley; as explained on page 118. For this reason Ezekiel was told to make it into barley cake, meaning the truth came by the power of the Holy Spirit, and not by the aid of men.

"I WILL LAY BANDS UPON THEE"

Quoting verse 8 , we read: "And, behold, I will lay *bands* upon thee, and thou shalt *not* turn thee from one side to another, till thou hast *ended* the days of thy siege." The prophet was to lie on is *left* side 390 days. During this time he was to *eat* the varieties of food. But why on the left side? Why not on the right? Because the symbol would not have been perfect had he lain on his right side while eating. The stomach of a man is shaped something like a crescent, with a narrow neck to the right as an outlet. If a man lies on his left side, the outlet is upward, against gravity, and consequently would be difficult to empty itself, which would cause the food to remain within it. *Had it not been for the bands* the Lord put around Ezekiel, he would have turned to his right side, thus spoiling the symbol. The meaning is that even though the great enemy tried to *force out* every truth by *prejudice* and *insinuations,* and casting out of the church those who were teaching these new truths as it has been in each instance in the past, yet God saw to it that every truth would remain until He has put them in *one vessel,* and so it is.

"THOU SHALT DRINK ALSO WATER"

"Thou shalt drink also water by measure, the sixth part of an hin: From time to time shalt thou drink." Verse 11. Water, when taken in, gives life; without it, existence would be impossible. Christ, speaking to the woman at the well, said: "But the water that I shall give him shall be in him a well of water springing up into everlasting life." John 4:14. Christ referred to "water" as a symbol of everlasting life. The meaning of the symbol of drinking the water with the barley cakes is that souls were to be saved by each new truth (the Spirit of life).

MEAT BY WEIGHT—WATER BY MEASURE

Verses 10, 11: "And thy meat which thou shalt eat shall be by weight. . . . Thou shalt drink also water by measure." The "measure" and "weight" are symbols signifying that God would only give truth by measure, a little at a time. As the prophecy reads, "from time to time shalt thou eat and drink", and so has God given light a little at a time as we could grasp it. It has come in its exact Biblical order: Faith, Spirit, grace, baptism, time of the end, and the Sabbath (Rest).

Abraham, the father of the faithful, is the symbol of faith; Isaac, the symbol of Spirit of truth (as the Bible says he was born after the Spirit); Jacob, the symbol of grace, (for as he was a sinful man, had it not been for the grace of God, he could not have prevailed.) The Exodus movement is the symbol for baptism, for we read in 1 Cor. 10:2, "And were all baptized unto Moses in the cloud and in the sea." The wilderness life is the symbol of the sanctuary question at the end of the 2300 days; it was in the wilderness that the heavenly sanctuary was described by the earthly. "The promised land" is a symbol of the Sabbath rest. In the promised land they were to rest had they driven out the heathen, but because of national pride and disbelief, they failed to obtain the promised rest. The disobedience of Israel in the promised land is a symbol of our failing to obey God at the present time.

EXPLANATION OF VERSES 12, 14, 15

Wonderful prophecy as it is, the saddest part is now to be told.

The scripture about to be quoted has perhaps never been read publicly, or reproduced in any literature, but if it was never to be studied out, read in public, or published, God would never have placed it in the Bible. However, it is there, no doubt for a purpose, and must be considered. The quotation as found in verses 12, 14, 15, reads as follows: "And thou shalt bake it with dung that cometh out of a man, in their sight. Then said I, Oh Lord God! behold, my soul hath not been polluted: For from my youth up even till now have I not eaten of that which dieth of itself, or is torn in pieces; neither came there abominable flesh into my mouth. Then he said unto me, Lo, I have given thee cow's dung for man's dung, and thou shalt prepare thy bread therewith."

The prophet was told that he could not use wood, or coal to bake the cakes upon, but that he should use "dung that cometh out of a man". To Ezekiel it was too repulsive, and he pleaded to be excused. The Lord made an allowance, not by compulsion, but for Ezekiel's sake only, by telling Ezekiel to bake it with "cow's dung". The 13th verse gives an explanation of the symbol as follows: "And the Lord said, 'Even thus shall the children of Israel eat their defiled bread among the Gentiles'." The symbol is: Every portion of truth that has come so far, has been polluted, including the last one (Sabbath), notwithstanding all the instructions given us, line upon line, and precept upon precept. The picture tells the story; symbols do not lie. Instead of being offended because we are told of our failings, we should only praise God that in His mercy He has made a call for reformation, that we may not be left to perish in our sins, but are given an opportunity to choose whom we will serve.

The question may be asked, How have we polluted God's truth? Only one of the many references will be quoted here. Volume 1, pages 471, 472: "A great mistake has been made by some who profess present truth, by introducing merchandise in the course of a series of meetings, . . . Ministers have stood in the desk and preached a most solemn discourse, and then by introducing merchandise, and acting the part of a salesman, *even* in the house of God. . . . The burden of selling our publications should not rest upon ministers who labor in word and doctrine." Volume 8, page 250: "I saw our Instructor [Christ] pointing to the garments of so-called righteousness. Stripping them off, He laid bare the defilement beneath. Then He said to me: 'Can you not see how they have pretentiously covered up their defilement and rottenness of character? "How is the faithful city become an harlot?" *My Father's House* is made a house of *merchandise,* a place whence the divine presence and glory have departed! For this cause there is weakness, and strength is lacking'." Thus we have the proof that every truth thus far has been polluted, including the Sabbath.

THE 40 DAYS AND WHAT TRANSPIRES WITHIN

Thus far, the 390 years have been explained, and we shall now consider the 40 days,—or years. After Ezekiel had accomplished the 390 days, he was told to turn now to his right side and lie on it 40 days. Unlike the 390 days, he is not to eat anything, but fast the entire forty days, and during this period of time he must lie on his right side. As we have explained before, if one should lie on his left side, the stomach can not empty itself; but now he must lie on his right side. This position would give his stomach a chance to empty itself. Naturally, if the stomach would empty and could not take other food, he would become hungry (symbol of spiritual hunger).

The symbol is, that the church has been on a spiritual decline for forty years, and has had no new spiritual food to feed upon. Some may say, "We have the Bible and the Testimonies and we feed on them." It is true we have had them, but they have been closed to us, for we did not make proper use of the truth we have had, and it is a fact that the church has had no new light upon scriptures that were not understood forty years ago.

The forty-year period began in 1890, according to the chart on pages 112-13, at which time the 390 years ended. The time has about elapsed, and now we must have food or else we shall die, and God in

His mercy has remembered His people and is sending them an invitation to draw near for another good feast.

Would you, brethren, draw near for the great supper? Or will you make an excuse? Will you say, "I have bought a piece of ground, and I must needs go and see it: I pray theee have me excused." Or will your answer be, "I have bought five yoke of oxen, and I go to prove them." Or will it be that you have "married a wife and therefore, I cannot come." Remember that "the poor, and the maimed, and the halt, and the blind": From the "highways and hedges" will not hestitate; the house will be filled. "For I say unto you, That none of those men which were bidden shall taste of my supper." See Luke 14:16-24.

SEVEN—PERFECT NUMBER

In this prophecy we find there are only six portions, and only six steps have been made. Luther, Knox, Wesley, Campbell, Miller and White. The number "six" is not a perfect number. It is evident then, that there is still another portion to follow, and a step to climb. "Seven" is the perfect, Biblical number. The question is, Why was not the seventh portion included in this prophecy? Because the *six* were *polluted;* defiled with man's preparation, man's thoughts; and plans *have been* injected and followed, which, in God's sight are as "dung". It is not to be so with the seventh, for it is the last; it must be pure. This last portion, pure and undefiled, is represented by the angel of Rev. 18:1, "And after these things I saw another angel come down from heaven, having great power; and the earth was lightened with his glory." It is at this time that Isaiah's prophecy will be fulfilled. Isa. 52:1, 2: "Awake, awake; put on thy strength, O Zion; put on thy beautiful garments, O Jerusalem, the Holy City: For henceforth there shall no more come into thee the uncircumcised and the unclean. Shake thyself from the dust; arise, and sit down, O Jerusalem: Loose thyself from the bands of thy neck, O captive daughter of Zion [God's pure church]."

Note the last part of the first verse: "For henceforth there shall no more come into thee the uncircumcised and the unclean." There has always been in the church the uncircumcised, the unclean, and unconverted, in all her history, but here the prophet declares there shall be "no more". Let us give thanks to our God for this precious promise, and for the revelation of His Word. Zephaniah also declares, "The remnant of Israel shall not do iniquity, nor speak lies; neither shall a deceitful tongue be found in their mouth: For they shall feed and lie down and none shall make them afraid." In Prophets and Kings, page 725, we read: "Clad in the armor of Christ's righteousness, the church is to enter upon her final conflict. 'Fair as the moon, clear as the sun, and terrible as an army with banners', she is to go forth into all the world, conquering and to conquer."

It could be explained that this brings us to the opening of the seventh seal of Rev. 8:1. The church on the seventh step, under the seventh seal, and in the seventh trumpet. By this we know we are on the borders of Eternity. Would the lips of any of us utter the words, "The harvest is past, the summer is ended, and we are not saved?" But how shall we attain this perfection? It will not be easy. Unless we make an effort we shall never reach the mark, for the enemy is not leaving one string loose. He has interfered all the way, in every step, and every part of the truth, and his plans are stronger now than ever before. Nevertheless, prophecy has declared that the 144,000 have not bowed a knee to Baal, "and in their mouth was found no guile: For they are without fault before the throne of God." At the present time the denomination employs about 10,000 evangelical workers, but what will it be when 144,000 without guile, spot or wrinkle, or any such thing, filled with the Spirit of God, compass the globe? Such is the beginning of the seventh step. No wonder the prophet declared, "the uncircumcised and the unclean shall no more come into thee". "And I shall make her a strong nation." Micah 4:7.

While the prophecy of the 430 years finds its beginning with the Reformation by Luther, and others, the lesson is for this time, and the people of this age. Never before has this prophecy been understood, and, until now, no one ever received much from it, but when the time is fulfilled, God makes it known. Thus has He lead His people on and on. The verses not commented on will be considered now.

THE SIEGE

"Thou also, son of man, take thee a tile, and lay it before thee, and portray upon it the city, even Jerusalem." Eze. 4:1. The Hebrew translation reads: "Engrave" upon it a city; *namely* "Jerusalem", (the city: A symbol of the church membership). Ezekiel was told to engrave a city, and call it Jerusalem, and it must be engraved upon a tile. Paper or skin would not do, for it would not be as durable as tile. If it is engraved on a tile it cannot be erased. The thought is that the prophecy will surely come to pass, and after it once becomes history, one cannot erase the things portrayed; it is there to stay through all ages. (The tile mentioned here is not manufactured. It is a natural luminar tile, and quarried in large, self-separated slabs which in certain sections of that country is found in a great abundance. It is being largely or exclusively used for roofing and flooring.)

Verse 2: "And lay siege against it, and build a fort against it, and cast a mount against it, set the camp also against it, and set battering rams against it round about." "Lay siege against it": That is, invade the city (the church) by an army to compel its surrender; endeavor to obtain possession of the city,—the church. "And build a fort against it": A fort around a city makes it secure, so "build a fort against it" means to make sure that none escape. "And cast a mount": the word "mount" in the Greek translation is rendered (Prohómata), meaning "ramparts", which is an embankment surrounding a fort, thus making every effort and precaution to secure the city. "Set the camp also against it": That is, make temporary lodging places. The thought is,—make preparation to remain there until you have conquered the city. "And set battering rams against it round about": Or, as in margin, "chief leaders": Meaning an instrument with which to blow or strike. "Ram" is a male sheep, which is used as a symbol of God's men, and they are to batter around about until the city is taken. The instrument which they batter with is a clear, cutting, and convincing Bible Truth.

The "city" (Jerusalem) is God's church; namely, the Seventh-day Adventists (Israel). God Himself organized this church by a prophet, and there is a great deal of difference between this church, and the churches during the Reformation from Luther's time onward. God permitted His people to be voted out of the church by the majority in times past, and they were compelled to start another movement until the next step they were to make, and so on. In this case, God is to deal with the entire body. Those who sigh and cry for the abominations that are done in the church will be sealed by the man with the writer's inkhorn. Those who are determined to do evil, that is, do contrary to the rules laid down by the Spirit of God through the Testimonies for the church will be destroyed by the five men with the slaughter weapons of Ezekiel 9. None can escape, for the city is besieged, fortified, and made sure. It is a fact, that in every age where God demonstrated His truth and purpose in clear lines, after being rejected, that people suffered the vengeance of the all-powerful and great God. For instance, the anti-diluvians, cities of Sodom, Egypt, Canaanites, Babylon, and ancient Jerusalem.

Separation in Principle

"Moreover take thou unto thee an iron pan, and set it for a wall of iron between thee and the city: And set thy face against it, and it shall be besieged, and thou shalt lay siege against it. This shall be a sign to the house of Israel." Verse 3. "Take thou an iron pan, and set it for a *wall of iron* between thee and the city [church]": A symbol of an impregnable separation between the two classes. This does not mean that they do not see, or speak to one another, but a separation in principle, rule, or guide. "And set thy face against it": As a general of armies sets his face against another nation, with intent to conquer. "This shall be a sign to the house of Israel": The sign is to those who are marked or sealed; namely, the 144,000, for they are Israel, The True.

TIME OF SPIRITUAL HUNGER

"Moreover He said unto me, Son of man, behold, I will break his staff of bread in Jerusalem: And they shall eat bread by weight, and with care; and they shall drink water by measure, and with astonishment: That they may want bread and water, and be astonied one with another, and consume away for their iniquity." Verses 16, 17. The 13th verse applies to the time of the 390 years; verses 16, 17, to the time of the forty years. The beginning of the 16th verse shows that there is a break in the prophecy, for we read: "*Moreover* He said unto me", that is, besides, or furthermore. "I will break the staff of bread in Jerusalem" (I will cut down, or set it on the decrease). "That they shall eat bread by weight and with care, and drink water by measure and with astonishment": That is, sparingly, until their supply of bread is exhausted, and they become hungry. "Astonied" (astonishment) : That is, we would say that we have the truth, or are God's people, but we do not understand why thus and so; power is lacking, and there is something wrong.

The 17th verse is the fulfillment of the prophecy contained in verse 16. The Douay version seems to make it clearer from which verse 17, is here quoted: "So that when bread and water fail every man may fall against his brother, and they may pine away in their iniquity." The beginning of the verse in the Greek, and Bulgarian are the same with the exception that the word "people" is used instead of "brother". The Hebrew translation renders: "In order that they may want bread and water, and be confounded one with the other and pine away for their iniquity." "So that when bread and water fail every man may fall" (Douay) : That is, in the time of the forty-year period, they will exhaust their supply of bread, and water (spiritual) and become real hungry, so that they may discover their mistake. Quoting Testimonies to Ministers, page 419: "God requires certain things of His people; if they say, I will not give up my heart to do this thing, the Lord lets them go on in their supposed wise judgment without heavenly wisdom, until this scripture (Isa. 28:13) is fulfilled. You are not to say, I will follow the Lord's guidance up to a certain point that is in harmony with my judgment, and then hold fast to your own ideas, refusing to be molded after the Lord's similitude. Let the question be asked, Is this the will of the Lord? Not, Is this the opinion or judgment of ————?" "But the word of the Lord was unto them precept upon precept, precept upon precept; line upon line, line upon line; here a little, and there a little; that they might go, and fall backward, and be broken, and snared, and taken." Isa. 28:13.

Testimonies to Ministers, pages 105-107: "We are not to think, as did the Jews, that our own ideas and opinions are infallible; nor with the papists, that certain individuals are the sole guardians of truth and knowledge, that men have no right to search the Scriptures for themselves, but must accept the explanations given by the Fathers of the church. . . . Those who allow prejudice to bar the mind against the reception of truth can not receive the divine enlightenment. Yet, when a view of Scripture is presented, many do not ask, *Is it true,—in harmony* with God's word? but, By *whom* is it advocated? and unless it comes through the very channel that pleases *them*, they *do not* accept it. So thoroughly satisfied are they with *their own ideas,* that they *will not* examine the Scripture evidence, *with* a desire to learn, but *refuse* to be interested, merely because of their prejudices.

"The Lord *often* works where *we least* expect Him; He surprises us by revealing His power through instruments of *His own* choice, while He passes by the men to whom *we* have looked as those through whom light should come. God desires us to *receive* the truth upon *its own* merits,—because it is *truth.* . . . But *beware* of rejecting that which is *truth.* The great danger with our people has been that of *depending upon men,* and making flesh their arm. Those who *have not* been in the habit of searching the Bible *for themselves,* or weighing evidence, have confidence *in the leading men,* and *accept* the decisions *they* make; and thus *many will reject the very messages God sends* to His people, if these leading brethren do not accept them.

"*No one* should claim that he has *all the light* there is for God's people. The Lord *will not* tolerate this. He has said, 'I have set before thee an open door, and *no man* can shut it.' Even if all our leading men should *refuse* light and truth, that door *will still* remain open. *The Lord will raise up men who will give the people the message for this time.* . . . Suppose a brother held a view that *differed* from yours, and he should come to you, proposing that you sit down with him and make an *investigation* of that point in the Scriptures; should you rise up, filled with *prejudice,* and *condemn* his ideas, while *refusing* to give him a candid hearing? The only right way would be to sit down as Christians, and *investigate* the position presented, *in the light of God's word,* which will reveal truth and unmask error. To ridicule his ideas *would not* weaken his position in the least if it were false, or strengthen *your* position if it were true. If the pillars of our faith will not stand the *test* of investigation, *it is time that we knew it.* There must be no spirit of Pharisaism cherished among us." Though one may stubbornly dispute the direct application of the scriptures quoted here, certainly none would question the lesson taught in this publication and yet claim to be in harmony with the movement.

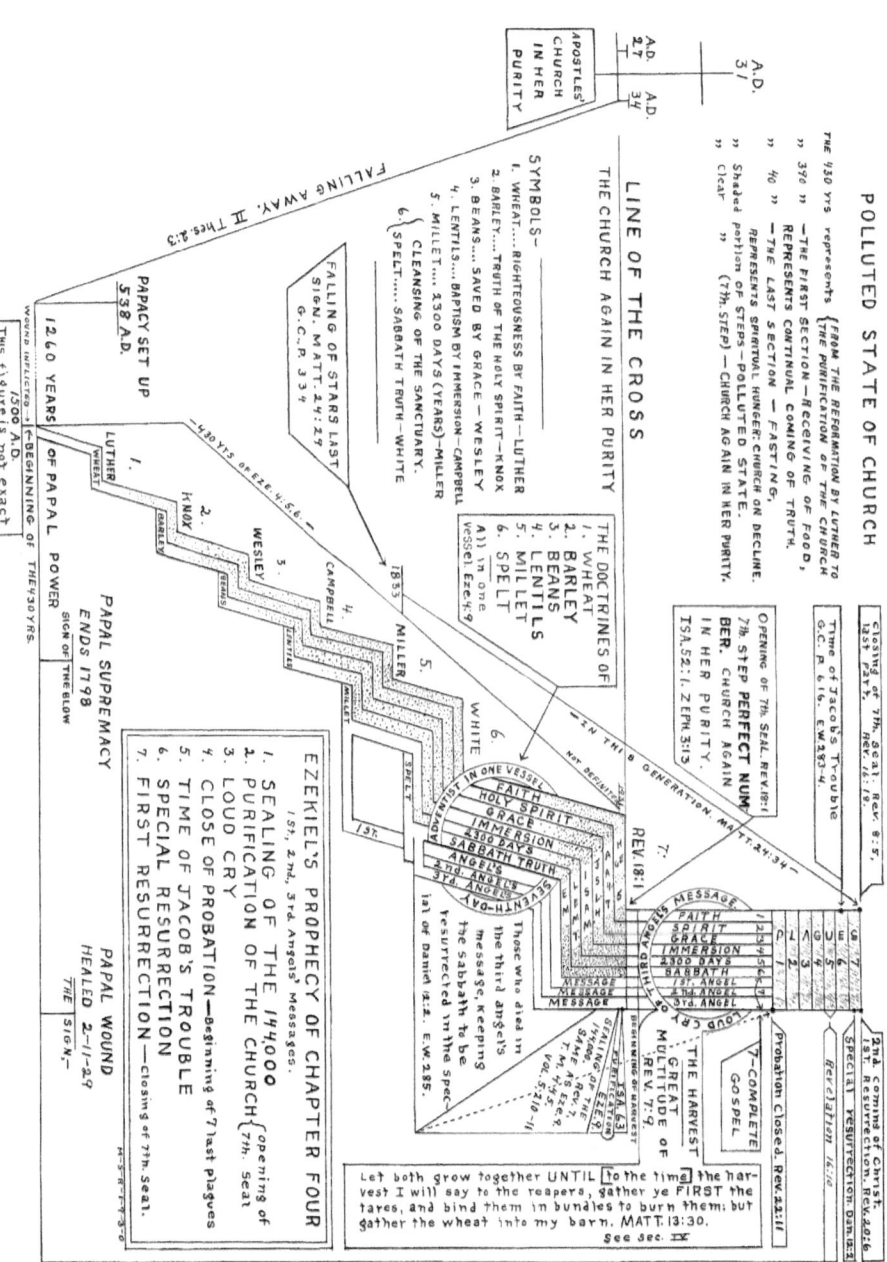

POLLUTED STATE OF CHURCH

LINE OF THE CROSS

THE CHURCH AGAIN IN HER PURITY

THE 930 YRS represents {FROM THE REFORMATION BY LUTHER TO THE PURIFICATION OF THE CHURCH}

„ 390 „ —THE FIRST SECTION — RECEIVING OF FOOD, REPRESENTS CONTINUAL COMING OF TRUTH.

„ 40 „ —THE LAST SECTION — FASTING, REPRESENTS SPIRITUAL HUNGER, CHURCH ON DECLINE.

„ Shaded portion of STEPS — POLLUTED STATE.

„ Clear „ (7TH. STEP) — CHURCH AGAIN IN HER PURITY.

FALLING AWAY, II Thes. 2:3

SYMBOLS—
1. WHEAT....RIGHTEOUSNESS BY FAITH—LUTHER
2. BARLEY....TRUTH OF THE HOLY SPIRIT—KNOX
3. BEANS....SAVED BY GRACE—WESLEY
4. LENTILS....BAPTISM BY IMMERSION—CAMPBELL
5. MILLET....2300 DAYS (YEARS)—MILLER
6. {SPELT.....SABBATH TRUTH—WHITE}
   {CLEANSING OF THE SANCTUARY.}

FALLING OF STARS LAST
SIGN. MATT. 24:29
G.C. p. 334

PAPACY SET UP
538 A.D.

1260 YEARS

WOUND INFLICTED
1500 A.D.
THIS figure is not exact

OF PAPAL POWER

BEGINNING OF THE 930 YRS.

LUTHER
WHEAT

1.

2.
KNOX
BARLEY

3.
WESLEY
BEANS

4.
CAMPBELL
LENTILS

5.
MILLER
MILLET

6.
WHITE
SPELT

1st.

THE DOCTRINES OF
1. WHEAT
2. BARLEY
3. BEANS
4. LENTILS
5. MILLET
6. SPELT
All in one
vessel Ezek. 4:9

7th. STEP PERFECT NUM-
BER. CHURCH AGAIN
IN HER PURITY.
ISA. 52:1. ZEPH. 3:13

OPENING OF 7th. SEAL REV. 18:1
IN THIS GENERATION. MATT. 24:34

Time of Jacob's Trouble
G.C. p. 616. EW. 283-4

Closing of 7th. Seal.
last part.
Rev. 16:19.

2nd coming of Christ.
1st. RESURRECTION.
SPECIAL RESURRECTION. Dan. 12:1

PAPAL SUPREMACY
ENDS 1798
SIGN OF THE BLOW

PAPAL WOUND
HEALED 2-11-29
THE SIGN.

EZEKIEL'S PROPHECY OF CHAPTER FOUR
1st, 2nd, 3rd Angels' Messages.
1. SEALING OF THE 144000
2. PURIFICATION OF THE CHURCH {opening of 7th. Seal}
3. LOUD CRY
4. CLOSE OF PROBATION—Beginning of 7 last plagues
5. TIME OF JACOB'S TROUBLE
6. SPECIAL RESURRECTION
7. FIRST RESURRECTION—Closing of 7th. Seal.

FAITH
HOLY SPIRIT
GRACE
IMMERSION
2300 DAYS
SABBATH TRUTH
1st. ANGEL
SECOND ANGEL
3rd. ANGEL

SEVENTH-DAY ADVENTIST IN ONE VESSEL

FAITH
SPIRIT
GRACE
IMMERSION
2300 DAYS
SABBATH
1st. ANGEL
2nd. ANGEL
3rd. ANGEL

THIRD ANGEL'S MESSAGE
FIRST ANGEL'S MESSAGE
SECOND ANGEL'S MESSAGE

Those who died in
the third angel's
message, keeping
the sabbath will be
resurrected in the spec-
ial of Daniel 12:1. E.W. 285.

PLAGUE
1 2 3 4 5 6 7

Probation Closed. Rev. 22:11

Revelation 16:10

THE HARVEST

COMPLETE
GOSPEL

GREAT
MULTITUDE OF

Let both grow together UNTIL to the time the harvest I will say to the reapers, gather ye FIRST the
tares, and bind them in bundles to burn them; but
gather the wheat into my barn. MATT. 13:30.
See Sec. IX

(THE TERMINATION OF PAPAL LINE IS NOT YET CLEARLY REVEALED)

APOSTLES'
CHURCH
IN HER
PURITY

A.D.
27

A.D.
34

A.D.
31

SECTION VI.

SYNOPSIS OF ISAIAH, CHAPTERS 54-66 INCLUSIVE

This call for reformation as set forth here is the direct result of the study of the thirteen chapters in the book of Isaiah, as devised by the Seventh-day Adventist denomination, and presented to the churches in the entire organization throughout the world. These lessons were taught in the Sabbath School department during January, February, and March of the year 1929, and beginning with the 54th chapter, ended with the 66th. We believe the hand of God was leading, and that these particular lessons came at an appointed time by divine direction, with intention to arouse His people to action from the lukewarm Laodicean condition, and spiritual feebleness.

In Volume 3, page 492, we read: "General Conference, which is the highest authority that God has upon earth." ("General Conference" spoken of here is not one man's opinion, but a General Conference of brethren assembled from all parts of the field, as described in Gospel Workers, page 489: "But when, in a General Conference, the judgment of brethren assembled from all parts of the field is exercised. Private independence and private judgment must not be stubbornly maintained, but surrender"). For this reason, God honored the General Conference, and sent the lessons through that channel, with the intention to bring forth a reformation in the entire denomination in one single quarter of Sabbath School studies.

These thirteen chapters of Isaiah are one continuous letter written for the church. Though they have been in the Bible for many centuries, they were intended for us at this present time, and stand as a direct epistle to the church now. The 54th chapter is the beginning of the letter, and it ends with the 66th. The following reasons are given for believing thus.

Isaiah 54—Beginning of Letter
"The God of Comfort"

"Sing, O barren, thou that didst not bear; break forth into singing, and cry aloud, thou that didst not travail with child: For more are the children of the desolate than the children of the married wife, saith the Lord." Isa. 54:1. Chapter four of Galatians says the woman spoken of here, the "barren", "she who travailed not with child", "desolate", is Sarah. The other, called the married wife, is Agar. Sarah is desolate, because she stepped aside and gave her husband to Agar, thus Agar is the married wife. Sarah was barren, without child, while Agar had Ishmael.

"For it is written, Rejoice, thou barren that bearest not; break forth and cry, thou that travailest not: For the desolate hath many more children than she which hath an husband." Gal. 4:27. Gal. 4:25, says Agar represents the Old Testament church, or Jerusalem in Palestine. "For this Agar is Mount Sinai in Arabia, and answereth to Jerusalem which now is, and is in bondage with her children." "But Jerusalem which is above is free, which is the mother of us all. So then, brethren, we are not children of the bondwoman, but of the free." Gal. 4:26, 31. Thus Sarah (the free) is the symbol of Jerusalem which is above, or the church of the New Testament.

Ishmael represents the children of the Old Testament church, but Isaac, the children of the New Testament (Christian) church. "Now we, brethren, as Isaac was, are the children of promise. But as then he that was born after the flesh persecuted him that was born after the Spirit, even so it is now." Gal. 4:28, 29. As Abraham did cast out the bondwoman (Agar) and her son (Ishmael), just so God did cast out the Old Testament church, or Jerusalem which now is. Gal. 4:30: "Nevertheless what saith the scripture? Cast out the bondwoman and her son: For the son of the bondwoman shall not be heir with the son of the freewoman." The Scripture makes the subject too plain to be misunderstood. Sarah is the symbol of the Christian church, and Agar, of the Jewish church.

Turning to the 54th chapter of Isaiah, it will be noticed that this chapter is addressed to the barren, childless, desolate woman,—Sarah, who is the symbol of the Christian church. The Spirit of Prophecy, commenting on this chapter, says the prophecy is for the gospel church at this time. We read in Prophets and Kings, pages 374, 375: "Looking on still farther through the ages, the prophet beheld the literal fulfillment of these glorious promises. He saw the bearers of the glad tidings of salvation going to the ends of the earth, to every kindred and people. He heard the Lord saying of the *gospel church,* 'Behold, I will extend peace to her like a river, and the glory of the Gentiles like a flowing stream;' and he heard the commission: 'Enlarge the place of thy tent, and let them stretch forth the curtains of thine habitations: Spare not, lengthen thy cords, and strengthen thy stakes; for thou shalt break forth on the right hand and on the left; and thy seed shall inherit the Gentiles.' Jehovah declared to the prophet that He would send His witnesses 'unto the nations, to Tarshish, Pul, Lud, . . . to Tubal, and Javan, to the isles afar off.' The prophet heard the voice of God *calling His church* to her *appointed work,* that the way might be prepared for the *ushering in of His everlasting kingdom."*

The prophecy could not have been for the early part of the Christian church, for we read in verse 17: "No weapon that is formed against thee shall prosper; and every tongue that shall rise against thee in judgment thou shalt condemn. This is the heritage of the servants of the Lord, and their righteousness is of me, saith the Lord." "No weapon that is formed against thee shall prosper": If this scripture had a reference to the early part of the church, or prior to the dark ages, then God would have failed to carry out His promise. Note that from the beginning of the Christian church the stones, swords, crosses, ropes, fires, and many other cruel instruments which were formed against the church did prosper, and continued to prosper up till about the middle of the 18th century, therefore the prophet could have had no reference to the early part of the church. The following quotation will prove the time to which the scripture applies: "Whosoever shall gather together against thee shall fall for thy sake. . . . 'No weapon that is formed against thee shall prosper; and every tongue that shall rise against thee in judgment thou shalt

condemn.' . . . Clad in the armor of Christ's righteousness, the church
is to enter upon her final conflict. 'Fair as the moon, clear as the sun,
and terrible as an army with banners.' . . . The darkest hour of the
church's struggle with the powers of evil, is that which immediately
precedes the day of her final deliverance. But none who trust in
God need fear; for 'when the blast of the terrible ones is as a storm
against the wall,' God will be to His church 'a refuge from the
storm'." Prophets and Kings, page 725.

Again we read in Early Writings, pages 284, 285: "As the saints
left the cities and villages, they were pursued by the wicked, who
sought to slay them. But the swords that were raised to kill God's
people *broke and fell as powerless as a straw.* Angels of God shield-
ed the saints. As they cried day and night for deliverance, their cry
came up before the Lord." Thus we have proof that the chapter
was written for the people of God who shall live at the time of the
end. The intention in this article is not to explain all the chapter
contains, but to point out the time it was intended for, with a few
instructive remarks. In another study we may take all these chapters
separate of each other, verse by verse.

In verses 14 and 15, there is great encouragement for the people
of God, and it ought to strengthen our faith. "In righteousness shalt
thou be established: Thou shalt be far from oppression; for . . . they
shall surely gather together, but not by me: Whosoever shall gather
together against thee shall fall for thy sake." The time of the fulfillment of these verses is well portrayed in Early Writings, pages
282, 283: "I saw the saints leaving the cities and villages, and associating together in companies, and living in the most solitary places.
Angels provided them food and water, while the wicked were suffering from hunger and thirst. Then I saw the leading men of the
earth consulting together, and Satan and his angels busy around them.
I saw a writing, copies of which were scattered in different parts of
the land, giving orders that unless the saints should yield their peculiar faith, give up the Sabbath, and observe the first day of the
week, the people were at liberty after a certain time, to put them to

death . . . . but angels in the form of men of war fought for them. Satan wished to have the privilege of destroying the saints of the Most High; but Jesus bade His angels watch over them. . . . Next came the multitude of the angry wicked, and next a mass of evil angels, hurrying on the wicked to slay the saints. But before they could approach God's people, the *wicked must first pass this company of mighty, holy angels.* This was impossible. The angels of God were causing them to recede, and also causing the evil angels who were pressing around them to fall back."

Verses 11 and 12, contain another wonderful promise, and show the purity and holiness of God's people. "O thou afflicted, tossed with tempest, and not comforted, behold, I will lay thy stones with fair colors, and lay thy foundations with sapphires. And I will make thy windows of agates, and thy gates of carbuncles, and all thy borders of pleasant stones." This scripture could hardly refer to the New Jerusalem,—the Holy City, for there is no reference made of the walls of the city having windows, nor could there be any necessity for them, for twelve gates only are mentioned. Furthermore, the gates are made of one great pearl, and not of carbuncles. ("And the twelve gates were twelve pearls: Every several gate was of one pearl." Rev. 21:21.) The verses being considered at this time refer to a spiritual house of which Solomon's temple was a symbol. This spiritual house is referred to by Paul in Eph. 2:20-22, "and are built upon the foundation of the apostles and prophets, Jesus Christ himself being the chief corner stone; In whom all the building fitly framed together groweth unto an holy temple in the Lord: In whom ye also are builded together for an habitation of God through the Spirit."

Note that this spiritual house has foundations, windows, gates, and borders (enclosures). The foundations refer to the apostles, Jesus Christ Himself being the chief corner stone. See Eph. 2:20. The windows of a house are used to give light. This has reference to the prophets who foresee things in advance and give the light upon the subject as in 1 Sam. 9:9. ("Beforetime in Israel, when a man went to enquire of God, thus he spake, Come, and let us go to the seer: For he that is now called a Prophet was beforetime called a *seer.*") The "gates" of a house serve the purpose to let in those who have the right, and to keep out all others. This could have no other meaning than the watchmen on the walls of Zion (the ministry). The "borders" (or enclosures) mean the church members the "lively stones". 1 Pet. 2:5, "Ye also, as lively stones, are built up a spiritual house, an holy priesthood, to offer up spiritual sacrifices, acceptable to God by Jesus Christ."

Note the kind and quality of material used here in this spiritual house. It is the most precious known to humanity—"I will lay thy stones with fair colors" (Isa. 54:11). Foundations of sapphires, windows of agates, gates of carbuncles, and borders of pleasant stones. Think of Jesus as the precious corner stone; the apostles, who sacrificed their lives, as the wonderful foundations; the prophets (many of whom were killed by cruelty, even to the extent of being sawed between two logs), as the windows to give light to this beautiful house; and those in the church during the dark ages, who suffered and were tortured by the cruel persecutors, to beautify the borders of this most glorious, spiritual house.

Let each one ask himself, Am I fitted to be used in this spiritual structure whose stones are of fair colors? Am I willing to trust in God, and suffer for Him, whatever He may permit for my good? Or do I want the world, and heaven, too? Can we serve God and Mammon? Can we in any way disregard the instructions given to us by the Spirit of God, and expect to be fitted among those who would rather die, than disobey in the smallest of His commands? How fearful the thought. Can the church supplant the instructions of God with wise plans of men?

God Calls To Return—The Word That Transforms
Isaiah 55

"Ho, every one that thirsteth, come ye to the waters, and he that hath no money; come ye, buy, and eat; yea, come, buy wine and milk without money and without price. Wherefore do ye spend money for that which is not bread? And your labor for that which satisfieth not? Hearken diligently unto me, and eat ye that which is good, and let your soul delight itself in fatness." Verses 1, 2. The word "Ho" signifies "whosoever", or "anyone that will hear". It was not so in the Old Testament time, for the Jew then thought the Bible was for the descendants of Abraham only.

"Come ye to the waters, and he that hath no money". Water is the most essential article to sustain life; both human, animal, and vegetable. It is the most abundant substance, and without it life is impossible. In this verse it is meant to represent spiritual life, which is bounded by Eternity. Jesus, speaking to the woman at the well, said, "Whosoever drinketh of the water that I shall give him shall never thirst; but the water that I shall give him shall be in him a well of water springing up into everlasting life." John 4:14.

Water is composed of two elements; namely, oxygen and hydrogen. Without hydrogen life cannot exist, and without oxygen, life would cease in less than fifteen minutes. Water is never sold; it is free. The price we pay in the cities is not for the water, but for the service rendered in bringing this necessity to us for daily use. Neither is it for sale in the Scriptures, but is offered free. No price can be set for life eternal. If it was sold, no one could buy it, therefore the symbol used here is perfect. It would be impossible to substitute any other earthly article to represent spiritual life.

WINE

"Yea, come, *buy* wine and milk without money and without price." Though the water is free, the wine and the milk are sold, but there is no set price on it, nor is the exchange made with money. Something must be given in trade to make the transaction. What must it be? The answer is found in the seventh verse, as follows: "Let the wicked forsake his way, and the unrighteous man his thoughts: And let him return unto the Lord, and he will have mercy upon him; and to our God, for he will abundantly pardon." We must forsake our ways and our thoughts, and in exchange, take God's thoughts and follow His ways. Verse 8: "For my thoughts are not your thoughts, neither are your ways my ways, saith the Lord." Not until *after* this transaction is made can one please, serve, or understand God, nor can he enter heaven. When this transaction is made, the thoughts, ways, desires, actions, and the whole human being is changed. How do we get God's thoughts? Only in one way may they be attained. God's thoughts and ways are found in His Word (the Bible). The man who will follow the complete instructions by the Spirit of God is in a heavenly atmosphere, and walks with God as Enoch of old.

What is the wine, and the milk? We shall first speak of the wine. While the water is rich in oxygen, the wine is rich in iron. With the absence of iron in the system, oxygen would be of no essential value to the human body, for iron is the train by which oxygen is transported throughout the human anatomy. As soon as oxygen enters into the lungs, the agency of iron takes the element and carries it through the entire system. Thus, whatsoever the wine represents, without it, the water (life) would be of no importance, as well as the water without the wine (as symbol) would be altogether useless. The wine represents the blood of Christ. Therefore, the wine is used in connection with the Lord's supper; a symbol of the spilled blood of Christ. If you must have life eternal (water), you must also have the blood of Christ (the wine), for one would be of no value without the other. Again we see that no other earthly article, substance, or element could be used to represent the blood of Christ.

THE MILK

The next symbol mentioned is the milk, and it, too, must be perfect in itself in order to point out the truth intended by the Spirit of God. The human body is made up of sixteen different elements. If we should exhaust our supply of one of these elements, and life did not cease immediately (depending on the element lacking), there would be trouble somewhere within the human system. If milk contained all the elements required to keep the human body, the meaning of the symbol would indicate that the first two symbols, or doctrines are of no great importance. Since milk does not contain all the necessary elements, it signifies that the doctrine represented by the milk only is not sufficient. (The element of iron is absent from milk. Though a trace of iron is found in the milk, it is so infinitesimal, that it may be expressed in the following language: "The amount of iron found in ten gallons of milk could be put in the corner of one's eye.") That which is not found in the milk is supplied by the wine. Therefore the three doctrines taught here cannot be separated one from the other.

What is the doctrine taught by the milk? This symbol is simple to understand. The milk represents the Word of God as found in the Bible. 1 Pet. 2:2, "As newborn babes, desire the sincere *milk of the word,* that ye may grow thereby." God's Word is perfect, and it will supply all the doctrines (elements) needed for the human heart to make us perfect, but without the shedding of the blood of Christ, it would not profit us at all. Neither would the Word and the blood help us much if there was no life in the Son of God. Thus, the water, wine, and milk are combined, and can not be separated one from another and still maintain life eternal. Perfect symbols are they not?

Suppose you would add an element to the milk, would it not be a strange one? And if it be a strange one to the milk, would it be foreign to the human system? If this be true, we must conclude it would be poison to the human body. "But," you say, "suppose I add the element of iron, it would not then be poison." By adding another element, it would put the milk out of balance, and it would be milk no longer. It is impossible for human wisdom to improve on God's work. Just so, it is impossible for us to neglect one of God's words and yet maintain spiritual life, neither can we add, though the thing may be good, as we may see it. It would throw the Word out of balance, and it would be God's Word no longer, just as the milk would be milk no longer. God's Word must be kept in the human heart, pure and unadulterated, if we must live by it. "This robe, woven in the loom of heaven has in it not one thread of human devising." Christ's Object Lessons, page 311.

(One may say, if milk is not a balanced diet, how then can a babe be raised on milk and yet be perfectly healthy? God, who made the milk, knew what the baby requires for its growth, and what the milk could supply, so He has made provision before the babe is born. Between the stomach and the small intestine, in that part of the bowel, is found a large "lump". This "lump" is placed there to supply the iron. The opening to the small intestine, as well as to the stomach, is too small for the "lump" to pass through. Thus it is compelled to remain there. Each time nourishment passes by, it absorbs part of the iron; thus the element is supplied, and the babe has suffered no lack. As the baby grows older, the "lump" gradually decreases in size. Just as it is with the human babe, so it is with the animal life.) Truly our God is infallible, and who can comprehend His wisdom?

Why Spend Money For That Which Is Not Bread?

"Wherefore do ye spend money for that which is not bread? And your labor for that which satisfieth not? hearken diligently unto me, and eat ye that which is good, and let your soul delight itself in fatness." Isa. 55:2. When we spend our money for food which does not contain all the required elements, or if it is of an unbalanced proportion, then it is not as the Creator made it. In such a case we have spent our money for that which is not "bread".

When buying food we must be very careful in our selection and make sure that it is free from adulteration, or disjunctive manufacturing processes. In such foods, the elements required to sustain physical health are not found. It would be only a waste of money in buying such foods. The worst harm done by the use of these baser products is not to one's pocketbook only, but to his health in reducing his physical powers. The upkeep of the human body depends on the food supply we give it.

BLESSINGS TO JEW AND GENTILE—BLIND WATCHMEN
ISAIAH 56

In the beginning of this chapter God asks His people, "keep ye judgment and do justice". The reason given is that His salvation is near to come, and His righteousness to be revealed. The thought is that the scroll is soon to make a turn, and the present order of things must change. If the watchmen to whom God is speaking would not commence a general housecleaning, God would have to get watchmen who would lift their voice like a trumpet and show His "people their transgression, and the house of Jacob their sins". God, in this chapter, asks His people for a strict Sabbath observance, regardless who they are, without distinction of class, race, or people. Thus they shall have the promise of His covenant, and their offerings and sacrifices shall be accepted upon His altar.

There is a severe charge against *His watchmen* of their *failure* to deal with the sins in the church, and the result is that *His people* are *devoured* by the enemy. "*His* watchmen are blind: They are all ignorant, they are all dumb dogs, they cannot bark." Verse 10. The phrase "dumb dogs" is not to humiliate them, but is used here as a symbol. Of all animals, a dog is a man's best friend, and it is a dog's business to protect his master, or warn him of the danger by the sound of his barking. But if that dog becomes dumb, and fails to give the sound, then he is not only useless to his master but dangerous, for he can not be depended upon. Thus, a "dog" is a perfect symbol of a watchman over God's people.

A good faithful minister is man's best friend by warning him of the danger involved in sin, but if that minister will not sound the alarm and give the warning, then he has become as a "dumb dog": Not only useless but dangerous, for thus the sheep are devoured by the enemy. The watchmen are not only charged with failure to deal properly with existing sins in the church, but they are greedy as well. "Come ye, say they, I will fetch wine, and we will fill ourselves with strong drink." Verse 12. This refers to the same watchmen or servants as in Matt. 24:48-50, who are gluttonous, disregard health reform, and do not see the danger. Read "Isaiah the Gospel Prophet", page 25, first paragraph. The watchmen mentioned by the prophet are not those in Babylon (popular churches), but.*"His* watchmen" in His true church. According to Testimonies to Ministers, page 445, Ezekiel 9, is the sealing of the 144,000. Speaking of Ezekiel's prophecy in Volume 5, page 211, we read: "The ancient men, those to whom God had given great light, and who had stood as guardians of the spiritual interests of the people, had betrayed their trust. They had taken the position that we need not look for miracles and the marked manifestation of God's power as in former days. Times have changed. These words strengthen their unbelief, and they say, The Lord will not do good, neither will he do evil. He is too merciful to visit his people in judgment. Thus peace and safety is the cry from men *who will never again* lift up their voice like a trumpet to show God's people their transgressions and the house of Jacob their sins. *These dumb dogs,* that would not bark, are the ones who feel the just vengeance of an offended God. Men, maidens, and little children, all perish together."

THE RIGHTEOUS AND THE WICKED IN THE DAY OF TROUBLE
ISAIAH 57

The entire 57th chapter deals with idolatry in God's church. God's people were called to come out of Babylon. The reason why we are called out is that we are to depart from the customs of Babylon. This chapter reveals the truth. Though we came out, we brought the customs and idolatry into the house of God. The evil spoken of in this chapter is Christmas-keeping, and Christmas gifts one to another. The 9th verse says, we have honored the king (the devil) by doing this, and "debase" ourselves "even unto hell". This surely is true. We as a people spend the Lord's money in telling the public that Christmas is not the birthday of Christ, and then turn about and do the same thing the world is doing. By such methods we are implicated in the highest form of hypocrisy.

Verses 4, 5, and 6, tell of the evil practices of Israel of old, and are written in this chapter to make a comparison with the people now, in as much as to say, we are doing the same as they back there, and are no better. Quoting Volume 1, page 129: "I saw that many who profess to believe the truth for these last days, think it strange that the children of Israel murmured as they journeyed; that after the wonderful dealings of God with them, they should be so ungrateful as to forget what he had done for them. Said the angel, 'Ye have done worse than they'." To explain the entire chapter, it must be taken verse by verse, but being too lengthy, it can not be done at this present time.

TRUE FASTING—THE SABBATH RESTORED
ISAIAH 58

Verse 1: "Cry aloud, spare not, lift up thy voice like a trumpet, and shew my people their transgression, and the house of Jacob their sins." God asks His watchmen to cry aloud and not to leave one thing undone; to lift up their voices like a trumpet, and fear not how far the sound may reach; to show the transgressions and sins to His people, by a general housecleaning, "for His salvation is near to come, and His righteousness to be revealed". Quoting Testimonies to Ministers, page 427, we read: "Cleanse the camp of this moral corruption, if it takes the highest men in the highest positions. God will not be trifled with."

The second verse describes the people to whom He wishes to speak. The first part of the third verse tells of the complaints His people are making. "We have fasted", they say, "and have afflicted our souls, but our prayers are not heard." He takes no knowledge of them, is their cry. The last part of the verse tells where the trouble lies: "Behold, in the day of your fast ye find pleasure, and exact *all* your labors." This fast cannot be a fast for food, for when one is fasting of food he is permitted to find pleasure, and exact all his labor. In fact, one must go about his daily duties as usual, so that he would show no outward appearance of fasting. Our Saviour requires that this duty be performed in sincerity, and not in hyprocrisy, for the glory of God, and not for attraction and appearance to men.

Jesus said, "Moreover when ye fast, be not, as the hypocrites, of a sad countenance: For they disfigure their faces, that they may appear unto men to fast. Verily I say unto you, they have their reward. But thou, when thou fastest, anoint thine head, and wash thy face; That thou appear not unto men to fast, but unto thy Father, which is in secret: And thy Father, which seeth in secret, shall reward thee openly." Matt. 6:16-18.

Turning back to Isaiah 58, verse 13, tells the kind of fast this is. "If thou turn away thy foot from the Sabbath, from doing thy pleasure on my holy day; and call the Sabbath a delight, the holy of the Lord, honorable; and shalt honor him, not doing thine own ways, nor finding thine own pleasure, nor speaking thine own words." Therefore, the fast mentioned here is not a fasting of food, but of pleasure, labor, and our own ways and thoughts, and that we must honor God and keep His Sabbath holy. The charge is, that we exact *all* our labor on the Sabbath day. As a people we have forgotten the true meaning of Sabbath keeping. We have come to suppose that anything which pertains more or less to religion is permissable on God's holy day. It is said, It is the Lord's work. But God has never said anywhere in the Scriptures that His people are at liberty to do all manners of work (that pertain to religion) on the Sabbath day. Work which can be done on a day other than the Sabbath is not a work for the Sabbath. "Six days shalt thou labor and do all thy work: But the seventh day is the Sabbath of the Lord thy God: In it thou shalt not do *any* work."

Note the way the commandment reads: *"Any work"*. God does not mean that we can do our work in the six days, and His on the Sabbath. He says it is a day of rest: Not physical, but spiritual rest. For instance, it would be wrong for one to sell good religious books on the Sabbath, even if he turned all the proceeds to the church. It would be wrong for a surgeon to perform surgical operations on patients on the Sabbath day if it can be done at another time. It would be wrong for a nurse to give treatments to patients on the Sabbath day if it was not absolutely necessary. Read Volume 7, page

106. It would be wrong for a church council to meet on the Sabbath and discuss church business, or make plans of any kind. It would be wrong for a Sabbath keeper to load himself with evangelical announcements for a series of meetings, and distribute them from house to house on the Sabbath day. All this manner of work could be done on a day other than the Sabbath.

When we do this kind of work on the Sabbath, we do it to save ourselves an hour or so of time for the next day, thus we rob God of His time and add it to our secular pleasure. If it is wrong for one to go and sell good religious books on the Sabbath, though he turns all the proceeds to the Church, it would be doubly wrong to sell that same book in the house of God on the Sabbath day, regardless of what is done with the income. If all of this is true, then it would be wrong to go out with Harvest Ingathering papers and receive contributions for missions on the Sabbath. It is time for God to call our attention to these things.

Quoting Patriarchs and Prophets, pages 313, 314: " 'Ye shall keep the Sabbath therefore; for it is holy unto you. . . . Whosoever doeth *any* work therein, that soul shall be cut off from among his people.' Directions had just been given for the immediate erection of the tabernacle for the service of God; and now the people might conclude, because the object had in view was the glory of God, and also because of their great need of a place of worship, that they would be justified in working at the building upon the Sabbath. To guard them from this error, the warning was given. Even the sacredness and urgency of that special work for God must not lead them to infringe upon his holy rest day."

The balance of chapter 58, teaches that we must take care of our poor and sick, instead of sending them to the county farm, or hospital, if we are to delight in the Lord. There are many lessons that we can draw from the services of ancient Israel. God gave them the seventh-day Sabbath as a day of rest for praise and thanksgiving. Though the sacrificial was a sacred, religious service, requiring much labor, they were not permitted to do it on the seventh-day Sabbath.

For this reason God gave them the monthly Sabbaths in which they were to do that sacred work. If God did not allow every kind of religious service to be performed on the seventh-day Sabbath *then,* will He now? "I the Lord change not." Read Lev. 23.

A Redeemer Promised To A Penitent People
Isaiah 59

Verses 2-8, tell how terrible and grievous our sins are in God's sight. The first verse contains the wonderful promise: "Behold, the Lord's hand is not shortened, that it cannot save; neither his ear heavy, that it cannot hear." If we would repent of our sins and turn to Him with fasting and prayer, He will have mercy upon us, and will hear our prayers. Though our sins are unspeakably great, verses 9-13, are of a good report. Some of the people are conscious and repenting from their sins. In 16-19, is a prophecy too sad to speak of. It applies to those upon whom the responsibility rested to bring about reformation by presenting the lessons to the church in their true light, calling every sin by its right name instead of applying it to other people and times, and thereby diverting the instructions intended for the church. The admonitions in the Scriptures were overlooked and unheeded, and what God expected of His people during the first three months of 1929, was not accomplished, simply because those in responsible positions failed to discharge their duty.

Verse 16, first part: "And he saw that there was no man, and wondered that there was no intercessor." God "was astonished". Moses and Aaron "stood between the dead and the living". Num. 16:48. God used Elijah on Mount Carmel. 1 Kings 18. In the crisis here brought to view, God finds no man (Eze. 22:30), so He Himself interposes.

Isa. 59:16-18: "Therefore his arm brought salvation unto him; and his righteousness, it sustained him. For he put on righteousness as a breast plate, and an helmet of salvation upon his head; and he put on the garments of vengeance for clothing, and was clad with zeal as a cloke. According to their deeds, accordingly he will repay, fury to his adversaries, recompence to his enemies; to the islands he will repay recompence." God clothes Himself with His own attributes, and advances to set things right. Had there been a man, God would have let the man do the work, but as there was none, He does it Himself. This reveals one of God's working principles. He will use one man, or a nation, to help correct or punish another. When that cannot be done, God steps in. While God will come with vengeance to some, He comes with salvation to others. Verse 20: "And the Redeemer shall come to Zion." This is not referring to the second coming of Christ in the clouds, for it takes place before probation closes. He is not coming with vengeance to the ungodly in the world, but coming to the church. And when He comes, He will do the work mentioned in Mal. 3:1-3.

Verse 19: "So shall they fear the name of the Lord from the west, and his glory from the rising of the sun." God will make this coming as an example to the nations, just as He did with Sodom and Gomorrah. Verse 19, last part: "When the enemy shall come in like a *flood,* the Spirit of the Lord shall lift up a standard against him." John, in Rev. 12:15, refers to this incident. "And the serpent cast out of his mouth water as a flood after the woman, that he might cause her to be carried away of the flood." The woman here mentioned is God's church (Seventh-day Adventist) "which keep the commandments of God, and have the testimony of Jesus Christ." The "flood" is not the blue Sunday law, or any persecution in the past. The blue law has a different setting, and is described in Revelation 13, as a persecuting power to enforce the mark of the beast.

"Flood" is the same as "water", which means people (in the church) unconverted, whom Satan is using to cause the church to be carried away in a very quiet manner, so that no one would be suspicious of the great deception. In this way he attempts to deceive the *very elect* (144,000) if it were possible. Being impossible, Christ Himself interposes and delivers His people (those who sigh and cry for all the abominations in the church) and then makes an example of the others.

Rev. 12:16, "And the earth helped the woman, and the earth opened her mouth, and swallowed up the flood which the dragon cast out of his mouth." The meaning is that they die, being buried in the earth, as in Num. 16:32, "And the earth opened her mouth, and swallowed them up, and their houses, and all the men that appertained unto Korah, and all their goods." Thus "the Spirit of the Lord shall lift up a standard against him." Isa. 59:19, last part. This will fulfill Matt. 13:29, 30: "Let both the wheat and the tares grow together *until* the harvest." The separation will mark the beginning of the harvest, which is the Loud Cry of the third angel's message. Rev. 18:1. The spirit of God is poured upon His people (those who escape the ruin), and the promise is, that it shall never depart from them. Isa. 59:21, "As for me, this is my covenant with them, saith the Lord; my spirit that is upon thee, and my words which I have put in thy mouth, shall not depart out of thy mouth, nor out of the mouth of thy seed, nor out of the mouth of thy seed's seed, saith the Lord, from henceforth and forever." Read "Isaiah the Gospel Prophet", Volume 3, pages 43-49.

As soon as the separation is finished, and Satan has lost out with his deceptive scheme, the church finds herself in a great conflict with the enemy. Rev. 12:17, "And the dragon was wroth with the woman, and went to make war with the remnant of her seed [those who are left], which keep the commandments of God, and have the testimony of Jesus Christ." (The war against the woman is the blue law.)

THE FINAL TRIUMPH OF THE RIGHTEOUS
ISAIAH 60

This chapter begins with the words "Arise, shine; for thy light is come, and the glory of the Lord is risen upon thee." The Latter Rain, the Spirit of God, and the glory of His power. The chapter tells of the ingathering in the time of harvest. A great multitude composed of all nations, and classes of people, rich and poor alike, from all walks of life; kings and rulers among them, and also the wealth of the Gentiles, shall come to the church. The nation and the kingdom that will not serve them (the church) shall perish. The multitude gathered here are the ones with the palms in their hands. Rev. 7:9.

Isa. 60:19, 20, tell of the purity of God's church and His care over His people. Verse 21, says, "Thy people also shall be all righteous." The unclean and unconverted will not be permitted in the church. "Awake, awake; put on thy strength, O Zion; put on thy beautiful garments, O Jerusalem, the holy city: For *henceforth* there shall *no more* come unto thee the uncircumcised and the unclean." Isa. 52:1. "The remnant of Israel shall not do iniquity, nor speak lies; neither shall a deceitful tongue be found in their mouth: For they shall feed and lie down, and none shall make them afraid." Zeph. 3:13. Verse 22, of Isaiah 60: mentions their success in winning souls to Christ.

BUILDERS OF THE OLD WASTE PLACES
ISAIAH 61

The first verse and part of the second apply to Christ Himself at the beginning of His ministry. The Spirit of Prophecy says it will repeat itself with the people of God. This would find its fulfillment in the time of harvest, with the 144,000 (those who escape the ruin of Isaiah 59, and 63), by whose effort the great multitude of Rev. 7:9, is made.

Isa. 61:2, "To proclaim the acceptable year of the Lord, and the day of vengeance of our God." The acceptable *year* cannot be a prophetic time, for it would mean 365 years. It must be a literal year of twelve months. There is good reason for believing that this must be that year in which the lessons came, and the truth in them made known. Had this not been the prophetic year, the call would not have come, for God keeps accurate time. To Ninevah, God gave forty days to repent. Now to His people He gives one year to make good, otherwise He would have to spue them out of His mouth, and this applies to those upon whom the responsibility rests. "And unto the angel of the church of the Laodiceans write; . . . I know thy works, that thou art neither cold nor hot: I would that thou wert cold or hot. So then because thou art lukewarm, and neither cold nor hot, *I will spue thee out of my mouth."* Rev. 3:14-16. "The call to this great and solemn work was presented to men of learning and position; had these been little in their own eyes, and trusted fully in the Lord, he would have honored them with bearing his standard in triumph to the victory. But they separated from God, yielded to the influence of the world, and the Lord *rejected* them." Volume 5, page 82.

The *day* of vengeance in Isa. 61:2, follows the year. The day may be prophetic, which in that case, would mean a literal year. Thus, it would mean a year in each case. This year of vengeance is not the seven last plagues, nor is it the destruction of the wicked at the second coming of Christ. It takes place before the close of probation, for in the fourth verse we read: "And they shall build the old wastes, they shall raise up the former desolations, and they shall repair the waste cities, the desolations of many generations." The meaning of this verse is to restore the truth of God which has been trodden down under foot for many generations. The 144,000—the true Israel of God—are the builders. Thus, we see that after the day of vengeance, God's truth is to be restored and revealed to the people. Therefore, it must be before the close of probation. The balance of the chapter confirms the same thought.

The "day of vengeance" is the same as in Ezekiel 9; Isaiah 63; and Isaiah 59; as previously explained. Verse 6, meaning the 144,-000, says they are priests, as explained on pages 37, 38.

THE HOLY PEOPLE—THE LORD'S REDEEMED
ISAIAH 62

In Volume 3, page 65, of "Isaiah the Gospel Prophet", we read: "I will not rest." God is speaking. He has determined that the righteousness of His people shall become evident, and He will not rest until it is accomplished. The words indicate not only determination, but also that there has been delay, that now the crisis has come, and that God is tremendously in earnest to see the work finished. God intends to exhibit His people to the world. He wants to demonstrate what can be done in human flesh; and He will not rest satisfied until His people reflect His image fully. When that is done, the earth will be lightened with the glory of God. Rev. 18:1."

Verse 2: "A new name." Indicative of the new experience they have passed through, which is the separation, or sifting, as explained. God Himself with His own mouth gives the name so it can not be counterfeited. The time the name is received is at the end of the 430 year period as explained on the chart on pages 112-13. Thus, the church is reorganized under a new name. The old name, being polluted, could no longer be retained. There is no one to go by the old name, for the ones who were not worthy of having the new name have perished under the figure of the five men with the slaughter weapons of Ezekiel 9. The name only remains for a curse. In Isa. 65:15, we read: "And ye shall leave your name for a curse unto my chosen: For the Lord God shall slay thee, and call his servants by another name." The old order of things being changed. The watchmen who were unfaithful have perished.

"I have set watchmen upon thy walls, O Jerusalem, which shall *never hold their peace day nor night:* ye that make mention of the Lord, keep not silence." Isa. 62:6. (These are the watchmen under the new name.) Verses 8 and 9, reveal God's care and protection over His church. In the 10th verse is God's command to His people: "Go through, go through the gates; prepare ye the way of the people; cast up, cast up the highway; gather out the stones; lift up a standard for the people." In the 11th verse God says He has proclaimed to the people who shall live at the end of the world: "Behold, the Lord hath proclaimed unto the *end* of the world, Say ye to the daughter of Zion, Behold, thy salvation cometh; behold, His reward is *with* Him, and His work *before* Him."

AFFLICTED FOR HIS PEOPLE'S SAKE

ISAIAH 63

Verses 1-3, "Who is this that cometh from Edom, with dyed garments from Bozrah? This that is glorious in his apparel, traveling in the greatness of his strength? I that speak in righteousness, mighty to save. Wherefore art thou red in thine apparel, and thy garments like him that treadeth in the winefat? I have trodden the wine press alone; and of the people there was none with me: For I will tread them in my anger, and trample them in my fury; and their blood shall be sprinkled upon my garments, and I will stain all my raiment."

The last part of the preceding chapter speaks of "the holy people, the redeemed of the Lord". The first part of this chapter concerns those who have rejected the Lord (those who are to leave the name for a curse). To them the day of vengeance has come. The picture is not a pleasant one to look at, but it is true. It is God's "strange work". Edom is another name for Esau. See Gen. 25:30. Esau had his name changed because he sold his birthright for a bowl of pottage. The class here are termed Edom because they have sold their birthright for self-gratification to satisfy lust, the god of appetite (disregard of health reform), as explained on pages 59, 60. "Bozrah" is the name of a city. The name means "sheepfold", a symbol of the church.

Verse 4: "For the day of vengeance is in mine heart, and the year of my redeemed is come." Note, "the day of vengeance" the Lord says is in His "heart", but the "year of His redeemed is *come*". Note the verb "come" is in present tense, just as in Rev. 14:7, "Saying with a loud voice, Fear God, and give glory to Him; for the hour of His judgment is *come.*" We, as a people, hold that the verb "come" was inscribed in present tense because the *judgment* in heaven took place (at the end of the 2300 days of Daniel's prophecy) in 1844, but it was not understood until after the prophetic period had passed, therefore God did not intend to make the judgment known until after the hour had come. For this reason Inspiration inscribed the occurrence in present tense, *"is come"*, in order to be grammatically correct. Thus William Miller made the mistake of the event to transpire at the end of the 2300 days; namely, the sanctuary truth, Jesus entering the Most Holy place, and the beginning of judgment.

If the preceding scripture is true, then the one in Isa. 63:4, is just as dependable as any. This chapter, or the incident recorded in it, has never been understood, therefore God must have preserved the prophecy for a given time. Now the prophecy is understood, and being in present tense, we must believe, then, that "the year of His redeemed is *come*". If one should disbelieve the interpretation given, then he means to say God has made a mistake in inscribing the verb in present tense. This may be said if not by words, then by action.

His Redeemed

What is meant by "His redeemed"? "For the day of vengeance is in mine heart, and the year of my redeemed is come." Verse 4. You are here referred to Ex. 15:13, which is the song that Moses and the children of Israel sang after being delivered out of Egypt, and the Red Sea. "Thou in thy mercy hast led forth the people which thou has *redeemed*: Thou hast guided them in thy strength unto thy holy habitation." Ex. 15:13. Inspiration uses the same word "redeemed" in the song of deliverance. The experience of Israel being a type of Israel, the true, (the 144,000), and a duplicate of the church now, as explained in Section 4, we too, must be redeemed as well as they. For this reason, the prophet used the phrase "the year of my *redeemed is come*". According to the scripture, this must be the year (in which the lessons came—1929), when God began to deliver His people from the corruptions in the church. This is why they sing the song of Moses and the Lamb. Had this not been the prophetic year the call would not have come, for God keeps accurate time.

Quoting Ex. 15:14-16, "The people shall hear, and be afraid: Sorrow shall take hold on the inhabitants of Palestina. Then the dukes of Edom shall be amazed; the mighty men of Moab, trembling shall take hold upon them; all the inhabitants of Canaan shall melt away. Fear and dread shall fall upon them; by the greatness of thine arm they shall be as still as a stone; till thy people pass over, O Lord, till the people pass over, which thou hast purchased." The land of Canaan represents the land into which the church at this present time came into existence; namely, the United States of America. The name "Palestina" means "land of strangers". The United States is composed of strangers; people from many nations, and races. "Dukes of Edom" refers to the same class as those mentioned in Isa. 63:1, as previously explained. The name "Moab" means "progeni", or fore-fathers.

Quoting Isa. 63:5, "And I looked, and there was none to help; and I wondered that there was none to uphold: Therefore mine own arm brought salvation unto me; and my fury, it upheld me." This part of the prophecy has surely met its fulfillment. The lessons came to the church through the proper channel, and were presented by the Sabbath School department, but they were rushed through. The sins mentioned were applied to other people, no corrections of any kind were made, and the lesson intended was lost. The entire thing is forgotten and no one cares, therefore, "there was none to help". God "wondered that there was none to uphold". We wonder too. The scripture is plain, and in the helps to the lesson was admitted that the slaughter is in the church before the second coming of Christ in the clouds. Read "Isaiah the Gospel Prophet", pages 49, 70-73; also the quarterly of the same lesson. If such a message as this would not arouse the people, then may the question be asked, What else could have done it? Thus heaven "wondered". Indeed, the people have said in their hearts, "The Lord hath forsaken the earth, and the Lord seeth not: He will do neither good nor evil."

Verse 6: "And I will tread down the people in mine anger, and make them drunk in my fury, and I will bring down their strength to the earth." A. R. V., "poured out their life blood." Verses 7-9, speak of the Lord's goodness, mercies, and multitude of loving kindnesses. "In all their affliction He was afflicted." These verses bring to view the wonderful and blessed thought of God's suffering with His people. Verse 10, draws out a comparison that when we rebel against God, He turns to be our enemy. From the 11th verse and onward, including chapter 64, is a prayer of some one of God's children. Seeing the evil approaching, he has poured out his soul to God in prayer, to save His people. Remembering God's dealings with His chosen people and the wonderful deliverance of Israel out of Egypt, the one who offers the prayer evidently understands the situation.

The experience of Israel in Egypt is a duplicate, and the request is for a man like Moses. Verses 11-13: "Then he remembered the days of old, Moses, and his people, saying, Where is he that brought them up out of the sea with the shepherd of his flock? Where is he that put his holy Spirit within him? That led them by the right hand of Moses with his glorious arm, dividing the water before them, to make himself an everlasting name? That led them through the deep, as an horse in the wilderness, that they should not stumble?"

Verse 16: "Doubtless thou art our father, though Abraham be ignorant of us, and Israel acknowledge us not: Thou, O Lord, art our Father, our Redeemer; thy name is from everlasting." The language used in this verse proves beyond a doubt that the person is not an Israelite (Jew) after the flesh. The people in trouble here are not from the stock of Abraham, "though Abraham be *ignorant* of *us* and Israel *acknowledge us* not". It would have been impossible for the prophet Isaiah, or any other of his nation to utter the words while they boasted over the fact that they were of Israel, the stock of Abraham, which to them was a great honor.

Verse 17: "O Lord, why hast thou made us to err from thy ways, and hardened our heart from thy fear? Return for thy servant's sake, the *tribes* of thine inheritance." This verse reveals the reason for God's displeasure with His people: Error; hard-hearted, not fearing God. "Why hast thou made us to err?" This is not a charge against God that He has caused them to sin, but rather a wish that God might have used even harsher punishment to bring them back to their senses.

Verse 18: "The people of thy holiness have possessed it but a little while: Our adversaries have trodden down thy sanctuary." Their "adversaries": Isa. 59:18, tells that *their* adversaries are the *Lord's* adversaries. They have trodden down the sanctuary with the multitude of merchandise, laughter, whispering, common talking, manicuring, and other forms of idolatry to dishonor God to His face (in His church). Verse 19: "We are thine: Thou never barest rule over them; they were not called by thy name." They have not followed God's instructions. Though they identify themselves among the people of God in His house of prayer, they are not in reality called by His name.

"Isaiah the Gospel Prophet", page 73 (Lessons for Today) commenting on "Verses 1-6", says, "These verses should bring serious thoughts to every soul. There is no more dreadful picture in all the Bible than this section presents. The figure of God's striding forth to tread the wine press of His wrath is an awful one. Yet it is true. Esau had all the opportunity that any one could have to know right from wrong. He willfully chose wrong, and became a persecutor of the true people of God. We conceive that there are none upon whom God's wrath will be visited more completely than upon those who have *known* the truth, are closely related to it, as it were, and yet turn from it to become persecutors of those who do *right*. Even as it is a blessed thing to accept the truth, so it is a fearful thing to reject it. And rejection need not include all truth. To reject a part may be just as fatal as to reject the whole. So all should beware." Read Volume 5, page 492; Volume 8, pages 248-250; Volume 1, page 190; Volume 1, pages 471-472; Volume 5, pages 207-216; Testimonies to Ministers, page 380; Volume 2, page 708; Testimonies to Ministers, pages 206, 407, 408.

A PEOPLE PREPARED FOR A NEW HEAVEN AND A NEW EARTH
ISAIAH 65

Verse 1, "I am sought of them that asked not for me; I am found of them that sought me not: I said, Behold me, behold me, unto a nation that was not called by my name." The language used in this verse is in the past tense. However, there is a chance for an argument as to whether it be in past or present tense, as it is translated in the King James' version. The following, which is altogether in past tense, is quoted from the Hebrew translation by Isaac Lesser. "I *allowed* myself to be *sought* by those that *asked* not; I let myself be *found* by those that *sought* me not: I *said,* here am I, unto a nation that *called* itself not by my name." The Greek, also the Bulgarian are in past tense, but let us quote the same verse which was quoted by Paul to the Romans, as it is in the King James' version. Rom. 10:20, "But Esaias is very bold, and saith, I *was found* of them that *sought* me not; I *was made* manifest unto them that *asked* not after me."

Certainly no one can dispute the language used by Paul, for he was well educated in both Hebrew and Latin tongues. Furthermore, Paul made the translation under the inspiration of the Holy Spirit, therefore we must believe this scripture as it is translated by him— from the Hebrew to the Greek,—in past tense. We shall speak of verse 2, and then come back with the thought. *"I have* spread out my hands all the day unto a rebellious people, which walketh in a way that was not good, after their own thoughts." Note that while the first verse is in past tense, the second is in present. Paul applies the first verse to the Gentiles in his time, but the second to Israel,—after the flesh. Here is an opportunity for concentration of thought upon the subject. Paul is applying the scripture in past tense to present time in his day, but the scripture in present tense he applies to a people in the past. The way the application was made certainly does not sound grammatically correct, but we cannot say Paul made a mistake. The application and translation must be right, as well as grammatically correct.

The wisdom used in this scripture is amazing, and it should cause us to give glory to our God. Paul, under the Spirit of Inspiration made the application, so as to clear the scripture from the apparent complication. The chapter was not written for Israel, nor for the Gentiles in Paul's day, but directly for the church at the pres-

ent time.   If this can be proven, we must accept it as present truth
direct from God.   The scripture being grammatically incorrect of
the application proves that the *time* for this chapter was not yet ripe,
the same as other scriptures and prophecies.   It could not be understood, nor correctly applied until the time appointed.   Then God reveals His Word to His people in the manner He will choose, but it
may come in an unexpected way.

The first verse rightfully applies to the Gentiles, the second was
applied to Israel after the flesh, which is a type of Israel by the
promise (the 144,000, the church at this present time; namely, the
Seventh-day Adventist).   For this reason, Paul had to apply the
scripture to the type, for the true was not yet in existence.   Now, the
time being ripe, the scripture is grammatically correct, the first verse
in past tense to the Gentiles in Paul's time, the second to the church
at this present time, in present tense.   Thus we have the positive
proof of the application and the time to which this scripture applies.
This should turn our hearts to God, and cause us to search diligently
the prophecy contained in this chapter.

Space will not permit to present here all this chapter contains.
Only an outline of some of the things will be given.   The charge
against the church is not a pleasant one, but it ought not to discourage
any one of us, for our God is merciful and willing to forgive us of
our sins if we would but acknowledge our guilt.   Had it not been so,
He would not have sent the message.   The last part of verse 3, is
quoted here: "That sacrificeth in gardens, and burneth incense upon
altars of brick."   We must understand that these are symbols, but
they are not hard to decipher.   Had it been impossible to be understood, no one could profit by it, therefore the symbol would not have
been used in the chapter.   "Gardens" are used for a display.   "Sacrifice" is the same as gift.   "Incense", according to Rev. 8:3, 4, is the
way prayers are sent to God.   Nowhere in the Bible can we read of
any of God's people building altars of brick.   Altars to God were
always built with *stones.*

The difference between brick and stone will now be considered.

Brick is the product of man, but stone is the workmanship of God. Let us now consider the lesson intended here. "Gardens", display; "Sacrifice", gifts; "Incense", prayers; "Bricks", man-made proposition. The charge is, we sacrifice for display, we offer our prayers to God (upon altars of *brick*); we follow after man instead of God's pure word, as given to the church.

Verse 4: "Which remain among the graves, and lodge in the monuments, which eat swine's flesh, and broth of abominable things is in their vessels." "In the graves"; "in the monuments", meaning man-made devices of which there is no resurrection. "Swine's flesh", "broth of abominable things": Means disregard of health reform; man eats whatever his lustful appetite craves for.

Verse 5: "Which say, Stand by thyself, come not near to me; for I am holier than thou." While this class is not living the truth, yet they think they are better than others, and being so high-minded, by their action they say, "we are holier than thou". In the 6th verse, God says, He will "recompense into their bosom". By the information already given, the reader can determine the meaning of the seventh verse.

Verse 8: "Thus saith the Lord, As the new wine is found in the cluster, and one saith, Destroy it not; for a blessing is in it: So will I do for my servants' sakes, that I may not destroy them all." "Cluster" is composed of many grapes, and is a symbol of the church as a body. The Lord says He will not destroy them all. The "wine" in the cluster represents the blood of Christ, and for this reason, all are not destroyed. The tenth verse speaks of the promise to those who shall escape. The 11th and 12th verses speak of the class that shall perish. The slaughter here is the same as that of Ezekiel 9. Quoting Isa. 65:12,—"Therefore will I number you to the sword, and ye shall all bow down to the slaughter: Because when I called, ye did not answer; when I spake, ye did not hear; but did evil before mine eyes, and did choose that wherein I delighted not."

Verses 13 and 14, show God's care over His people and the suffering of the other class. Verse 15: "And ye shall leave your name for a curse unto my chosen: For the Lord God shall slay thee, and call his servants by another name." This verse has been previously explained in connection with the 62nd chapter of Isaiah, page 68. The class mentioned here is the same as in Volume 5, page 155: "The call to this great and solemn work was presented to men of learning and position; had these been little in their own eyes, and trusted fully in the Lord, he would have honored them with bearing his standard in triumph to the victory. But they separated from God, yielded to the influence of the world, and the Lord *rejected* them."

Verse 16: "That he who blesseth himself in the earth shall bless himself in the God of truth; and he that sweareth in the earth shall swear by the God of truth; because the former troubles are forgotten, and because they are hid from mine eyes." "Bless himself in the God of truth": Many people will bless themselves, but not in the God of truth. That is, they obtain riches, or some other blessing, but not by honesty. Some "sweareth", but not by the God of truth. That is, they will tell a falsehood, but after God purifies His church all these things shall pass away, and be forgotten.

Verses 17-19, speak of the new earth. Verse 20, is here quoted from the Hebrew translation by Isaac Lesser. "There shall no more thence an infant of few days, nor an old man that shall not have the full length of his days; for as a lad shall one die a hundred years old; and as a sinner shall be accursed he who (dieth) at a hundred years old." It seems this translation makes the meaning of the verse just a little plainer than the King James'. The scripture speaks of the time at the end of the 1000 years (millennium) after the resurrection of the wicked. At that time there will not be any births to infants. "There shall *no more* thence an infant of days." The lesson therefore is not so difficult for one to comprehend. All the wicked are called forth in the second resurrection, whether old or young (at the time of death). All come up at the same time. This hour becomes the birth of all the wicked in the second life. There is to be no natural, or unnatural death, for all must live to the time of the second death, which is by "fire come down from God out of heaven and devoured them". Read Rev. 20:7-10. "And as a sinner shall be accursed he who (dieth) at an hundred years old." This scripture predicts the span of life of the wicked after they are resurrected as being 100 years. "For as a lad shall one *die a hundred years old;* and as a sinner shall be accursed he who (dieth) at a hundred years old." During this 100 year period, the wicked make preparation for their attack on the holy city. Read Rev. 20:8, 9.

Verses 21-25, speak of the saints in the earth made new. Here is another evidence that the chapter is intended for the people at the time of the end, for the closing verses speak of the earth made new.

THE INGATHERING FROM THE GENTILES:
WORSHIP IN THE NEW EARTH
ISAIAH 66

Verse 1: "Thus saith the Lord, The heaven is my throne, and the earth is my footstool: Where is the house that ye build unto me? And where is the place of my rest?" The house mentioned here is a spiritual house as in Eph. 2:20-22, of which Solomon's temple was a symbol. The following quotation is found in Prophets and Kings, pages 35, 36: "Thus as the building on Mt. Moriah was noiselessly upreared with 'stone made ready before it was brought thither: So that there was neither hammer nor ax nor any tool of iron heard in the house, while it was in building', the beautiful fittings were perfected according to the patterns committed by David to his son."

The lesson intended here is that the spiritual stones (the members of the church) are to be made ready before they are brought thither. Why, then, are candidates so often granted baptism and membership in the church without being instructed in all the advent truth? It is surprising to know the large number of so-called Seventh-day Adventists who do not believe in the writings of the Spirit of Prophecy, and altogether ignorant of the truth in health reform. Are not these the fundamental principles in the church? Is not health reform the right hand and arm of the third angel's message? Has not this continual practice drifted the church into the world?

That beautiful temple reveals God's desire for His church. For this reason, God lavished so much wealth upon this palatial structure upon Mt. Moriah. According to estimates given in the monthly bulletin of the Illinois Society of Architects, it reached the tremendous total of more than eighty-seven billion dollars. The several estimates show the total cost to have been $87,212,210,840. This sum represents a nation's wealth. The question is, How did Israel ever raise such an enormous sum of money to lavish on one single structure? God never asks us to do anything unless He Himself makes it possible.

The tremendous amount of wealth expended on this magnificent temple represents God's care and love for His people, as well as the glory of the church. Solomon recognized that this temple was but a symbol of a temple which he was not able to build. In 2 Chron. 2:6, we read: "But who is able to build him an house, seeing the heaven and the heaven of heavens cannot contain him? Who am I then, that should build *Him* an house, save only to burn sacrifice before him?" God asks His people at this present time, "Where is the house which ye build unto me?" (Isa. 66:1). Douay version reads: "That *ye* will build to me?" The Hebrew translation reads: "A house that *ye can* build unto me?"

"The heaven is my throne, and the earth is my footstool." This scripture shows the impossibility for a human mortal to do anything for God, except He does it through him. How offensive it must be to heaven when we say *we* are to finish God's work in this generation, or attempt to build Him a house by the plans of men. We have said it, and have acted like it, but we have failed. Now God asks us, "Where is the house that *ye* will build unto me?" One may say, See this great denomination we have built. If there is any greatness about it, it is not to man's credit. Though we have boasted much of our efforts, God lets us go on according to our supposed wise judgment until we fall and discover our mistake. True, it is a great denomination, but God does not see it the way we do. At the rate we are going it would take us hundreds of years to finish the work, and the fact of the matter is, *we* never can. Furthermore, as great a denomination as it is, it is not ready for translation, therefore we can ask ourselves, Where is the house *we* have built? The thirteenth chapter of Ezekiel is written for the church at this present time from which we quote verse 5: "Ye have not gone up into the gaps, neither made up the hedge for the house of Israel to stand in the battle in the day of the Lord."

"And where is the place of my rest?" We call ourselves Sabbath keepers and boast much of keeping the commandments of God, but here we are asked "where is the place of my rest?" We have polluted God's holy day, and desecrated the Sabbath with merchandise, as previously explained on pages 147-8. See also page 124. A good minister of God, after being questioned as to the authority in selling our publications on the Sabbath day in the house of God, said, "It is a question just how much of our publications are to be sold on the Sabbath." The confliction in this minister's mind was answered in three short words: "None of it". But this answer did not satisfy the man in the sacred position, and he added, "Ancient Israel killed the lamb and sacrificed it on the Sabbath. Therefore, we can sell our books." The answer given to this was, "If Israel did sacrifice the lamb on the seventh-day Sabbath they were told to do so, but you are told *not* to, and that is the difference." The fact of the matter is that God did not give the seventh-day Sabbath to ancient Israel for sacrifices, but for a day of rest. Monthly Sabbaths were added for the sacrifices. Read Leviticus 23.

In the second verse of Isaiah 66, God tells us that all these things which we boast of, He has made and they have been, "but to this man will I look, even to him that is poor and of a contrite [penitent] spirit, and trembleth at my word." Verse 3: "He that killeth an ox is as if he slew a man; he that sacrificeth a lamb, as if he cut off a dog's neck; he that offereth an oblation, as if he offered swine's blood; he that burneth incense, as if he blessed an idol. Yea, they have

chosen their own ways, and their soul delighteth in their abominations." The scripture is unmistakably plain that our sacrifices, offerings, prayers, and whatever form of religion we may have, is not
only an abomination to Him, but it is the most offensive. "Yea, they
have chosen their own ways, and their soul delighteth in their abominations."

Verse 4: "I also will choose their delusions, and will bring their
fears upon them; because when I called, none did answer; when I
spake, they did not hear: But they did evil before mine eyes, and
chose that in which I delighted not." God did call by these lessons
when they came to the church through the Sabbath School department, but they came, and went, and are forgotten. So then, because
they have chosen their own ways, and did evil before God, and delighted not in following the instructions given to the church, now, He
says He will choose their delusions, and will bring their fear upon
them. It is a fearful thing to turn a deaf ear to the voice of God.
While this verse speaks of a class who are determined to follow their
own choice in preference to God's way, the next verse speaks of a
class who *do* fear God, and dare serve Him. Thus, it is unmistakably clear that there are two classes of people in the church.

Verse 5: "Hear the word of the Lord, ye that tremble at his
word; Your brethren that hated you, that cast you out for my name's
sake, said, Let the Lord be glorified: But he shall appear to your joy,
and they shall be ashamed." This verse shows that though the call
in the lessons was turned down by those in responsible positions, God's
Word never returns void to Him, for the class in this verse fear God,
and tremble at His Word, and the result is that there is division in
the church. The class who are in opposition to God are either the
majority, or, those who have a stronger influence upon the members
of the church, for the verse says they cast out their brethren (the
godly class) for His name's sake. The class who are casting out
God's people think they are doing His service, for the scripture reads:
[they] "Said, Let the Lord be glorified."

It is bad enough for one to turn down God's Word, but it is far worse when such a one is so blinded, that by turning down the heavenly call, thinks he is doing God's service. The verse holds an encouraging promise for the God-fearing ones, for it says, "He shall appear to your joy," and when the Lord fulfills His promise, the oppressors of God "shall be ashamed". It has been one of Satan's tricks *throughout the history of the church* to flood her with his agents, and unconverted, so that when truth comes to the church, as soon as God's people respond to the call, he stands ready to vote them out by the majority of his followers. The result has been that necessity gave birth to a new movement or denomination, but, according to verses 4 and 6, God is to deal entirely different in this instance. The reason being, because God organized this denomination Himself by a prophet, and has given us special light of present truth. Thus, it leaves us without excuse and God deals accordingly with the people.

Quoting Volume 3, page 265: "But if the sins of the people are passed over by those in responsible positions, His frown will be upon them, and the people of God, as a body, will be held responsible for those sins. In His dealings with His people in the past, the Lord shows the necessity of purifying the church from wrongs." The "voice of noise", the sixth verse, has reference to the class who have chosen their own way in preference to the Lord's way, whom He calls His enemies.

Verses 7 and 8: "Before she travailed, she brought forth; before her pain came, she was delivered of a man child. Who hath heard such a thing? Who hath seen such things? Shall the earth be made to bring forth in one day? or shall a nation be born at once? for as soon as Zion travailed, she brought forth her children." In these two verses a comparison is made with the church at the first coming of Christ (Jewish), and the church just prior to His second coming. "Before she travailed, . . . before her pain came." This refers to the church at the time Christ came. She did not expect Him (travailed not), nor did she feel, or know when He came. Though she was not worthy, "she was delivered of a man child."

The church referred to in the eighth verse is the opposite of the one in the seventh verse. The time is ripe for a mighty movement, in which thousands will be converted in a day. This is the church in the time of the latter rain, the loud cry of the third angel's message. The church is become thoroughly in earnest. As soon as there is a real travail for purity of sinners, the work is finished, almost at once. "Shall the earth bring forth in one day? or shall a nation be born at once? for as soon as Zion travailed, she brought forth her children."

The ninth verse shows that God is the one who does the work. The tenth verse says those who love her (the church) and mourn for her now, will rejoice and be glad. The eleventh verse shows why they will rejoice and be delighted: Because of truth and light in God's Word which will come to the church represented by the milk. "That ye may suck, and be satisfied with the breasts of her consolations; that ye may milk out, and be delighted with the abundance of her glory." Isa. 66:11. Verses 12-14, tell of God's care over His people, and the church's love for her members, the Lord's favor toward His servants, and indignation toward His enemies.

Verses 15-17: "For, behold, the Lord will come with fire, and with his chariots like a whirlwind, to render his anger with fury, and his rebuke with flames of fire. For by fire and by his sword will the Lord plead with all flesh: And the slain of the Lord shall be many. They that sanctify themselves, and purify themselves in the gardens behind one tree in the midst, eating swine's flesh, and the abomination, and the mouse, shall be consumed together, saith the Lord." The coming of the Lord "with fire . . . . to render his anger with fury," is not the coming of Christ in the clouds to receive His people. It is before the close of probation, and in the time of the purification of the church. See Mal. 3:1-3. He comes with vengeance to those who claim His name, but follow man instead of Christ, and the result is that they do not keep His truth. (The class who do not investigate for themselves but accept the decisions of others who are following after man, and are in the clutches of the devil.)

"Behind one tree": Margin reads, "one after another". The

reading here justifies the translation: "Following the leader". That
is, people are inclined to follow a man in high position instead of
searching in the Word for themselves and demand a "thus saith the
Lord". "In the gardens behind one tree": This phrase also suggests the "tree of knowledge of good and evil". The partaking of
the forbidden fruit in the garden of Eden brought sin into existence.
The charge here is similar, only worse. Men have chosen for their
food the things God has forbidden, and "spend money for that which
is not bread". "By His sword will the Lord plead with all flesh".
This has no reference to those outside the church, for we read in the
nineteenth verse, "And I will set a sign among them, and I will send
those that escape of them unto the nations." Last part: "And they
shall declare my glory among the Gentiles." It is plain here that
those who shall escape the ruin, God shall send to all the nations, and
declare His glory to the Gentiles. Therefore, it must be in the
church only, and some length of time before the close of probation.
The "nations" mentioned in the verse is simply to show the large
territory covered by His servants (in all nations).

The destruction mentioned in verses 15-17, and Isaiah 63, is the
same. Thus, God makes them an example, or sign to all nations, for
we read in the last part of the eighteenth verse, and the first part of
the nineteenth: "It shall come, that I will gather all nations and
tongues; and they shall come, and see my glory. And I will set a
sign among them."

Verse 20: "And they shall bring all your brethren for an offering
unto the Lord out of all nations upon horses, and in chariots, and in
litters, and upon mules, and upon swift beasts, to my holy mountain
Jerusalem, saith the Lord, as the children of Israel bring an offering
in a clean vessel into the house of the Lord." This verse shows the
ingathering of the Gentiles to the church by His servants (the 144,-
000). "His holy mountain" means His denomination; "Jerusalem"
means the leading part.

Verse 21: "And I will also take of them for priests and for
Levites, saith the Lord." We have previously explained that the

144,000 are to be priests and Levites, but in this verse the Lord says He will take also of the Gentiles "for priests and Levites". The reason for this is given in the next two verses. Verse 23: "And it shall come to pass, that from one new moon to another, and from one Sabbath to another, shall all flesh come to worship before me, saith the Lord." There is to be a system of worship, therefore a need of priests and Levites.

Verse 24: "And they shall go forth, and look upon the carcasses of the men that have transgressed against me: For their worm shall not die, neither shall their fire be quenched; and they shall be an abhorring unto all flesh." "For their worm shall not die, neither shall their fire be quenched:" Man's body is consumed by worms, and the meaning is that these consuming worms will not die until the body is reduced to dust. Neither will the fire be quenched till "the carcasses" are reduced to ashes. The reason why the worm and fire are mentioned here is told in the sixteenth verse: "For by fire and by his sword will the Lord plead with all flesh". The destruction is accomplished by both, and where the sword is used, the worm will do its work. "The worm shall not die, . . . the fire shall not be quenched", means that the prophecy is sure, and the destruction foretold will be accomplished.

SECTION VII.
WHAT IS THE MEANING OF THE FOURTH CHAPTER OF MICAH?

"But in the last days it shall come to pass, that the mountain of the house of the Lord shall be established in the top of the mountains, and it shall be exalted above the hills; and people shall flow unto it." Micah 4:1. The scripture is unmistakably clear; that it was intended for the last days, for it reads: "But in the *last days* it shall come to pass". It is also positive that this scripture would be fulfilled, for it says: "it *shall come to pass*".

It is an accepted fact that nearly all Bible students agree that the "mountain" spoken of in this chapter is a symbol of God's church (denomination), of which the temple built on Mount Moriah was a type. The prophet declares that God's church would be established in the top of the mountains (denominations), and it shall be exalted above the hills (sects, or organizations). Exalted, not by the world, but by the Spirit of God in power, truth, and righteousness, and people will flow unto it. God has spoken it by His holy prophet, therefore it would be foolish, and deceptive for one to argue, or try to explain away the meaning of the sacred word.

This same prophecy is also described in the second chapter of Isaiah from which we quote. "The lofty looks of man shall be humbled, and the haughtiness of men shall be bowed down, and the *Lord alone shall be exalted in that day*." Isa. 2:11. If everything that is human would be made low and bowed down, and the Lord alone exalted in that day, one can clearly see that the prophecy is to meet its fulfillment, for the Lord is exalted on earth by His church as portrayed by the prophet Isaiah. "Thou shalt also be a crown of glory in the hand of the Lord, and a royal diadem in the hand of thy God. Thou shalt no more be termed Forsaken; neither shall thy land any more be termed Desolate: But thou shalt be called Hephzibah, and thy land Beulah: For the Lord delighteth in thee." Isa.

62:3, 4. When the mountain of the Lord is thus "established on the top of the mountains, and exalted above all hills", then doubtless "people shall flow unto it".

This glorious time spoken of by the prophet, Micah, is none other than the loud cry of the third angel's message. The 60th chapter of Isaiah is a prophecy of the church in the time of the "latter rain", from which we quote: "Arise, shine; for thy light is come, and the glory of the Lord is risen upon thee. For, behold, the darkness shall cover the earth, and gross darkness the people: But the Lord shall arise upon thee, and his glory shall be seen upon thee. And the Gentiles shall come to thy light, and kings to the brightness of thy rising. Lift up thine eyes round about, and see: All they gather themselves together, they come to thee: Thy sons shall come from far, and thy daughters shall be nursed at thy side." Isa. 60:1-4.

"And after these things I saw another angel come down from heaven, having great power; and the earth was lightened with his glory." Rev. 18:1. "The remnant of Israel shall not do iniquity, nor speak lies; neither shall a deceitful tongue be found in their mouth: For they shall feed and lie down, and none shall make them afraid." Zeph. 3:13. "For, behold, the darkness shall cover the earth, and gross darkness the people: But the Lord *shall* arise upon thee, and *His glory* shall be seen *upon thee."* Isa. 60:2. Such a glorious time is ahead of God's church.

Verse 2, first part: "And many nations shall come, and say, Come, and let us go up to the mountain of the Lord, and to the house of the God of Jacob; and he will teach us his ways, and we will walk in his paths." The words just quoted are spoken by the nations. When the church of God is purified and filled with the Holy Spirit, "clad in the armor of Christ's righteousness, the church is to enter upon her final conflict. 'Fair as the moon, clear as the sun, and terrible as an army with banners,' she is to go forth into all the world, conquering and to conquer." Prophets and Kings, page 725.

Indeed, people will inquire and invite one another, saying, Come, and let us go up to the mountain of the Lord and to the

house of the God of Jacob." "Therefore, thy gates shall be open
continually; they shall not be shut day nor night; that men may bring
unto thee the forces (margin, wealth) of the Gentiles, and that their
kings may be brought . . . . and I will make the place of my feet glorious. The sons also of them that afflicted thee shall come bending
unto thee; and all they that despised thee shall bow themselves down
at the soles of thy feet; and they shall call thee, The city of the Lord,
The Zion of the Holy One of Israel." Isa. 60:11, 13, 14. Indeed,
this is the harvest time spoken of by the prophets, and the great ingathering from all nations. "The house of the God of Jacob" meaning the church into which the 144,000 are sealed,—Israel the true.

Verse 2, last part: "For the law shall go forth of Zion, and the
word of the Lord from Jerusalem." When the law of the Lord is
proclaimed by His church, you can clearly see what is meant by a
righteous church: Righteous people who would obey the voice of the
Lord. Zephaniah, looking down through the ages by the prophetic
eye, foresaw this glorious church. "The remnant of Israel shall
not do iniquity, nor speak lies; neither shall a deceitful tongue be
found in their mouth: For they shall feed and lie down, and none
shall make them afraid." Zeph. 3:13. None need misunderstand
this scripture. It will be fulfilled just as it is written. Though
some may think this prophecy is empty talk because the *people* are saying, "come, and let us go up to the mountain of the Lord".

We read in Counsels to Teachers: " 'This shall be the covenant
that I will make with the house of Israel: After those days, saith the
Lord, I will put My law in their inward parts, and write it in their
hearts; and will be their God, and they shall be My people. And
they shall teach no more every man his neighbor, and every man his
brother, saying, Know the Lord: For they shall all know Me, from
the least of them unto the greatest of them, saith the Lord: For I
will forgive their iniquity, and I will remember their sin no more."
Jer. 31:33, 34.'

" 'And many nations shall come, and say, Come, and let us go up
to the mountain of the Lord, and to the house of the God of Jacob;

and He will teach us of His ways, and we will walk in His paths: For the law shall go forth of Zion, and the word of the Lord from Jerusalem.' Micah 4:2." Counsels to Teachers, pages 454, 455. Note that the Spirit of Prophecy applies Micah 4:2, as a sure prophecy that will come to pass and find its fulfillment with the people of God, by associating the verse with Isa. 54:11-14; Jer. 31:33, 34; which scriptures find their fulfillment in the time of the "Loud Cry of the Third Angel's Message".

Verse 3, "And he shall judge among many people, and rebuke strong nations afar off; and they shall beat their swords into plowshares, and their spears into pruninghooks: Nation shall not lift up a sword against nation, neither shall they learn war any more." "And he shall judge among many people, and rebuke strong nations afar off." In Isa. 60:10, 12, we have the explanation of the text. "And the sons of strangers shall build up thy walls, and their kings shall minister unto thee: . . . For the nation and kingdom that will not serve thee shall perish; yea, those nations shall be utterly wasted."

"And they shall beat their swords into plowshares, and their spears into pruninghooks: Nation shall not lift up a sword against nation, neither shall they learn war any more." This verse reads exactly the opposite of Joel 3:10, "Beat your plowshares into swords and your pruninghooks into spears: Let the weak say I am strong."

These scriptures reveal two classes of people. One class shall flow into the church by great groups: Kings, and great army leaders who have been building destroying weapons and preparing for war. Now the gospel has conquered them. While they are joining the church they gather their war implements, beating them into *plowshares and pruninghooks.* "Violence shall *no more* be heard in thy land, wasting nor destruction *within thy borders;* but thou shalt call thy walls Salvation, and thy gates Praise." Isa. 60:18. The other class, outside of the church, prepare for war, beating their plowshares into *swords,* and their pruninghooks into *spears.* One people is preparing for translation, while the other is getting ready for conquest. Therefore both scriptures run parallel and will be fulfilled at the same time. Thus the world would be divided into two great separate and distinct classes: Separating the wheat from the chaff, the goats from the sheep.

Verse 4, "But they shall sit every man under his vine and under his fig tree; and none shall make them afraid: For the mouth of the Lord of hosts hath spoken it." The meaning of the verse is that God's church is in an absolute security, and none need fear. Remember that the 144,000 are sealed before this time, and their life is sure; none can harm them nor touch their present life, or the life to come, for they are living saints, to be translated. Having this assurance, none can make them afraid, and they shall triumph with victory. Quoting Isaiah 60:17, last part, and 18: "I will also make thy officers peace, and thine exactors righteousness. Violence shall no more be heard in thy land, wasting nor destruction within thy borders; but thou shalt call thy walls Salvation, and thy gates Praise."

Verse 5, "For all people will walk every one in the name of his god, and we will walk in the name of the Lord our God for ever and ever." The verse is unmistakably clear that the world would be divided into two great, and separate classes. God's people would have nothing in common with the wicked, and would say, "all people will walk every one in the name of *his* god". But *"we* will walk in the name of the *Lord our God* for ever and ever."

Verse 6, "In that day, saith the Lord, will I assemble her that halteth, and I will gather her that is driven out, and her that I have afflicted," meaning the church now, in this present condition. "I will make her a remnant": That is, after the separation (purification), those who are left,—the 144,000, being the remnant. The affliction is the time of purification.

Verse 7, "And I will make her that halteth a remnant, and her that was cast far off a strong nation: And the Lord shall reign over them in mount Zion from henceforth, even for ever." "Her that was cast far off",—the church at this present time was "cast off", or, as it reads in Rev. 3:16, "I will spue thee out of my mouth",— meaning the present Laodicean state. But in His mercy He will gather the remnant (those that are left) and make the church a "strong nation" by the ingathering of the Gentiles into the message. A great army of 144,000, filled with the Holy Ghost will fearlessly proclaim the message in all the world, going forth conquering and to conquer. "A little one shall become a thousand, and a small one a strong nation: I the Lord will hasten it in its time." Isa. 60:22. "And the Lord shall reign over them from henceforth even forever": Christ Himself takes charge of the flock once and forever. "God has promised that where the shepherds are not true he will take charge of the flock himself." Volume 5, page 80.

Verse 8, "And thou, O tower of the flock, the stronghold of the daughter of Zion, unto thee shall it come, even the first dominion; the kingdom shall come to the daughter of Jerusalem." This verse is familiar to all. A prophecy of Christ,—"O tower of the flock . . . . unto thee shall it come, even the first dominion." "The first dominion" is the dominion Adam lost. The promise is that Christ will restore it all, and in turn, by inheritance, it shall come to the church (His people). "The kingdom shall come to the daughter of Jerusalem."

Verse 9, "Now why dost thou cry aloud? is there no king in thee? is thy counselor perished? for pangs have taken thee as a woman in travail." This time of crying and pain could be no other but the time just before us, the time of purification. "Behold, I will send my messenger, and he shall prepare the way before me: And the Lord, whom ye seek, shall suddenly come to his temple, even the messenger of the covenant, whom ye delight in: Behold, he shall come, saith the Lord of hosts. But who may abide the day of his coming? And who shall stand when he appeareth? for he is like a refiner's fire, and like fullers' sope." Mal. 3:12.

This purifying process will not be an easy matter on the part of sinners, for "refiner's fire and fullers' sope" is being used, and when God gets through with this washing process, He will have a people pure and clean. Then there will be a glorious time with joy and gladness in the Lord, as it is with a woman in travail, but when a son is born there is great joy. But the question is asked, "Now why dost thou cry out loud? is there no king in thee? is thy counselor perished?" Though it may seem painful yet none need fear, for God's church has a King and a counselor who neither "slumbers nor sleeps". The furnace is watched closely. The sinner *shall* perish, but the godly shall be preserved.

Verse 10, "Be in pain, and labor to bring forth, O daughter of Zion, like a woman in travail: For now shalt thou go forth out of the city, and thou shalt dwell in the field, and thou shalt go even to Babylon; there shalt thou be delivered; there the Lord shall redeem thee from the hand of thine enemies." This verse shows that after the purification, the church is not immediately translated to the New Jerusalem in heaven, but is left to do her appointed work here on earth. "For now shalt thou go forth *out of the city,* and thou shalt *dwell in the field,* and thou shalt *go* even *to Babylon; there* shalt thou be delivered; *there* the Lord *shall redeem thee from* the *hand* of *thine enemies."*

'Be in pain and labor to bring forth, O daughter of Zion, like a woman in travail." The explanation of this scripture is found in Isa. 66:7, 8. We quote verse 7: "Before she travailed, she brought forth; before her pain came, she was delivered of a man child." This woman "brought forth before she travailed; before her pain came she was delivered of a man child". The woman is the Old Testament church in the days of Christ. Christ is the man child whom she brought forth, but she travailed not, neither did she have pain. That is, she knew Him not; she felt no pain of deliverance. As it would be a miracle for a woman to give birth to a child in this way, so it was a miracle that Christ was born to that unworthy mother (Jewish church: Because she had backslidden). Quoting the 8th verse: "Who hath heard such a thing? who hath seen such things? Shall the earth be made to bring forth in one day? or shall a nation be born at once? for as soon as Zion travailed, she brought forth her children." While it was a miracle for the Jewish church to give birth to Christ; there is a still greater miracle with the church mentioned in this verse, for while the latter travailed she brought forth her children. It would be a wonder for such a thing, as it is impossible for the earth to bring forth in one day, or for a nation to be born at once. Nevertheless it will be done, "for as soon as Zion travailed she *brought* forth her children".

Humanly speaking, to finish the work of the gospel in this generation (the generation being almost past) would be an impossible task; but prophecy declares that impossibilities will be accomplished. The church which travailed and brought forth her children is the church in the time of the loud cry of the third angel's message. There is a great ingathering to be accomplished in just a little while. "And after these things I saw another angel come down from heaven, having great power; and the earth was lightened with his glory." Rev. 18:1. "And many nations shall come, and say, Come, and let us go up to the mountain of the Lord and to the house of the God of Jacob."

Verse 11, "Now also many nations are gathered against thee, that say, Let her be defiled, and let our eye look upon Zion." As soon as God's church as a body (not as individuals) escapes the clutches of the devil (for the unclean shall not enter in), and becomes earnest, filled with the Spirit of God, the wrath of the old enemy will be aroused, and will bring about the fulfillment of Rev. 12:17. "And the dragon was wroth with the woman, and went to make war with the *remnant* of her seed, which keep the commandments of God, and have the testimony of Jesus."

This time of trouble is also described by the Spirit of Prophecy. Early Writings, pages 33, 34: "And at the commencement of the time of trouble, we were filled with the Holy Ghost as we went forth and proclaimed the Sabbath *more* fully. . . . The wicked thought that we had brought the judgments upon them, and they rose up and took counsel to rid the earth of us, thinking that then the evil would be stayed. In the time of trouble we all fled from the cities and villages, but were pursued by the wicked, who entered the houses of the saints with a sword." Also pages 282, 283. "I saw the saints leaving the cities and villages, and associating together in companies, and living in the most solitary places. Angels provided them food and water, while the wicked were suffering from hunger and thirst. Then I saw the leading men of the earth consulting together, and Satan and his angels busy around them. I saw a writing, copies of which were scattered in different parts of the land, giving orders that unless the saints should yield their peculiar faith, give up the Sabbath, and observe the first day of the week, the people were at liberty after a certain time, to put them to death." Jeremiah also describes this troublous time. "The shepherds with their flocks shall come unto her; they shall pitch their tents against her round about; they shall feed every one in his place." Jer. 6:3.

Verse 12, "But they know not the thoughts of the Lord, neither understand they his counsel: For he shall gather them as the sheaves into the floor." The wicked cannot understand God. While they seek to destroy His people they are but erecting the gallows to hang themselves upon. As the wicked Haman prepared the gallows to take the life of Mordecai, the Jew, only succeeded to hang his own neck on it, just so the wicked will be confused in the day of God, for they know not the thoughts of the Lord.

Verse 13, "Arise and thresh, O daughter of Zion: For I will make thine horn iron, and I will make thy hoofs brass: And thou shalt beat in pieces many people: And I will consecrate their gain unto the Lord, and their substance unto the Lord of the whole earth." God's church is to thresh, garner in, bind in bundles, burn and destroy. The wicked shall perish and be as though they had not been. "For the nation and kingdom that will not serve thee shall perish; yea, those nations shall be utterly wasted." Isa. 60:12.

SUMMARY OF LESSONS OF REFORM

What Makes Infidels?

The question is asked, What is it that makes infidels? First of all, we shall define the word. "Infidel",—"a person who has no religious faith." Standard Dictionary. If this is true, then one who has a religion, whatever kind it may be, is not an infidel. It is an accepted fact that those who are in some dark corner of the earth, away from civilization, or Christianity, are not irreligious people. That is, as a rule they believe in some kind of supreme being, or supernatural power. This being so, we must admit that heathendom does not contribute to this great degeneracy so rapidly sweeping through the nations. Infidelity has its beginning in civilized lands. An attempt shall be made here to designate who is directly responsible for this widespread evil, which, like cancer is eating away the morals of the nations.

The following argument was put forth to an audience in a certain metropolitan city recently by a man who was attired in Indian costume, and who claimed to be a half-breed Indian. This man said, "This earth of ours rotates on its axis once in every twenty-four hours. During the day we stand on top of the earth with the sun over head, but at night we stand underneath the earth, hanging by our feet with moon and stars below us in space. If you meet a Christian at midday," continued the Indian, "and ask him where he is going, he will tell you he is going to heaven. If you ask him, Where is heaven? he points up toward the sun, and says, 'There is heaven.' But you meet him twelve hours later, at midnight, while he is under the earth, and ask him then where heaven is. This time he points up toward the stars, thinking he is pointing in the same direction as he did at midday, and says, 'There is heaven'."

Then he added, "Christians do not know where heaven is, neither do they know which way they are going. No matter at what time of day or night it is, they always point straight up. Furthermore, astronomers have been photographing suns and planets for many years. Some of these suns are so far out in space it would take millions of light years to get there, but they have not yet photographed heaven [where the throne of God is], so if there is any heaven, it must be so far away that if these Christians would travel as fast as light (186,000 miles a second), it would take them millions upon millions of years to get there. This would be impossible for the human span of life is limited to only a few years."

What this Indian has said is true, as far as his objection is concerned, and of the impossibility for one to get to heaven, that is, humanly speaking. It would take a fairly good Bible student to give a satisfactory answer to this kind of infidel, but the thought intended here, is that the Christian's contact with the Indian made him (the Indian) an infidel instead of a Christian. The evil did not stop there, for in turn, this Indian is now making infidels of hundreds and thousands of people by the use of the so-called light he has received of a so-called Christian. The experience of this Indian teaches that anyone professing the name of Christ, his course of action and conversation when in contact with the world, has a decided influence for the better or worse, and in turn, as the waves of the sea, one wave carries another, and another still another. "Throw a pebble into the lake, and a wave is formed, and another, and another, and as they are increased the circle widens until it reaches the shore. So with our influence; beyond our knowledge or control it tells upon others in blessing or in cursing." C. O. L.

Evidently there are two classes of Christians. One class makes disciples for Christ, while the other class contribute infidels against Christ. We may well ask ourselves, Which class do I belong to? 2 Cor. 13:5, "Examine yourselves, whether ye be in the faith; prove your own selves. Know ye not your own selves, how that Jesus Christ is in you, except ye be reprobates?" Quoting 2 Tim. 2:15, "Study to show thyself approved unto God, a workman that needeth not to be ashamed, rightly dividing the word of truth." This commandment is as good as any Bible commandment. At least it ought to be as good as the fifth commandment of the decalogue. "Honor thy father and thy mother: That thy days may be long upon the land which the Lord thy God giveth thee." Ex. 20:12.

If a father commands his son to do a certain thing and that son refuses to obey, he has dishonored his earthly father, and is become a transgressor of the fifth commandment. But if one is asked to do a certain thing by his heavenly Father and should refuse to respond to the call, such a person has dishonored his heavenly Father, and is become a transgressor of the first commandment, "Thou shalt have no other gods before Me." In fact, he is breaking the first four commandments which are honor to God, while the last six are love for man. "For whosoever shall keep the whole law, and yet offend in one point, he is guilty of all." Jas. 2:10.

Quoting the first part of 1 Pet. 3:15, "But sanctify the Lord God in your hearts." The meaning is that God alone should dwell in the heart and nothing else should interfere. It is possible for one to obey the commandment in 2 Tim. 2:15, as previously quoted, but without a sanctification of his heart to the Lord God, if he would spend a life time in studying, it would be in vain as far as spiritual things are concerned, of which we speak. On the other hand, if one would obey these two commandments (1 Pet. 3:15 and 2 Tim. 2:15), then he must be able to fulfill the last part of the verse, "and be ready always to give an answer to every man that asketh you a reason of the hope that is in you with meekness and fear". 1 Pet. 3:15. The kind of answer we give to every man will prove whether we keep God's commandments or not. If our answer is like the above-mentioned Christian, then we too know not where heaven is, neither do we know where we are going. Our influence would be such as to make infidels against Christ instead of disciples for Christ. The Christian who has sanctified the Lord God in his heart can give a better answer to the above-stated Indian than a so-called Christian.

Quoting Isa. 14:13, "For thou hast said in thine heart, I will ascend into heaven, I will exalt my throne above the stars of God: I will sit also upon the mount of the congregation, in the sides of the north." Lucifer wanted to ascend to the sides of the north because that is where God's throne is, and where the throne of God is, there heaven is also. Had this Christian pointed toward the north at mid-day the same as the compass, and in the same direction at midnight, or at any time, the extreme ends of all lines would meet at the same point. This answer would have been proper and instructive as well. The whip against heaven as well as the confusion would have been avoided, and the amount of good derived from a wise answer could not be estimated. An answer to this Indian, and the directions to heaven are given at the close of this chapter.

Lucifer said he will ascend to the sides of the north. He could have ascended had he obeyed the commandment of the Lord. But no, Lucifer thought he knew better than his God, and wished to make an improvement in heaven. Honest in his deception, he at-tempted the impossible task. In Isa. 14:15, we read: "Yet thou shalt be brought down to hell, to the side of the pit." The result was instead of ascending to the sides of the north where he desired to go, he descended down in the sides of the pit (in the opposite direc-tion). Just so, many Christians now, like Lucifer, think they are going to ascend up in the sides of the north (Heaven) but in their own way, wishing to improve on the wisdom of the Living God. They are more interested to go to heaven than they are to study and obey the explicit instruction given them in the Word of God. Though honest in their misconception of the heavenly direction, they will find themselves down in the sides of the pit (hell). The disappointment to such a one would be greater than we can realize. Experience only can tell the sorrow and grief at such a time. This class of Chris-tians are not only a detriment to themselves, but are injurious to others, and are the ones of whom our Lord said, "Ye are of your father the devil, and the lusts of your father ye will do." John 8:44.

Quoting 2 Cor. 13:5, "Examine yourselves, whether ye be in the faith; prove your own selves. Know ye not your own selves, how that Jesus Christ is in you, except ye be reprobates?" We, as Seventh-day Adventists, would do no wrong to heaven nor injustice to ourselves if we would take an account of our Christian experience so that we may be able to tell where we are headed for. We, as a people, have been honored by heaven with a special message for the world in this generation. We call this message the "Third Angel's Message" which is a combination of the first, second, and third angel's messages of Rev. 14:6-12. The substance of the message we bear may be classified into five subjects: (1) the time of the end; (2) the judgment (day of atonement, since 1844); (3) the second coming of Christ in *this generation;* (4) the restoration of the true Sabbath; (5) calling God's people out from Babylon (idolatry) which we define to be Sunday, Easter, and Christmas keeping, etc. Because they have refused to acknowledge and renounce the practice of these so-called Christian institutions or festivals is the chief cause of the downfall of Babylon. The call is to depart from these pagan practices to the true worship of Jehovah.

We teach tithing for the support of the gospel. We claim we are the people who keep the *commandments* of God and have the *testimony* of Jesus, the latter being the gift of the Spirit of Prophecy; also the doctrines of health reform, dress reform, etc. The chief and only purpose of these doctrines being to prepare a peculiar people to God's own glory and honor; a people to meet the Lord without tasting death, or, to rise in the special resurrection of Daniel 12. "But ye are a chosen generation, a royal priesthood, an holy nation, a peculiar people; that ye should shew forth the praises of him who hath called you out of darkness into his marvellous light." I Pet. 2:9.

This message is to penetrate into the uttermost parts of the earth, for by it shall the world be judged. Rejectors being condemned to death, it is a far more fearful message than we can even realize. This is the substance and the object of the message we bear to every kindred, tongue, and people, and its presentation before the public in all its wonders has a great effect. The people listen with intense interest and give their undivided attention, eager to grasp every thought expressed. Becoming interested in the truth, they begin to search deeper in the Word. They supply themselves with the books of the Spirit of Prophecy, and with great interest commence to search through the sacred pages.

Believing as they have been taught that this is the day of judgment, they expect to see God's people rid themselves from all sin by obedience to His divine Word, and especially to the instructions given to the church by His messenger in this generation. As they search through the writings by the Spirit of Prophecy, they naturally come to the following passages: Counsels on Health, page 277: "Our ideas of building and furnishing our institutions are to be molded and fashioned by a true, practical knowledge of what it means to walk humbly with God. *Never* should it be thought necessary to give an appearance of *wealth*. *Never* should appearance be depended on as a means of *success*. This is a *delusion*. The desire to make an appearance that is not in every way appropriate to the work that God has given us to do, an appearance that could be kept up only by expending a large sum of money, is a merciless tyrant. It is like a canker that is ever eating into the vitals.

"Men of common sense appreciate comfort above elegance and display. It is a mistake to suppose that by keeping up an appearance, more patients, and therefore more means, would be gained. But even if this course would bring an increase of patronage, *we would not consent* to have our sanitariums furnished according to the luxurious ideas of the age."

Volume 5, page 188, speaking of Abraham, Isaac and Jacob: "They lived only for God's glory, and declared plainly that they were strangers and pilgrims on earth, seeking a better country, that is, an heavenly. Their conduct proclaimed their faith. . . . But how are the professed people of God today maintaining the honor of his name? How could the world infer that they are a peculiar people? What evidence do they give of citizenship in Heaven? . . . As *your* course was presented before me, I was pointed to the dwellings recently erected by our people in that city. These buildings are so many *monuments of your unbelief* of the doctrines which you profess

to hold. They are preaching sermons more effective than any delivered from the pulpit. I saw worldings point to them with jesting
and ridicule, as a denial of our faith. They proclaim that which the
owners have been saying in their hearts,—'My Lord delayeth his
coming'."

Volume 7, pages 59, 91, 92: "The Lord has instructed me to
warn those who in the *future* establish sanitariums in new places, to
begin their work in humility, consecrating their abilities to His service. The buildings erected *are not* to be *large or expensive. Small*
local sanitariums are to be established in connection with our training-schools". . . . "We must also remember that our work is to cor-
respond with our faith. We believe that the Lord is soon to come,
and should not our faith be represented in the buildings we erect?
Shall we put a large outlay of money into a building that will soon be
consumed in the great conflagration? Our money means souls, and
it is to be used to bring a knowledge of the truth to those who, because of sin, are under the condemnation of God."

Volume 9, page 71: "God designs that we shall learn lessons
from the failures of the past. It is not pleasing to Him to have *debts*
rest upon His institutions. We have reached the time when we must
give character to the work by *refusing* to erect large and costly buildings. We are not to copy the mistakes of the past, and become more
and more involved in debt."

It is the privilege of the reader to inquire from God's people
why the instructions given by one whom we believe to be the prophet
of God for the present time have not been carried out. Now we are
confronted face to face with our text, "And be ready always to give
an answer to *every man* that asketh you a reason of the hope that is
in you with *meekness* and *fear*." 1 Pet. 3:15. What answer can
we give that would demonstrate meekness and fear within the hearts
of God's people? Would our answer give a character to God's work
and His people? Would that answer establish the confidence of the
inquisitor in the message and the people that bear this great responsibility? What shall we say? Whether by word or by silence, that

answer can only be, "Yes, that is what the prophet says, but it is not what we do." Would such an answer give one the impression that we believe this is the day of atonement, and that every man must confess his sin? Would that person now accept the truth and be a Christian? Or would he, with the previously-mentioned Indian become an infidel? Most likely the latter would be accepted, and the truth rejected. But this is not where the evil ends.

Another comes with the following question: "You preach that Christmas is not the true birthday of Christ; that it is the birthday of an imposter, a day of pagan institution, and idolatrous worship. You have told us that Christians must not take part in it, and for this reason are supposed to come out from fallen Babylon. Why then do you do the same as those who are in Babylon? You give gifts and receive gifts, you send and receive Christmas greetings as well as those who do not know the difference." What answer shall we give to this second inquisitor that would establish his faith in what we believe?

Whether we answer the question or not, our works have declared, "Yes, that is what we preach, but that is not what we practice." Is not this hypocrisy of the highest form? Has our answer now compelled this poor soul to accept, or to reject the truth? Most likely he would reject the truth and join the ranks of infidelity now if never before. What is true of Christmas, the same is true of Easter, etc., but the current does not stop here.

The third person in line comes with the following passages: Volume 6, pages 215, 216, "Our conferences look to the schools for educated and well-trained laborers, and they should give the schools a most hearty and intelligent support. Light has been plainly given that those who minister in our schools, *teaching* the word of God, *explaining* the Scriptures, *educating* the students in the *things* of God, should be supported by the tithe money. . . . *The same* principles which, if followed, will bring success and blessing to our training-schools and colleges, should govern our plans and work for the church schools." This prophet whom you say is a prophet of God says thus and so. Why then do you not pay your school teachers by the tithe as God has commanded? Why do you desecrate the Sabbath by raising the teacher's salary in the hour of worship? If this is a prophet of God, why have you lightly esteemed the instructions given? Do you not fear God? Now what can be said to this man? We may not say anything. But that will not hide the evil for our works have revealed the following secret, "Yes, that is what God has said by His prophet, but that is not what we do."

How much tithe do you think this man would pay after he knows that we have misused it? Would such practices establish his confidence in the message and in the people? Would he now sacrifice a day in a week and one-tenth of his income and perhaps his position? His soul is at stake, and of whom shall it be required? Fearful, is it not?

The fourth one arrives with Volume 1, pages 471, 472: "A great mistake has been made by some who profess present truth, by introducing merchandise in the course of a series of meetings, and by their traffic diverting minds from the object of the meetings. If Christ were now upon earth, he would drive out these peddlers and traffickers, whether they be ministers or people, with a scourge of small cords, as when he entered the temple anciently. . . . 'And said unto them, It is written, My house shall be called the house of prayer, but ye have made it a den of thieves'." These traffickers might have pleaded as an excuse that the articles they held for sale were for sacrificial offerings. But their object was to get gain, to obtain means, to accumulate. . . . Ministers have stood in the desk and preached a most solemn discourse, and then by introducing merchandise, and acting the part of a salesman, even in the house of God, they have diverted the minds of their hearers from the impressions received, and destroyed the fruit of their labor. . . . Their time and strength should be held in reserve, that their efforts may be thorough in a series of meetings. Their time and strength should not be drawn upon to sell our books when they can be properly brought before the public by those who have not the burden of preaching the word."

This newly-interested person asks the question, "Why do you sell your publications in the church? Why do you desecrate the Sabbath with your merchandise? Is not the morning hour of the Sabbath sacred and for worship only? You have told me this was the prophet of God for this generation. Why have you disregarded the warning? Is not this book written by that prophet in whom you claim to believe?" What shall we tell this man? Is there anything we can say that would excuse us from the guilt? Whether we answer by word, or by silence, our works have manifested the following act, "Yes, that is what the prophet of God has said, but that is not what we do." We have sung our song, but what about the soul of this man?

The next person comes with Volume 8, pages 141, 142: "Those who are steadfast to the truth should not be set aside in favor of worldlings. Prices should not be set so high to meet current expenses that the poor will, to a large extent, be excluded from the benefits of the Sanitarium."

"This book which is claimed to be the inspired word of God, and which is said to contain all the instructions for the church at this present time says the denominational institutions must not set their prices so high as to meet current (running) expenses. The latest report according to the General Conference Bulletin in 1930 is: The denomination has received a net income of some $116,000,000 in four years from these institutions. If this prophet of God has said, "You are not to set your prices so high as to meet your current expense", how then did you make all these millions of dollars in just four short years? Why have you not followed the instructions? Does not your God mean what He says?"

What shall our answer be this time? Shall we say it is better to sacrifice than to obey? Is this what we teach? Or shall we say God has changed and cares but little whether His Word is respected or not? Will we hear the "well done" for losing the sheep and bringing the dollars? Is He after the gold more than the sheep? What shall we say? Shall we say our institutions are facing sunshine, and our judgment is better than God's? We may not say this by words, but our works have revealed that which is in our hearts. But what about this poor soul? Will he cast his lot with the people of God, or with the rank of infidelity? Oh! who shall pay the price of his blood?

The line has not yet reached its end, for another interested one comes with a large number of references, both from the Bible and the Spirit of Prophecy, wishing to inquire in regard to the instructions for the church respecting health reform. These books, which it is claimed are written for the people of God for this last generation, teach a strict health reform. This prophet has charged the church to establish health institutions everywhere, consisting of the manufacturing of health foods, health food stores, health cafeterias, schools and teachers for the art of cooking; also that the members of the church must refrain from foods which are considered by health authorities to be unhealthful.

Health reform is to be agitated everywhere, and it seems this prophet is right in the matter. The prophet also claims that those who disregard health principles can not enter in through the pearly gates of the Holy City, according to the following statement from Volume 5, page 197: "Rather than sit at a table where wholesome food is provided, he will patronize restaurants, because he can there indulge appetite without restraint. . . . That man is worshipping at the shrine of perverted appetite. *He is* an *idolater.* The powers which, sanctified and ennobled, might be employed to honor God, are weakened and rendered of little service. An irritable temper, a confused brain, and unstrung nerves are among the results of his disregard of nature's laws. *He is inefficient, unreliable.* . . . *Thus* the God of Israel is dishonored, while Satan's power is revered and exalted."

Volume 2, page 69: "A wrong course of eating or drinking destroys health, and with it the sweetness of life. . . . Thousands have indulged their perverted appetites, have eaten a good meal, as they called it, and as the *result,* have brought on a fever, or some other acute disease, and certain death. That was enjoyment purchased at immense cost. Yet many have done this, and these *self-murderers* have been eulogized by their friends and the minister, and carried directly to Heaven at their death. What a thought! *Gluttons in Heaven! No, no; such will never enter the pearly gates of the golden city of God."*

"If these things are written by the prophet of God, as claimed, why have you so lightly esteemed the counsel of the Lord? Why do most of your people eat flesh foods? The prophet writes that God's people must leave flesh food alone. If these things are so, then how do you expect to gain entrance through the pearly gates? Does not your God mean what He says?" Have not our deeds already given the following answer to this earnest soul? "Yes, that is what the prophet says, but that is not what we do." One may say, It is the duty of the ministry to instruct the people in the church, and what I do not know I can not be responsible for. For the benefit of such a one we quote the following scripture: "So thou, O son of man, I have set thee a *watchman* unto the house of Israel; therefore thou shalt hear the word at *my mouth*, and *warn* them from *me*. When I say unto the wicked, O wicked man, thou shalt surely die; if thou doest not speak to warn the wicked from his way, *that wicked man shall die* in his iniquity; but *his blood* will I require *at thine hand."* Ezekiel 33:7, 8.

The seventh one, next in line with a great number of references both from the Bible and the Testimonies, wishes to inquire about certain things which are a question in his mind. "Do not these references plainly teach that God's people can not and must not follow the fashions of the world, and that ornaments be discarded by the members of the church?" Volume 1, page 270: "The prophecy of Isaiah 3, was presented before me, as applying *to these last days;* and the reproofs are given to the *daughters of Zion* who have thought only of appearance and display. Read verse 25: 'Thy men shall fall by the sword, and thy mighty in the war.' I was shown that this scripture will be *strictly fulfilled.* Young men and women professing to be Christians, yet having no Christian experience, and having borne no burdens and felt no individual responsibility, are to be proved. *They will be brought low in the dust,* and will long for an experience in the things of God, which they have failed to obtain."

Isa. 3:16-24, "Moreover the Lord saith, Because the daughters of Zion are haughty, and walk with stretched forth necks and wanton eyes, walking and mincing as they go, and making a tinkling with their feet: Therefore the Lord will smite with a scab the crown of the head of the daughters of Zion, and the Lord will discover their secret parts. In that day the Lord will take away the bravery of their tinkling ornaments about their feet, and their cauls, and their round tires like the moon, the chains, and the bracelets, and the mufflers, the bonnets, and the ornaments of the legs, and the headbands, and the tablets, and the earrings, the rings, and nose jewels, the changeable suits of apparel, and the mantles, and the wimples, and the crisping pins, the glasses, and the fine linen, and the hoods, and the vails. And it shall come to pass, that instead of sweet smell there shall be stink; and instead of a girdle a rent; and instead of well set hair baldness; and instead of a stomacher a girding of sackcloth; and burning instead of beauty."

"Why, then, are the members of your denomination wearing these things, and are permitted to take an active part in the church even to the extent of serving in office, also being members of your church council? The instructions by your prophet are, that church members in dressing their children should have the clothing evenly distributed, covering all necessary parts of the body." This prophet claims that these instructions must be closely followed to safeguard the health and maturity of your children. You claim this is a prophet of God and these volumes contain the instructions for the church for this generation. Why have you slighted the advice of your prophet? Do you not believe in these writings, or do you think these instructions are not good? If you do not care for the welfare of your children, do you not fear your God?"

Numerous questions have been asked, but let us answer them by the following: When your God appears with vengeance upon the wicked, and if he should question you with all the foregoing questions, what would you answer Him? Matt. 22:12-14 will here be quoted: "And he saith unto him, Friend, how camest thou in hither not having a wedding garment? And he was *speechless.* Then said the king to the servants, Bind him hand and foot, and take him away, and cast him into outer darkness; there shall be weeping and gnashing of teeth. For many are called, but few are chosen."

Still another wishes to find the truth and earnestly presents his question this time from Testimonies to Ministers, page 475: "Prophecy must be fulfilled. The Lord says: 'Behold, I will send you Elijah the prophet *before* the coming of the great and dreadful day of the Lord.' *Somebody is to come* in the spirit and power of Elijah, and when he appears, men may say: 'You are too earnest, you do not interpret the Scriptures in the proper way. Let me tell you how to teach your message'." "This prophet whom you say is a prophet of God claims that another prophet, or a message, is to come to the church, but you say that you have all the truth and that you need no more truth or prophets. Why have you not educated your people to expect a message before the end? Do you not fear that the result now may be the same as in the time of Christ with the Jews?" This question will be answered by the following scripture. We quote Christ, speaking to the Jews, "Wherefore ye be witnesses unto yourselves, that ye are the children of them which killed the prophets. Fill ye up then the measure of your fathers." Matt. 23: 31, 32.

After all these questions are asked without receiving proper answers, have we complied with the text, "and be ready always to give an answer to every man that asketh you a reason of the hope that is in you *with* meekness and fear"? We must not be surprised if the inquisitor expresses his personal opinion in the following manner: "You people teach one thing but do another. You have departed from the fundamentals of your doctrine. Your doctrines as they are written in your books are beautiful and in harmony with the law and the testimony, but your personal testimony and practice is contrary to anything that is printed in your books." Doubtless these are some of the reasons why out of 104,000 baptized in the last four years, fifty-two some thousands left the truth, and only forty-eight some thousands remained in the church. Note that a larger number of them went out than those who stayed in. These are some of the causes which are apt to make infidels.

GOD REVEALS SECRETS TO HIS PROPHETS

If the Testimonies for the church have any connection with the Spirit of God, and if these things written in this article are true, then we must believe God has made the thing known to His servant the prophet, (the founder of this denomination). The following vision is quoted from Testimonies to Ministers, page 469: "As the Spirit of the Lord rested upon me, I seemed to be present in one of your councils. One of your number rose; his manner was very decided and earnest as he held up a paper before you. I could read plainly the heading of the paper; it was the *American Sentinel*. Criticisms were then passed upon the paper and the character of the articles therein published. Those in council pointed to certain passages, declaring that this must be *cut out,* and that must be *changed.* Strong words were uttered in criticism of the methods of the paper, and a strong un-Christlike spirit prevailed. Voices were decided and defiant. My guide gave me words of warning and reproof to speak to those who took part in this proceeding, who were not slow to utter their accusations and condemnation. In substance this was the reproof given: The Lord has *not* presided at this council, and there is a spirit of strife among the counselors. The minds and hearts of these men are not under the controlling influence of the Spirit of God."

The *American Sentinel* was one of the denominational papers in the early days of the movement. The changes that were suggested to be made does not necessarily mean that the things contained in that particular paper were to be changed or cut out. We must remember that it is only a vision, and it can mean any denominational paper that contains God's truth. We read at the top of this same page from which this vision is quoted: "Do not think that you will be found as vessels unto honor *in the time of the latter rain,* to receive the glory of God, if you are lifting up your souls unto vanity, speaking perverse things, in secret cherishing roots of bitterness." From this it is clear that the vision is touching the time just before the latter rain.

The prophecy in this vision has met its fulfillment, and who would dare doubt the authenticity of the Spirit of God? Who would dare support an open violation of sacred things against his own hurt? God has set His hand to redeem His people. Pharaoh and his host cannot prevail against the all-powerful God. "And it shall come to pass in that day, that the Lord shall set his hand *again* the *second time* to recover the remnant of His people, which shall be *left,* from Assyria, and from Egypt, and from Pathros, and from Cush, and from Elam, and from Shinar, and from Hamath, and from the islands of the sea. And the Lord shall utterly destroy the tongue of the Egyptian sea; and with his mighty wind shall he shake his hand over the river, and shall smite it in the seven streams, and make men go over dryshod. And there shall be an highway for the remnant of his people, which shall be left, from Assyria; *like as it was* to Israel in the day that he came up out of the land of Egypt." Isa. 11:11, 15, 16.

God will yet have a clean people and a pure church, and the gates of hell cannot prevail against it. "Awake, awake; put on thy strength, O Zion; put on thy beautiful garments, O Jerusalem, the holy city: For henceforth there shall no more come into thee the uncircumcised and the unclean." Isa. 52:1. "The remnant of Israel shall not do iniquity, nor speak lies; neither shall a deceitful tongue be found in their mouth: For they shall feed and lie down, and none shall make them afraid." Zeph. 3:13.

God's Law,—How Broken?

If an earthly father would ask his son to do a certain thing, and that son would refuse to do that certain thing, he has transgressed the fifth commandment, and that son, through his disobedience to the request, has dishonored his father. "Honor thy father and thy mother: That thy days may be long upon the land which the Lord thy God giveth thee." Ex. 20:12. But if our Heavenly Father has asked us to do a certain thing, and we refuse to obey, we have dishonored Him, and have become transgressors of the first commandment. In fact, we would be breaking the first four commandments, which are in honor to God. The obedient to these precepts are those who love God and keep His commandments. "Thou shalt have no other gods before me." Ex. 20:3. "And why call ye me, Lord, Lord, and do not the things which I say?" Lu. 6:46. "Not every one that saith unto me, Lord, Lord, shall enter into the kingdom of heaven; but he that doeth the will of my Father which is in heaven." Matt. 7:21.

Is The Church In An Excellent Condition?

In the General Conference Bulletin No. 2, of 1930, the statement is made that we are in an excellent condition. The increase in members and finances is being given as the reason in support of the statement. However, he who would believe the claim is saying in his heart the following quotations are false. Volume 3, pages 252-257, 260: "The message to the church of the *Laodiceans* is a startling denunciation, and is *applicable* to the people of God at the *present time.* . . . The people of God are represented in the message to the *Laodiceans* as in a position of *carnal security.* They are at ease, believing themselves to be in an exalted condition of spiritual attainments. 'Because thou sayest, I am rich, and increased with goods, and have need of nothing; and knowest not that thou art wretched, and miserable, and poor, and blind, and naked.'

"What greater deception can come upon human minds than a confidence that they are *right,* when *they are all wrong!* The message of the True Witness finds the people of God in a sad deception, yet *honest in that deception. They know not that their condition is deplorable* in the sight of God. *While* those addressed are *flattering* themselves that they are in an *exalted* spiritual condition, the message of the True Witness *breaks their security* by the startling denunciation of their true condition of spiritual blindness, poverty, and wretchedness. The testimony, so cutting and severe, *cannot be a mistake,* for it is the True Witness who speaks, and his testimony must be correct.

"*It is difficult* for those who feel *secure* in their *attainments,* and *who* believe themselves to be rich in spiritual knowledge, to *receive* the message which declares that *they are deceived* and in need of every spiritual grace. The unsanctified heart is 'deceitful above all things, and desperately wicked.' I was shown that many are *flattering* themselves that they are good Christians who have not a ray of light from Jesus. They have not a living experience for themselves in the divine life. They need a deep and thorough work of self-abasement before God, before they will feel their true need of earnest, persevering effort to secure the precious graces of the Spirit. . . . They think the testimony of the Spirit of God in reproof is uncalled for, or that it does not mean them. Such are in the greatest need of the grace of God and spiritual discernment, that they may discover their deficiency in spiritual knowledge. . . . But the message of the True Witness reveals the fact that a terrible deception is upon our people, which makes it necessary to come to them with warnings, to break their spiritual slumber, and arouse them to decided action. . . . Unbelief is closing their eyes, so that they are ignorant of their true condition. The True Witness thus describes their blindness: 'And knowest not that thou art wretched, and miserable, and poor, and blind, and naked.'

"Faith in the soon coming of Christ is waning. 'My Lord delayeth his coming' is not only said in the heart, but expressed in words, and most decidedly in works. Stupidity in this watching time is sealing the senses of God's people as to the signs of the times. The terrible iniquity which abounds calls for the greatest diligence and for the living testimony, to *keep sin out of the church.* . . . Those *who despise the warning will be left* in blindness to become self-deceived. But those who heed it, and zealously go about the work of separating their sins from them in order to have the needed graces, will be opening the door of their hearts that the dear Saviour may come in and dwell with them. *This class* you will ever find in *perfect* harmony with the *testimony* of the Spirit of God. Ministers who are preaching present truth should not neglect the solemn message to the Laodiceans. . . . The True Witness declares that when you *suppose* you are really in a good condition of prosperity, you are in *need* of everything.

"The people of God must see their wrongs, and arouse to zealous repentance, and a putting away of those sins which have brought them into such a *deplorable* condition of poverty, blindness, wretchedness, and *fearful* deception."

The fact that our brethren think that we are in an excellent condition proves that Inspiration tells the truth. We think we are right while we are all wrong. Quoting Volume 3, pages 270, 271: *"Those* who work in the fear of God to rid the church of hindrances, and to *correct* grievous wrongs, that the people of God may see the necessity of *abhorring* sin, and may prosper in purity, and that the name of God may be glorified, *will* ever meet with *resisting* influences from the *unconsecrated.* Zephaniah thus describes the true state of this class, and the terrible judgments that will come upon them." *"This is* the rejoicing city that dwelt carelessly, that said in her heart, I am, and there is none beside me: How is she become a desolation, a place for beasts to lie down in! Every one that passeth by her shall hiss, and wag his hand." Zeph. 2:15.

"Woe to her that is *filthy* and polluted, to the oppressing city! She obeyed *not* the voice; she received *not* correction; she trusted *not* in the Lord; she drew *not* near to her God. *Her* princes within her are roaring lions; *her* judges are evening wolves; they gnaw *not* the bones till the morrow. *Her* prophets are light and treacherous persons: *Her* priests have polluted the sanctuary, they have *done vio-*

lence to the *law*. The just Lord is in the midst thereof; he will not do iniquity: Every morning doth he bring his judgment to light, he faileth not; but the unjust knoweth *no* shame." Zeph. 3:1-5.

WHAT HAS BEEN GAINED DURING THE PAST QUADRENNIUM?

At the General Conference of 1930, held in San Francisco, Calif., the following statistics are reported with great enthusiasm and boasting over the excellency of the great denomination. The entire membership throughout the world four years ago was 250,988. Latest reports available in 1930, at the San Francisco Conference session says the membership has increased to 299,555. The increase in the four year period since the last General Conference held in Milwaukee, Wisconsin, is 48,567. Review and Herald, June 1, 1930, pages 39-41. The brethren think this is a tremendous increase in membership, and therefore, we are in an excellent condition, is the cry.

The story of a certain farmer's little girl has been told how she sold a few pounds of cherries to a stranger for a few pennies. She thought it would be wise to put her golden bracelet into the bag of cherries so that it would give her a better weight, and receive more money thereby. The child was overwhelmed with her supposed wise transaction, ran into the house, and happily exclaimed to her mother that she had received more money than the regular amount for her cherries by throwing the golden bracelet in with the cherries. On the child's part, it was a great increase, and a wise judgment, but to the mother's knowledge of the costly jewel being practically given away was a great disappointment.

The denomination's boasting of a so-called tremendous growth in members is as true as the supposed great increase in price of the cherries sold by the little girl. Let us take an account of the price we have paid for the little gain in members. We shall attempt to prove that the children born to this denomination in the past four years (were they saved to the church), the increase in members of a little over 48,000 would have been more than double, even though there had not been one added from outside of the church. If this is true, then more than one-half of the children born to the denomination are lost in the world, even if the entire gain of new members were the offsprings of the church. But if this increase is not entirely from within the church, then most all of the denomination's children are lost, and that would mean we have exchanged our jewels (children) for a few converts from the heathen lands, as the little girl exchanged her golden bracelet for the weight of the cherries.

How terrible the thought to lose your own children to the number of more than 97,000, and an expenditure of nearly \$165,000,000, all in four years' time to bring but few children from the world. If rightly realized the grief is heavier than one can bear. Think of such a tremendous loss of life, sacrifice, and labor inside of four years. But the worst part is that we are boasting instead of weeping, and therefore there is but little hope to remedy the great wound. Is it not true that Laodiceans are blind and asleep while they think they are rich and increased with goods? Now we shall bring the evidence that the charge made here is true.

The increase in membership in the last four years is just a little over 19%. This would mean that a church of 200 members should yield a little less than ten children per year, or about 39 every four years. This estimation is very low, from a church that is made up mostly of women as the Seventh-day Adventist church is. For an example, we shall consider Exposition Park church in Los Angeles, Cal. The present membership of this particular church is approximately 230. About 30 of these members are isolated and hardly ever attend church services on the Sabbath, so we shall consider only the 200 members who attend Sabbath services.

The denominational increase in members in the last four years being a little over 19%, therefore a church of the size stated above should yield about 39 children in four years or have about 39 children between two and six years of age in order to meet the increase we have made. The kindergarten in the Sabbath School of the said church takes the children from two to seven years of age. The lapse of time is five years instead of four.

The figures to meet the gain in members are less than ten per year of the fixed age, therefore in the span of five years the number of children of that age would not exceed 49 in the kindergarten of the Sabbath School if every child of that age attended the said department of this institution. In this particular church, only about one-half of the church membership attend the Sabbath School, but the other half may be present only for the preaching service, and where the parents are absent, the children are also. Therefore there must be less than half of the children from two to seven years of age present in the kindergarten department of the Sabbath School. The one-half of the children of kindergarten age should number less than twenty-five to meet the increased percentage of members in the four years. The number of children in the said institution attending the kindergarten department of the Sabbath School are about 35. The number required to meet the claim is less than 25; therefore we have 10 above the number estimated. These figures prove the percentage of children born each four years to this denomination to be not less than 35% of the membership. Therefore, if all the denominational children born each four years were saved to the church, without any evangelical effort for outside converts, the increase in the past four years would have been 35% instead of 19%. But the fact is, that the percentage of childbirths in the United States is much smaller than that in foreign lands. Where there is one child in an American home, there are three or more in a home of some foreign country, therefore the children born to this denomination each four years is much more than twice the total increase in members for the same period of time.

Where we have gained 48,567 new members, the children born to this denomination should have exceeded far above 97,000, and that above this figure would have taken care of the ones claimed by death, and some to spare. (It has been estimated those claimed by death in the same four years to be only about 3500.) Thus we have the proof that the "Lambs" which God has given to this people to raise for Him are lost in the world (devoured by the enemy), and no one cares. There is neither sorrow nor sadness in the camp of Israel, but instead, there is feasting and gladness and boasting with blindness.

"Where is the flock that was given thee, thy beautiful flock? What wilt thou say when he shall punish thee? for thou hast taught them to be captains, and as chief over thee: Shall not sorrows take thee, as a woman in travail?" Jer. 13:20, 21. "The living, the living, he shall praise thee, as I do this day: The father to the children *shall* make known thy truth." Isa. 38:19. "That the generation to come might know them, even the children which should be born; who should arise and declare them to their children." Ps. 78:6. "They that were full have hired out themselves for bread; and they that were hungry ceased: So that the barren hath born seven; and *she* that hath *many children is waxed feeble.*" 1 Sam. 2:5. May God help His people in this great day of deception where the shrewd enemy is trying to deceive even the very elect.

Answer To The Indian's Argument

On Pages 182-3

"Study to show thyself approved unto God, a workman that needeth not to be ashamed, rightly dividing the word of truth." 2 Tim. 2:15. "But sanctify the Lord God in your hearts: And be *ready always* to give an answer to *every man* that asketh you a reason of the hope that is in you with meekness and fear." 1 Pet. 3:15. The commandment in the Bible is that a Christian must study, and that he also must give an answer to every man. This Indian being one of the "every man", according to the Scriptures there must be a way, and it is the duty of a Christian to give him an answer with meekness and fear.

"For thou hast said in thine heart, I will ascend into heaven, I will exalt my throne above the stars of God: I will sit also upon the mount of the congregation, in the sides of the north." Isa. 14:13. Lucifer wished to ascend in the sides of the north because God's throne is there. Said the Psalmist, "Beautiful for situation, the joy of the whole earth, is mount Zion, on the sides of the *north,* the city of the great King." Ps. 48:2.

God's throne is in the *north.* One may point to the north at any time from any part of the earth, and the extreme end of each line would meet at the same point. Had the so-called Christian pointed to the north, the answer would have been proper and in harmony with the Bible; thus both the confusion and the whip would have been avoided. Pointing to the north does not mean that heaven is somewhere in the north corner of the celestial expanse of stellar bodies, for we understand that God's throne is in the *center* of the universe.

The axis of the earth tilts in a slanting direction in relation to its orbit. If we point in another direction than north or south at any time it would be either east or west. In the daytime, pointing in any direction (except with the axis of the earth) we are pointing to the *east* (the sun), and at night to the *west,* with no specific direction into space. Pointing to the sun constitutes east; the opposite direction to the sun is west, dealing with our solar system only, but the direction of north deals with the center of the universe.

There is no such thing as up and down in space. The only thing that would constitute *up* is the center of attraction (God's throne): Down (or south) is in the opposite direction from God's throne, (the great celestial expanse). The center of attraction is surrounded by island universes. The axis in each island universe (or suns, planets, and worlds) all point to one center of attraction (God's throne). This great and most supreme sovereign center stands as the highest peak on a great mountain around which all creation revolves, each suspended by an unseen power (chain) attached to its north axis similar to the pendulum hanging from a great clock.

How Can Christians Get To Heaven If The Distance Is So Great?

The fastest speed on earth known to modern science at this present time is light, which travels at the rate of 186,284 miles a second. If one was to take a flight on the wings of light to the great nebula Orion, it would take him 600 years to reach that far-distant wonder in the heavens which has drawn an earnest attention of modern science. Quoting from Early Writings, page 41, we read: "The atmosphere parted and rolled back; then we could look up through the open space in *Orion*, whence came the voice of God. The holy city will come down through *that open space.*" If the holy city is to come through that space, we may well suppose that that glorious open space in Orion is the gateway to that long-continued highway to heaven (God's throne). But think of the great distance to this most wonderful gateway. If it would take 600 light years to reach the entrance to that far-distant highway, then we ask ourselves, How many light years would it take to reach the other end of that heavenly highway to the city of the great King in the sides of the north?

We mortals can not give a direct answer to this great question only to say the distance from earth to the center of the universe (God's throne) is so vast that we finite beings only stand awestruck. We are amazed with the difficulty to compute mileage, or even light years. But if the distance is so vastly beyond human comprehension, then we, like the previously-stated Indian, ask the question, How would Christians ever get to heaven? Suppose that great wonder (train) which takes the redeemed would move at the tremendous speed of light, traveling 186,000 miles a second, it would take a good part of eternity to reach the city of the Great King (heaven).

Here we shall see what we consider a terrific speed. Heaven esteems it very dilatory. For an example, we shall consider Jesus after the resurrection. It was Mary who met Him first. As she reached for her Lord, Jesus said to her, "Mary, touch Me not; for I have not yet ascended to My Father." John 20:17. Eight days later Jesus again appeared to His disciples. "Then saith He to Thomas, Reach hither thy finger, . . . and *thrust* it into my *side;* and be not faithless, but believe." Verse 27. If Jesus would not let Mary touch Him because He had not yet been to His Father after

He had risen, we may not suppose He would let Thomas thrust His finger in His side except He had been to heaven by His Father. Jesus, in a week or less, made a round trip from earth to heaven.

Suppose this Indian wished to go to heaven, and chose to ride on the wings of light. Starting the same day Christ arose from the tomb, sweeping through space at the rate of 186,000 miles a second, he would still be on the way. More than that, the nebula,—which we are a part of is 300,000 light years in diameter. Therefore, he would still be inside the city limits of our own nebula. A certain writer, speaking of the center of the universe (God's throne), has described the distance in the following words: "But the solution of the mystery of the distance to the center of centers—to that remote point in space which is the center of gravity for all the tens of thousands of galaxies—will have to await the completion of our nebular survey which will take from ten to fifteen years or more; and it may never be solved."

The speed of light is altogether too slow a velocity for heavenly beings to span the immense universe of God. Daniel felt in need and offered a prayer to his God which is recorded in Dan. 9:4-19. This short prayer of only fifteen verses can be read in less than five minutes, but we may suppose he was very careful in his prayer and took his time: Perhaps ten or even twenty minutes. Quoting Daniel's own record: "And whiles I was *speaking,* and *praying. . . .* Gabriel whom I had seen in the vision . . . . being caused to fly *swiftly,* touched me . . . . and said, O Daniel, . . . at the *beginning* of thy *supplications* the commandment *came* forth, and I am *come* to show thee." Dan. 9:20-23. Here is a record of a rate of speed that is altogether beyond human comprehension. The prayer to heaven and the angel to earth was accomplished in less than twenty minutes. Heaven only knows how an angel can make that tremendous, unspeakable distance in but a few minutes. There would be no trouble, difficulty, or any delay on that most glorious journey after Christians once start on the way. But we surely are slow to start, and that is our only problem that we must solve in regards to the distance, and the journey from earth to heaven.

SUMMARY OF THE 144,000

THE DEADLY WOUND IS HEALED

"And I saw one of his heads as it were wounded to death; and his deadly wound was healed: And all the world wondered after the beast." Rev. 13:3. It is generally understood among Seventh-day Adventists that since the Italian government granted civil power to the pope on the 11th day of Feb., 1929, to be the event of the prophetic fulfillment, we shall grant that the interpretation is correct, and the "deadly wound" has been healed. Note the verbs "was" and "healed" are both in past tense. This being so, it is evident that this particular prophecy is to be fully understood after its fulfillment (as to when and how accomplished).

If the event of the above stated date fulfilled the prophecy, then we would make no mistake if we should suppose that the last part of the verse has as well met its fulfillment. "And all the world wondered after the beast." Quoting from Volume 6, page 14: "The prophecy of the Revelation is being fulfilled, that 'all the world wondered after the beast'. Rev. 13:3." The world being now at this present time in no better spiritual condition, but worse, we may conclude that the Scripture has fully met its fulfillment. The wound has been "healed" as well as the world has "wondered after the beast."

We need not assume that the world would have to enroll in the membership of that body of people in order to fulfill the prophecy. Note the world wondered *not* after the *wounded head* but after the *beast*. The scripture deals in the sense of spiritual matters. Again, quoting from Volume 6, page 15: "This demon-worship was revealed to him [John], and it seemed to him as if the whole world were standing on the brink of perdition." The world has partaken of the spirit of the beast, thus fulfilling the divine prediction.

"And I stood upon the sand of the sea, and saw a beast rise up out of the sea, having seven heads and ten horns, and upon his horns

Rev. 13:1-3.

ten crowns, and upon his heads the name of blasphemy." Rev. 13:1. Note this beast has seven heads and *ten horns.* In order to get a full understanding of the prophecy we must begin from the root up. (For the first time these ten kings (horns) are brought to our attention by the Scriptures, found in Dan. 2:41, 42, represented by the ten toes on the great image in Nebuchadnezzar's dream.) After revealing to the king the end of his golden empire, represented by the head of gold, and down through the stream of time to the second coming of Christ, Daniel says, "And *in the days* of *these* kings shall the God of heaven *set up a* kingdom which shall *never* be destroyed." Dan. 2.44.

In Daniel 7, this same prophecy of the world's history is repeated in symbols of beasts. The kings represented by the toes of the great image are this time represented by ten horns of the "fourth" and "non-descript" beast in verse 7. The reason for the duplicate is to bring the truth of the little horn (papal power, verse 8). The ten horns (kings) are repeated again in Rev. 13:1, to point out the *time* of the prophecy as explained by Daniel,—*"in* the *days* of *these* kings *shall* the *God* of heaven *set up* a kingdom."

Note that this (leopard) beast of Rev. 13:1-3, arises out of the sea, in like manner as the four beasts of Daniel 7, therefore, the process that brings about this beast on the stage of action is the same as those representing Babylon, Medo-Persia, Greecia, and Rome. If the ten horns of this beast represent the kings now in existence at which time "shall the God of heaven set up a kingdom" (quoting the words of Daniel), then the beast himself represents the period following Rome, as the breaking down of the Roman empire brought about the existence of these kings. It is also being termed "Rome in her broken state" symbolized by the great image of Dan: 2:42, the feet and toes of which are composed of iron and clay. Iron is the metal which represents Rome; the clay, the broken part.

"And I stood upon the sand of the sea, and saw a beast rise up out of the sea, having seven heads and ten horns, and upon his horns ten crowns, and upon his heads the name of blasphemy." Rev. 13:1.

The symbols given by Inspiration are perfectly capable of revealing the truth beyond a shadow of a doubt. Any interpretation of the prophecy that does not come up to the exact specification by the symbols is not the kind that can be depended upon, and sooner or later would be exploded.

It has been admitted that the ten horns represent the ten kingdoms into which Rome was divided. This interpretation is true, for you will note these ten horns are horns with crowns. The crowns denote these kings have received their kingdom, but note carefully the *heads* are *without* crowns, therefore these seven heads *cannot* represent kingdoms or civil governments. Thus it would be unwise and deceptive to even think that the heads could represent civil powers in the past or future.

All seven heads are alike without distinction one from another. If the head that was wounded represents a religious system, then we must conclude that the six represent religious bodies. The number of them being the Biblical number "seven", it means "all", or "complete".

Had the heads come one after another like the beasts of Daniel 7, and the little horn after which the three were "plucked up", it would denote a successive form of systems. Since all seven were in existence at the same time, the symbol reveals that all seven systems must rule during the same period.

These *seven heads* cannot represent anything at any time before the fall of the Roman monarchy, for that which represents what took place before the fall of Rome is symbolized in the composition of the beast, excluding the seven heads and ten horns (as set forth in the second verse). The leopard part represents Greecia (Dan. 7:6); the feet of a bear, Medo-Persia (verse 5); and the mouth of a lion represents Babylon (verse 4). The combination of the beast in Rev. 13: 1, 2, in his makeup, is the evidence that he comes on the stage of action after the four great universal empires; namely, Babylon, Medo-Persia, Greecia, and Rome. Thus, he becomes the fifth beast, representing the period which followed the fall of Rome. The ten horns of both beasts, Dan. 7:7, and Rev. 13:1, as well as the ten toes of Dan. 2:42, represent the same ten kingdoms into which Rome was divided. These ten kings personate the civilization in the fifth period, or the one which followed Rome to our own time, and on to the second coming of Christ, according to Dan. 2:44. "And in the days of these kings shall the God of heaven set up a kingdom which shall never be destroyed."

Furthermore, note that the ten horns on the non-descript beast of Dan. 7:7, are crownless, but the ones on the leopard beast of Rev. 13:1, *have* crowns. The symbol reveals that the horns on both beasts represent the same kings: Crownless on the first beast because those ten kings (horns) had no kingdom as yet before the fall of Rome. The fact that the leopard beast has the crowned horns is that he comes on the stage of action after the fall of Rome, at which time these kings received their kingdoms.

The little horn on the beast of Dan. 7:8, which came afterwards among the ten, and in place of which three fell has been interpreted to be the papal head, from 538 A. D. to 1798, and which was wounded in the fifteenth century. The deadly wound brought about the division and multiplied the head as pictured in Rev. 13:1. The six heads represent Protestantism, and the one which was wounded, Catholicism. The six Protestant, and the one Catholic head make the Biblical number "seven", meaning "complete" (all). The ten horns represent this present civilization under civil power; the heads are symbols of all Christendom.

This prophecy pictures the entire civilization which came out through the four universal empires by the fall of Rome. But it cannot include other nations and peoples, for the makeup of the beast is composed only of Babylon, Medo-Persia, Greecia, and Rome, as previously explained. Had the number of horns been "seven", it would have the Biblical meaning (all), but since the number "ten" is used, all other are excluded.

However, the nations and peoples who are excluded by the symbol "ten", and also by the composition of the beast are not altogether left out, for the fall of the three horns on the beast of Dan. 7:8, left a balance of the Biblical number "seven". Thus the fall of the three kings; namely, the Heruli, Ostrogoths, and the Vandals gave the signal for the present close union with the entire world by modern inventions. Therefore, the influence of the western civilization, both civil and religious (represented by the symbols,—horns and heads), involved the entire present civilization. Thus the symbolical prophecy has met its fulfillment.

The prophecy of Rev. 13:3, "And the world wondered after the beast", reveals a great apostasy. The Biblical number "seven" includes everything represented by the heads (riding on the beast and headed by the devil). Note the name of blasphemy is upon all seven heads,—symbols of impious religious leaders, mocking the personality or authority of God, under the cloak of Christianity. The intention of the complete satanic scheme is to deceive the whole world. The statement made by Christ is true, that he (Satan) will try to "deceive even the very elect [the 144,000] if it were possible". The Spirit of Prophecy, speaking on this scripture, says: "This demon-worship was revealed to him [John], and it seemed to him as if the whole world were standing on the brink of *perdition*. But as he looked with intense interest, he beheld the company of God's commandment-keeping people." Volume 6, page 15.

We must not be surprised if we should see that we have not heretofore fully understood the true meaning of the healing process. We repeat the definition of the verbs, being in the past tense: "as it *were wounded* to death; and his deadly wound *was healed*: and all the world *wondered* after the beast." It is evident that Inspiration foresaw that it would not be clearly understood until the divine prediction is fulfilled. The Spirit of Prophecy bears witness to this, by saying, "The mark of the beast is exactly what it has been proclaimed to be. *Not all* in regard to *this* matter is yet understood, *nor will it be* understood *until* the unrolling of the *scroll."* Volume 6, page 17. If the scroll has made a turn, then *only* may we expect the truth to unmask the scripture.

The exile of pope Pius VI, in 1798, and his death at Valence, France, August 19, 1799, is *not* the receiving of the wound, no more than the death of any other pope before or after. It only fulfilled Rev. 13:10,—"He that leadeth into captivity shall go into captivity." Also the great prophetic period of the 1260 years of Dan. 7:25. Neither was the election of another pope the healing of the wound. It was only a sign of the deadly blow being accomplished. Just so with granting back civil power to the pope in 1929, is not the thing which healed the wound, but only *a sign* that it has been healed.

Note carefully that the deadly wound was not inflicted by any one of the ten horns (like the little horn of Dan. 7:8, after which three fell). If any of the horns had inflicted the wound, it would indicate that it was to be delivered by a civil power (thus Berthier could be credited for delivering the blow). But since the horns had nothing to do with the head, it is evident that the infliction came from within the head, therefore Luther is the only one who can be credited for delivering the blow.

The exile of the pope in 1798, was only a sign of the material side of the wound, showing that the blow had been delivered, but the spiritual side of the truth has been altogether overlooked. Had not the head received the deadly wound by Martin Luther, the pope could not have been put in prison by Berthier, or by any other general, for before the sword was delivered, the pope reigned supreme. But Luther's blow weakened his power, thus the continual infliction began to iritate the "head". This irritation continued until 1870, when finally the temporal power of the pope was taken away. That being the last irritation on the "head", it shows that it was left to heal its "deadly wound". The idea established by Uriah Smith in "Daniel and Revelation" is correct as far as the material part is concerned.

The election of a new pope (the material) gave a signal that the deadly wound was to be healed. What we are interested in most is the spiritual part of the lesson, which we shall briefly endeavor to bring out at this time. The reason this prophecy is brought to our attention in this chapter is to reveal the truth of the *head* which received the deadly wound. Note that the beast has "seven" heads; the "one" was wounded but the "six" are not. The head which received the wound is being interpreted to be the papal head, wounded by "Martin Luther". The stroke being delivered by the true Biblical doctrine taught by Luther, the result was that Protestantism came on the stage of action in opposition to the "head". This is what made the "wound". The statement being true, then as long as Protestantism remains loyal to Bible principles, and the head in existence, that sore (wound) would remain open. But if Protestantism should depart from their pledge "the Bible, and the Bible only", or refuse new light, the wound would be healed, and the world would wonder after the beast (apostasy).

The head that was wounded was not much troubled because a pope had fallen under the sod, nor will it ever be as long as another can fill his place. The only thing that has worried the head and annoyed the beast is true Protestantism. The devil knows it and the head knows it, but God's people have allowed the old dragon to pull the wool over their eyes. Arise, brother! Arise, sister! Let not the shrewd enemy deceive you from a crown of life at the eleventh hour!

Is the death of the pope far more important than the birth of Protestantism? Is the exile of the pope of greater honor than the seclusion in Wartburg Castle? Is Berthier a greater hero for pulling the bars against the prison gates than the humble monk who swung them open to throw in the once-exalted pontiff? Has not the solidity of character, and stability of purpose, with faith in God, in the heavenly messenger made all these possible? If Luther is the greatest, and his act far more glorious, why should Inspiration inscribe a prophecy for the exile and death of the pope, rather than the act of Luther?

Why should Inspiration notice the taking away or restoring the temporal power of the pope, rather than the reclaim of the Bible, and the casting away of darkness? Has not God, by the hand of Luther, thrown asunder the doors of darkness, and caused light to shine on

His written Word? Has not the faith and effort of this heavenly messenger ended the terrible persecution and bloodshed of the saints of the Most High? The only rightful answer to all these numerous questions is: Luther's blow delivered the infliction on the head, and *only true Protestantism* can keep that sore open.

In 1844, when the announcement was made of the fall of modern Babylon by the preaching of the second angel's message of Rev. 14:8, the wound would have been healed, for Babylon had fallen, and would have brought about the fulfilment of,—"and all the world wondered after the beast". But "Seventh-day Adventists" came on the stage of action, thus keeping the thorn in the wound by being proclaimed the only true Protestants since that time. This being so, then as long as Seventh-day Adventists (as a body) remain true to the principles and doctrines which built this great movement, the wound *cannot* be healed, neither can it be said *"all* the world wondered after the beast".

As we have departed from the fundamentals,—strict obedience to God's Word, by which only can we keep His commandments as true Adventists,—then we have left the divine foundation, and wondered after the beast. If the wound is healed, then we, as a people, have partaken of the spirit of the beast (world). As the exile of the pope was a signal of the infliction accomplished, just so the granting of civil power to the pope in 1929, is a signal that true Protestantism has lost its power, thus the world wondered after the beast.

This wholesale apostasy headed by self deceived religious leaders cannot be after the purification of God's church, for that time is a time of harvest into which time the Gentiles of Isaiah 60, would be converted to the church. Speaking of the glorious harvest time, the prophet says: "And the loftiness of man shall be bowed down, and the haughtiness of men shall be made low: And the Lord alone shall be exalted in that day." Isa. 2:17. God's church would be exalted as prophesied by both Isaiah 2, and Micah 4; read pages 173-81. Therefore, the harvest time cannot be a time of apostasy for the church of God. If it was, God would have no church.

The prophet Isaiah, referring to this time of spiritual darkness, says: "And in that day seven women shall take hold of one man, saying, We will eat our own bread, and wear our own apparel: Only let us be called by thy name, to take away our reproach." It is an admitted fact that the women spoken of here represent churches. The Biblical number "seven" is used as a symbol, meaning "all", therefore the symbol does not exclude any, but means "all". The Spirit of Prophecy bears witness to this by saying the number "seven" indicates completeness. Acts of the Apostles, page 585. Naturally it would include Seventh-day Adventists as well, otherwise it would not be "all". While these women are refusing the instructions of Christ through His Word and His righteousness, symbolized by the bread and apparel, they wished to be called by His name (Christians), but while the world is on the brink of perdition, God immediately gets to work, and sets things in order, as foretold in the second verse.

"In that day shall the branch of the Lord be beautiful and glorious, and the fruit of the earth shall be excellent and comely for them that are *escaped* of *Israel.*" Isa. 4:2. Note that this glorious promise is for those that shall escape (Israel—the 144,000). This has no reference to the people in the world, but to those in God's church, for the third verse says, "he that is left in *Zion,* and he that remaineth in *Jerusalem,* shall be called holy". The fourth verse gives us the time very definitely, that it is the time of the purification of His church, for it says: "When the Lord shall have *washed away* the filth of the daughters of Zion, and shall have purged the blood of Jerusalem *from the midst* thereof by the spirit of judgment, and by the spirit of burning."

While the world has wondered after the beast, God has 144,000 who "have not bowed a knee to Baal". Though they seem to be lost without a shepherd, the arm of Omnipotence is watching over them. In the statement previously quoted from Volume 6, page 15, speaking of the terrible apostasy everywhere prevalent at this time, (in the sense that the world has wondered after the beast) says, "But as he [John] looked with intense interest, he beheld the company of

God's commandment-keeping people [the 144,000]. They had upon their foreheads the seal of the living God, and the faith of Jesus. . . . And I heard a voice from heaven saying unto me, Write, *Blessed* are the dead which die *in* the Lord from *henceforth.*" Note that after the sealing of the 144,000 there would be some who would die in the Lord (saved), for the scripture reads "from henceforth", meaning from the time this company was sealed.

The 144,000 are living saints, to be translated without seeing death. "The Lord has shut them in. Their destination is inscribed —GOD, NEW JERUSALEM." Testimonies to Ministers, page 446. Therefore, those who die "in the Lord" must be of those who are saved, after the separation (in the time of harvest) under which Isa. 52:1 and Zeph. 3:13, are fulfilled. Those who die at that time are perhaps those who cannot stand the hardship while the judgments of God are falling upon the land in the time of the plagues. While God clears the way for the seven last plagues by laying some of His people to sleep in the grave, He has done the same for the event to take place in 1931 (if that date be correct). For we read in Isa. 57:1, "The righteous perisheth, and no man layeth it to heart: And merciful men are taken away, none considering that the righteous is taken away from the evil to come."

Again, we call your attention to the past and future tense of the scripture; while Rev. 14:13, is in future tense, Isa. 57:1, is in past. This being present truth, it is easy to see that we, at the present time, stand between these two scriptures. The predicted event for the purification of God's church is by no means a small one. Those who cannot undergo the trial are laid in their graves, while 144,000 remain and will escape, but the balance in the church (now) shall perish in the ruin. May God help His people.

To the prophet Isaiah, this great apostasy, fostered by blind spiritual guides, was revealed, which he describes in the following scriptures: "And he saw that there was *no man*, and wondered that there was *no intercessor:* Therefore, *his* arm brought salvation unto him; and *his righteousness,* it sustained him." Isa. 59:16. "And I looked, and there was none to help; and I wondered that there was none to uphold: Therefore, *mine own* arm brought salvation unto me; and *my fury,* it upheld me." Isa. 63:5. Micah, looking forward to this wholesale deception, says: "Trust ye not in a friend, put ye not confidence in a guide." Micah 7:5.

There has never been given so much light on any *one* prophetic *event* since the world began, as the Lord has given on this particular subject that is set forth in this publication (the sealing of the 144,000, and the slaughter in the church in connection with the harvest, though it has not all been published). Therefore, it will leave the people without excuse. He who would neglect to make the needful preparation for this most solemn event would be committing the unpardonable sin. To such a one, that day is a fearful day. "Therefore thus will I do unto thee, O Israel: And because I will do this unto thee, prepare to meet thy God, O Israel." Amos 4:12.

"Awake, awake; put on thy strength, O Zion; put on thy beautiful garments, O Jerusalem, . . . Shake thyself from the dust; arise, and sit down . . . . loose thyself from the bands of thy neck, O captive daughter of Zion." Isa. 52:1, 2.

It would be of interest to note how perfectly God has portrayed our world by symbols. While the six Protestant and the one Catholic head make the Biblical number "seven", meaning all Christendom, God has the same prophecy confirmed by the prophet Ezekiel, and carried out by the reformers since Luther's time; namely, Luther, Knox, Wesley, Campbell, Miller, and Sister White. These godly men sacrificed all in an effort to lead God's church back to her standard of purity. But as the shrewd enemy succeeded to pull down the first, he proceeded to use the same method to the last. These six great reformers on the Protestant side established the six great denominations represented by the six heads, and the Catholic church (the mother of Protestantism), the seventh, thus including all Christendom in her polluted state. For this reason Inspiration gave the Biblical number "seven". (See the prophecy by Ezekiel on pages 114-32. We also have the "seven" churches of Revelation 2, and 3,

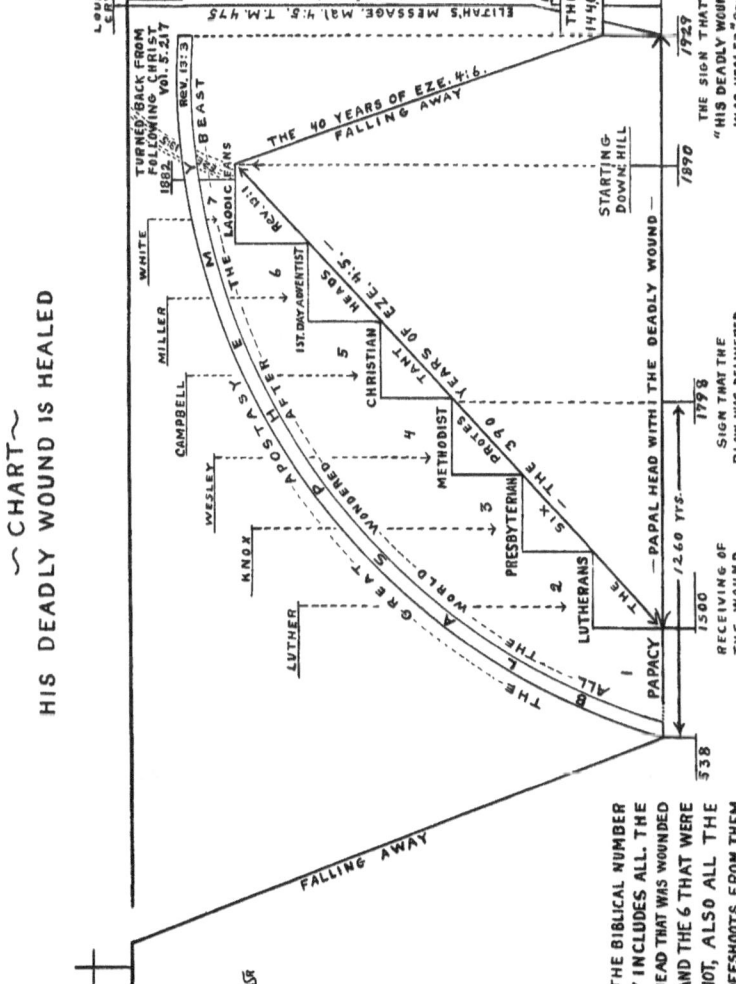

~ CHART ~
HIS DEADLY WOUND IS HEALED

beginning with the church of Ephesus, and on through the ages to our time (Laodiceans). This Biblical number "seven" includes the entire church history in the anti-typical period to the time of the separation of the tares from the wheat, as foretold by Christ in Matt. 13:30. Number "seven" is used to indicate the entire, or to the end of tares. See chart, page 224.

Though such great apostasy and blasphemy has gripped the world, *God's church,* 144,000 in number, scattered throughout the length and breadth of the earth without a shepherd, have not bowed a knee to Baal. While Laodiceans are shaken out (spued) by destruction, God takes charge of the flock Himself. Thus, the church and the message will triumph to the victory. See Volume 6, page 427; Testimonies to Ministers, page 300.

While the 430 year period which had to do with Israel in Egypt, and the 430 years of Ezekiel 4:5, 6, run parallel in our time, this chart (His Deadly Wound Is Healed) shows that one overlaps the other. For, the forty days (years), in which time Ezekiel was to fast while lying on his right side denoted a spiritual hunger (as explained on page 125, and chart on page 133) began in 1890, and ended in 1929. The application proves true by the event which took place on Feb. 11, 1929 (the healing of the wound), it being a signal that the prophetic period had ended. It is also proven by the truth that has come, for at the end of the forty days Ezekiel was to arise, and eat, and be free. If the prophetic forty years had not ended, we could not have received the truth published in this book, but the fact is that truth has come. Therefore, subtract from 1930, the forty prophetic years and you have 1890, the time when the church began to decline. See chart on page 221.

SUMMARY CHART

EXPLANATION OF TYPES

The intention and the purpose of this chart (on the following page) is to sum up both lessons (reform, and the 144,000). Through this chart we see a perfect harmony of what has been taught in this publication. It also enables us to check up on this most vital subject. God, who is so particular for the good of His church to reveal His truth to His people, has worked out most wonderful pictures of historical events. The evidence of everlasting love for Israel, His chosen, the first-fruits of His harvest. "The God of Jacob" for thousands of years in advance had laid His plans to present to His people an art of divine touch in a beauty of perfection.

Said the Psalmist, "The mighty God, even the Lord, hath spoken, and called the earth from the *rising* of the sun unto the *going down* thereof. Out of Zion, the perfection of beauty, God hath shined. Our God shall come, and shall not keep silence: A fire shall devour before him, and it shall be very tempestuous round about him. He shall call to the heavens from above, and to the earth, that he may judge *his people*. Gather my saints together unto me; those that have made a covenant with me by sacrifice. And the heavens shall declare his righteousness: For God is judge himself. Selah. Hear, O *my* people, and I will testify *against thee:* I am God, even thy God." Psalm 50:1-7.

OLD TESTAMENT (Section Two)

Speaking of section two in the summary chart, entitled "Patriarchate Types" is the section which gave birth to the patriarchs (for this reason we have given it that title), whom God preordained to be as monuments, and sign posts as it were, and examples for His church in their appointed time, to fulfill the divine purpose. Monuments? Yes; more than monuments. Their voices thunder by echoes, and re-echoes, onward through the ages, and in our own time they are heard the loudest.

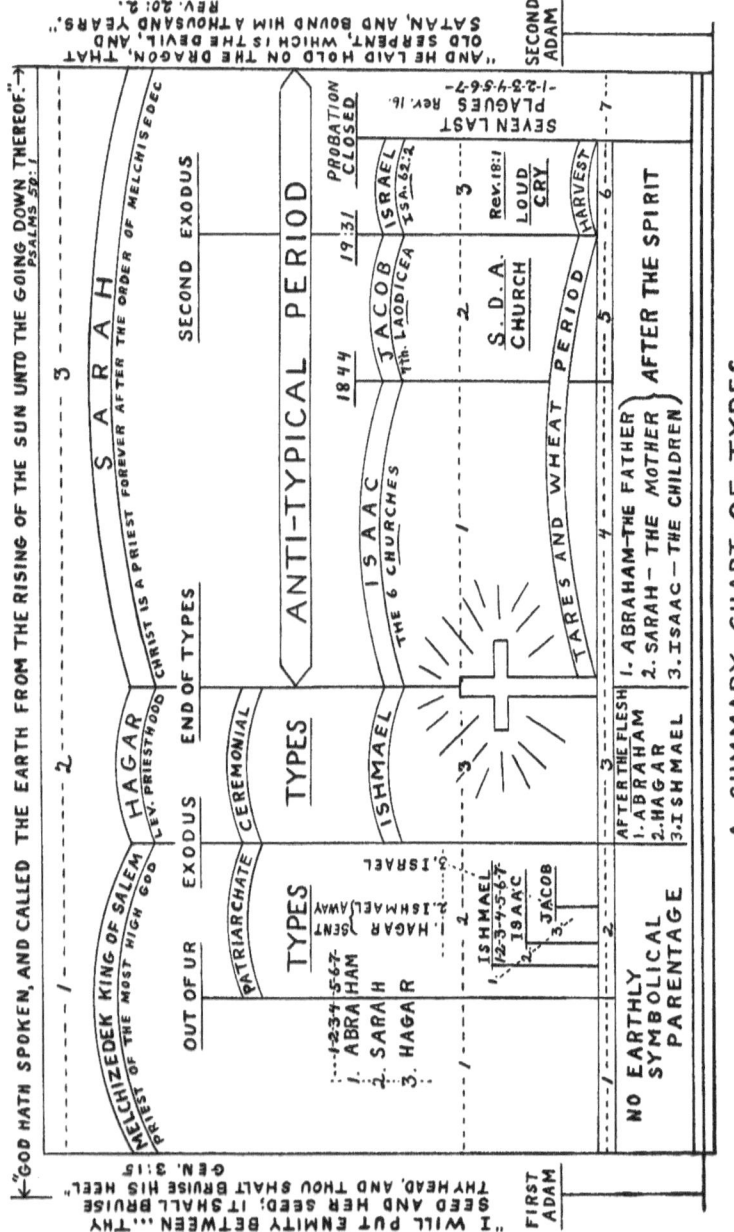

A SUMMARY CHART OF TYPES

Section number three, entitled "Ceremonial Types" is the section which, by the Tabernacle service in connection with the Sanctuary, has given us symbols of unmistakable, priceless lessons. Though they originated many centuries ago, their sweet melodies of salvation from the Father's love, onward through the avenue by the human race, have reached our own time without the loss of a single sounding note. These divinely appointed symbols were to reveal the Author of love to the human family in all ages.

True, we have reached an age of great knowledge, but it seems to be only of lesser importance, and very little in the knowledge of Him from whom all blessings come: In wisdom, knowledge, health, and strength to accomplish great things. Had not the people of God fallen into a drowsy, sleepy spell, many of these ancient symbols and types, with their true meaning of great importance to God's church, would have been revealed long ago. Much good could have been accomplished and the blessings derived from such knowledge cannot be estimated. While the world is making rapid progress in human wisdom and wicked devices, God's people have made no great advancement *for the better* in any line. For years we have been retracting from Him who is the Source of all true wisdom.

OLD TESTAMENT (Section Three)

The types ordained in section two immediately began to meet their anti-types as soon as the exodus movement gave way to section three. The passover night gave birth to this section (of ceremonial types). Hagar (the type) met anti-type which was celebrated and dedicated with great demonstrations, signs, and wonders. Said Paul, in Gal. 4:25, "For this Agar is mount Sinai in Arabia." Thus, Hagar became the symbolical mother of that church, with Abraham, the father after the flesh, and Ishmael, the symbol of the children from the stock of Abraham. The mother, the father, and the child are the types of Israel after the flesh (perfect symbols, are they not?). Thus, three of the types from section number two met anti-types in section three.

While the passover lamb gave way to Hagar, (symbol of the church under the Jewish economy), it also celebrated the commencement of the ceremonial system, thus section number three became the mother of the ceremonial types. The types themselves are not the true object, no more than a photograph is, but it is a representation which pictures an unmistakable evidence, the object in view. The passover lamb is a perfect type of the "Lamb of God, which taketh away the sins of the world" (John 1:29).

As the ceremonial section (number three) was ushered in by the typical passover lamb, it also closed with the anti-typical. As type met anti-type, said the apostle, "for even Christ our passover is sacrificed for us" (1 Cor. 5:7), thus, the reign of Hagar as a symbol of the typical church (Israel after the flesh) closed at the cross of Calvary. The putting away of the Old Testament church and her children, is as well symbolized in section number two. Quoting Gal. 4:29-31, "But as then *he* that was born *after the flesh* persecuted him that was born after the Spirit, even so it is now. Nevertheless what saith the scripture? *Cast out the bondwoman and her son:* For the son of the bondwoman shall not be heir with the son of the freewoman. So then, brethren, we are *not* children of the bondwoman, but of the free."

It is evident that Salvation is preached in types as well as by the word. There is a type for every church event and transaction in connection with the gospel of Christ. The termination of these types closed the typical, and ushered in the anti-typical period under which time every type must meet its anti-type.

While the parentage of the Old Testament church is "after the flesh", the New is of the Spirit, therefore Sarah became the symbol of the entire anti-typical period. Paul, writing to this church said, "For it is written, Rejoice, thou barren that bearest not; break forth and cry, thou that travailest not: For the desolate hath many more children than she which hath an husband." Abraham is the husband, and an earthly spiritual instead of a fleshly father. As there are three symbolical sections before Christ, there are also three after

Christ. Abraham's children by Sarah (Isaac and Jacob), being born by promise, are fitting symbols for the New Testament church.

New Testament (Section One)

As Isaac was the firstborn "after the spirit", naturally he must represent the first section, beginning at the cross of Christ. Quoting the words of Paul, he says, *"Now we, brethren, as Isaac was, are the children of promise."* Gal. 4:28. Isaac, then, represents that section from the cross to 1844, as there has been no other call before. The *commencement* of each previous section as well as their completion was marked by an important event; just so with the termination of the section represented by Isaac. 1844, is the only fitting time for that section to pass away and usher in the second, at which time the judgment in the heavenly Sanctuary began. Evidently the scroll had to make a turn, and again type met anti-type.

New Testament (Section Number Two)

Jacob, being the son of Isaac, naturally comes next in line. Jacob, then, is the symbol of the second section after Christ (as shown on the chart) beginning in 1844. The aim of the church since that time has been to make the 144,000. As Jacob was the father of the twelve tribes of Israel,—the type; just so he is the father in type of the anti-type (the 144,000,—the true). The section represented by Jacob is the only fitting symbolical period to give birth to the 144,-000. As soon as this number is made and sealed, this particular section is to pass away and usher in the next.

As there was an important event with each succeeding section (at the close of the one, and beginning of the other), there must be something of no lesser consequence that would make the change of this section with which we have identified ourselves. That important event is none other than the purification of God's church, and the separation of the tares from the wheat. Said Jesus, "Let both grow together *until* the harvest." The separation will mark the harvest. Note the verb "until", meaning "up to". *This* most solemn time for the one class (the tares), and glorious for the other (the 144,-000), *thrusts out* the section represented by Jacob, and *forwards* the other.

NEW TESTAMENT (Section Number Three)

Said Jesus, *"in* the time of harvest I will say to the reapers, Gather ye together *first* the tares, and bind them in bundles to *burn* them." The tares, therefore, are gathered just prior to the harvest, and burned in the time of the harvest (for note the prefix "in"). "But gather the wheat into My barn." Matt. 13:30. The wheat represents the 144,000; the "barn" is a symbol of security. This glorious company is saved and protected. Satan cannot harm them. They are to be translated without seeing death. John describes them as "being the firstfruits [of the harvest] unto God and the Lamb."

The tares are taken away by the five men with the slaughter weapons of Ezekiel's vision. This is the event that makes the change, and brings about God's church, in the *last* probationary section (Israel), as shown on the chart.

It was Jacob, the father of the twelve tribes, whose name was changed to Israel. Jacob's new name is a fitting symbol of the section entitled "Israel". Thus again would type meet anti-type.

It was *Jacob,* who, in the night, on the way to Padan-Aram had the dream of the great ladder which reached from earth to heaven, and "the angels of God ascended and descended upon it". This vision was a representation of the "Latter Rain", and the "Loud Cry" of the third angel's message in the time of harvest. The ladder, representing Christ; the angels, the messengers; God the Father at one end, and Jacob at the other, meaning a complete connection with heaven and earth.

Though the duration of this last section of probationary time (entitled Israel), is shorter than any of the periods before it, it is to be the most glorious time of God's church. The prophet Isaiah, looking forward to this time, says, "Awake, awake; put on thy strength, O Zion; put on thy beautiful garments, O Jerusalem, the holy city: for *henceforth* there *shall no more* come into thee the *uncircumcised and the unclean."* Never before this time in view, has God's church been kept entirely free from the unconsecrated and unconverted (tares: uncircumcised and unclean) in the midst of her, but now the time has come where He must purify His church and keep her as such. Zephaniah, referring to this time, says, "The remnant of Israel shall not do iniquity, nor speak lies." Zephaniah 3:13.

During this time of "harvest" (the Loud Cry), the third angel's message shall penetrate to the remotest parts of this sin-cursed world. John, pointing to this glorious harvest of ingathering, says, I beheld, and lo, a great multitude, which no man could number, of all nations, and kindreds, and people, and tongues, stood before the throne, and before the Lamb, clothed with white robes, and palms in their hands." Rev. 7:9. God "Will finish the work and cut it short in righteousness." Rom. 9:28. Thus God's church will be made ready to meet her Lord. Isaiah, looking forward to this church reflecting "the Divine", says, "Thou shalt also be a crown of glory in the hand of the Lord, and a royal diadem in the hand of thy God." Isa. 62:3. Glorious is God's church in the day of the Lord.

John, after seeing in vision the finishing work of the church, close of probation, and the judgments of God in the seven last plagues, says, "And I saw a *great white thone,* and *him* that sat on it, from whose face the earth and the heaven *fled away;* and there was found *no place* for them." Rev. 20:11.

OLD TESTAMENT (Section One)
MELCHIZEDEK, KING OF SALEM

The first main section in the chart entitled "Melchizedek" we have reserved for explanation until now. Note the following two main sections entitled "Hagar" and "Sarah" are the sections of church history with earthly parentage, the first being "after the flesh", and the second "after the Spirit", therefore, Hagar and Sarah are fitting symbols for these two main sections, with Abraham as the father. These two sections ("Hagar" and "Sarah") are unlike the first ("Melchizedek, King of Salem") which has none of these symbolical terms. It is a section of church history without earthly symbolical parentage.

In order to meet the divine standard of perfection, both in symbols as well as in figures, for the entire history of God's church, He must provide a fitting symbol for this particular section as He has provided for the two succeeding sections. Whatever that symbol is, it must be the kind to indicate church history without earthly parentage.

Paul gives us the information of the fitting symbol for this section in Heb. 7:1-3,—"For this Melchizedek, king of Salem, priest of the most high God, who met Abraham returning from the slaughter of the kings, and blessed him; To whom also Abraham gave a tenth part of all; first being by interpretation King of righteousness, and after that also King of Salem, which is, King of peace; Without father, *without mother, without descent,* having neither beginning of days, nor end of life; but made like unto the Son of God; abideth a priest continually." Though we mortals can not comprehend the existence of this man "Melchizedek, King of Salem", it must be true that he is "without father, without mother, without descent, having neither beginning of days, nor ending of life", thus making a perfect-fitting symbol of that section of God's church. Again we see God's perfection in perfect symbols for the entire history of His church.

As soon as sin entered in the beginning with the parents of the human family, and before they were driven out from their Eden home, the plans already devised for the return to their original home of eternal abode were made known to them as well as to the serpent. These pre-ordained plans of God are better understood by studying His wonderful divine dealings with the human family onward through the ages as pictured in this chart.

Our God has carried out His predestined plans without variation even to the minutest of details. Said Jesus, "These are the words which I spake unto you, while I was yet with you, that *all things* must be *fulfilled,* which *were* written in the law of Moses, and in the prophets, and in the psalms, concerning Me." Luke 24: 44. The Spirit of God led the psalmist to inscribe the words, "The Lord shall send the rod of thy strength out of Zion: Rule thou in the midst of thine enemies. The Lord hath sworn, and will not repent, Thou are a priest for ever after the order of Melchizedek." Psalm 110:2, 4.

Though we cannot comprehend such infinite wisdom, it gives us better understanding of God's love for sinners, and our misconception of so-called human knowledge of things. To the eternal "I AM", who inhabits eternity, before whom the darkness is light, and the remotest boundaries in space His footstool, who sees the end from the beginning, and to whom a thousand years are but as yesterday, all things are open and naked unto Him.

Said the Psalmist, " Whither shall I go from thy spirit? or whither shall I flee from thy presence? If I ascend up into heaven, thou art there. If I make my bed in hell, behold, thou art there. If I take the wings of the morning, and dwell in the uttermost parts of the sea; even there shall thy hand lead me, and thy right hand shall hold me. If I say, Surely the darkness shall cover me; even the night shall be light about me. Yea, the darkness hideth not from thee; but the night shineth as the day: The darkness and the light are both alike to thee. Such knowledge is too wonderful for me; it is high, I cannot attain unto it." Psalm 139:7-12, 6. The wisdom and knowledge of the infinite is beyond comprehension by the finite. The wonders we behold, and the events which make the history of our world are but duplicates from the blue-prints in heaven.

How To Check Up Contents Presented, If Authentic

"Which of you intending to build a tower, sitteth not down first, and counteth the cost whether he have sufficient to finish it? Lest haply, after he hath laid the foundation, and is not able to finish it, all that behold it begin to mock him." Luke 14:28, 29. The lesson that can be derived from this scripture is that he who does not check up on his plans and figures is not a wise man, therefore, it would not be wrong for us to suppose that Jesus wants us to check up on Bible truths before we accept them as such.

As God is infallible, all His works spell "perfection" even to "one jot or one tittle". The statement being true, He should have provided a way whereby we may check up and ascertain His truth. This chart (page 224), being the summary of the message this publication bears, should be able to tell whether it proves correct or not. If its contents prove 100% true, we must accept it as God's truth. By all Bible students, numbers "three" and "seven" are accepted to be the Biblical numbers to ascertain Scriptural truths. The Spirit of Prophecy bears witness to this as well as the Bible. "For there are three that bear record in heaven, the Father, the Word, and the Holy Ghost: And these three are one. And there are three that bear witness in earth, the Spirit, and the water, and the blood: And these three agree in one." 1 John 5:7, 8.

"In the revelation given to him there was unfolded scene after scene of thrilling interest in the experience of the people of God, and the history of the church was foretold to the very close of time. *In figures and symbols,* subjects of vast importance were presented to John, which he was to record, that the people of God living in his age and in future ages might have an *intelligent* understanding of the *perils* and conflicts before them." Acts of the Apostles, page 583. This being so, we shall apply the test on the contents of this book, as pictured in the chart.

Note that there are *"three"* main sections in the summary chart: namely, (1) Melchizedek, the priest of the Most High God; (2) Hagar; (3) Sarah. (I) Melchizedek, priest of the Most High God; (II) the Levitical priesthood; (III) the priesthood after the order of Melchizedek. Therefore, one priesthood links with another. Now count the sub-sections of probationary time in both before the cross and after. In each division we have *"three"* sub-sections. Again, count all the sections in both before and after the cross, including the plagues, and we have the number *"seven"*, meaning the end of the world.

Permit us to call your attention this third time to the types. I. The parent types; namely, Abraham (the father); Hagar and Sarah (the mothers) making the number "3". II. The children: —Ishmael, Isaac, and Jacob, making the number "3". III. Jacob's name changed to Israel, Hagar and Ishmael sent away again making the number "3". There is a fourth line of figures to call your attention to. The name "Abraham" contains "seven" letters, meaning complete, or a father for the entire future history of the church. Ishmael also has "7" letters; finished, or ended; meaning he is through; there are none of his descendants to succeed him.

Abraham's name at the time he was called out of Ur (before God added the two extra letters—H and A) spelled with five letters: (Abram). His son, Isaac, and his wives all have the same number of letters in their names. Naturally the question arises, why five? Why not three or seven? Had their names more or less than "5" letters, the picture would have been spoiled. Why? Because the "7" letters of Abraham and the "5" of Hagar make "12" in all,— a symbol of the twelve tribes of Israel after the *flesh*. Sarah and Abraham also number "12", meaning the twelve tribes of Israel after the *Spirit*. The same holds good with Isaac and Jacob, also meaning consecutive (one shall succeed the other).

Israel is spelled with six letters. Had this name been more or less it would spoil the picture. Why? Because the six letters indicate the sixth section. Israel the true (the 144,000) are sealed at the close of the fifth section. Had the name been of seven letters, it would denote "close of probation", instead of "beginning of harvest". Israel, in the time of harvest, will receive a new name by the mouth of the Lord. Read Isa. 62:2. Whatever that name may be, we are sure it will be perfect, to finish the picture of probationary time, as well as to indicate the end of all the redeemed, or close of probation. Woe to him who may think all these wonderful designs in the beauty of perfection are just a chance, or an accident. Such a one is denying the Master Mechanic of all creation. He is paying homage to evolution (chance). See chart on page 224.

The second system of checking up on truth is given by Isaiah, the prophet. "To the law and to the testimony: If they speak not according to this word, it is because there is no light in them." Isa. 8 :20. The contents in this publication are not only in perfect harmony with the text, but it does "exalt" the law and the testimony as well as all the writings of the Spirit of Prophecy.

Third :—The message presented here does not bring any new doctrines, or contradict the ones we have, but it does magnify them by showing their true magnitude and importance. Neither does it call for a new movement but it proves that this same movement would merge into a greater one.

As God foresaw all movements that would arise against, or for His church, He would have pointed out this message either as being false, or true. He foresaw that some movement would arise and claim that the church is "Babylon", so gave us the warning that it was false. Read Testimonies to Ministers, pages 49, 53. Again, God foresaw that some will come and call the ministry "priestcraft", and forewarned us that they are not sent from Him. Read Testimonies to Ministers, page 51. He also foresaw that some will announce the "day and the hour for the second coming of Christ", etc. Thus, God has forewarned the church all the way. Nowhere do we find any prophecy in contradiction against the message presented in this book. It is impossible to find opposition, seeing the entire message is derived from the Bible and the Testimonies, and predicted by them both.

If any should think this message for reformation is false, while he cannot find prophecy against it, would be saying, God has overlooked the danger and has failed to expose the scheme. Therefore, such a one means to say that God knows but little in predicting the future. But the matter of fact is that God knows it all from the beginning to the end. Thus, He has been able to present a message of warning such as this to His people inscribed in advance for thousands of years.

MICAH SIX AND SEVEN

PROPHECY OF THE BOOK, TIME DUE FOR PUBLICATION

The studies that comprise this volume were first typewritten into a book in manuscript form, which was entitled "The Shepherd's Rod". Thirty-three such copies were given to the leading men (ministerial association) of the Seventh-day Adventist denomination, —brethren of experience, ministers and conference presidents. This was done in order to comply with the instructions given to the church by the Spirit of God. We quote from Volume 5, page 293 : "There are a thousand temptations in disguise prepared for those who have the light of truth ; and the only safety for any of us is in receiving no *new* doctrine, no *new* interpretation of the Scriptures, without first submitting it to brethren of experience. Lay it before them in a humble, teachable spirit, with earnest prayer ; and if they see no light in it, yield to their judgment ; for 'in the multitude of counselors there is safety'."

Though the contents of this book introduces no new doctrines or new interpretation of scriptures that have been accepted by the denomination and divinely approved, we thought it best to submit this light to the ministry first.

These studies were presented in manuscript form to the leaders of this great movement for their inspection while assembled in a General Conference session in San Francisco, Calif., of 1930. It was done with an earnest pleading by the author of the said document. Requesting our dear brethren to investigate the contents in the said article by a close scrutiny, earnest prayer, and faith in Him who is merciful and more willing that we should know the truth of our salvation than we are ourselves ; who would reveal His word to all His children and unmask error for the good on both sides.

This appeal was made to God's servants with the request that they should ascertain the new light by God's book of all truth, and whatever their finding or intention with the article, to write us in a brotherly way as searchers for light. This they promised to do at their earliest possible convenience, being assured that whatever truth or error they could prove, by either Bible, or the Spirit of Prophecy, we were ready to accept. We felt certain that they, as shepherds of the flock, would have been earnest to do the right in the fear of the Lord. If they thought we were lead into error, we expected them as guardians of God's heritage to come to our assistance by the Word of God.

Since the document was placed in their hands, and at the time this publication goes to press, over five months have passed by. We now feel they have had ample time to at least write and give us some information in regards to the manuscript, and their intention. The elapse of time is an evidence that our brethren have failed to carry out their promise as well as their duty. Evidently these ministers of God and leaders of this great denomination must have overlooked the instructions respecting matters of this kind as given them by the Spirit of Prophecy. "If a brother is teaching error, those who are in responsible positions ought to know it; and if he is teaching truth, they ought to take their stand at his side. We should all know what is being taught among us; for if it is truth, we need to know it." Testimonies to Ministers, page 110.

If they have complied with the requirement quoted above, by an earnest searching in the document presented to them, and found error, their duty is, as representatives of Him who left the ninety-nine and went in search of the one lost sheep, to call on the writer either in person, or by correspondence seeking to make reconciliation for the erring one. Quoting Volume 6, pages 21, 22: "One soul is of more value to heaven than a whole world of property, houses, lands, money."

On the other hand, if they found no error, and yet refuse to make known their intention, even after making the second and the third appeal to our local conference, then it is perhaps that they wish to fulfill the following prophecy as found in Testimonies to Ministers, pages 106, 107. "But *beware* of *rejecting* that which is *truth*. The great danger with our people has been that of *depending* upon men, and making flesh their arm. Those who *have not been* in the habit of searching the Bible for themselves, or *weighing* evidence, *have confidence* in the *leading* men, and accept the decisions *they make;* and *thus* many *will reject* the very messages God sends to His people, *if these leading* brethren *do not accept* them.

"*No one* should claim that he has *all* the light there is for God's people. The Lord *will not* tolerate this. He has said, 'I have set before thee an open door, and *no man* can shut it.' Even if *all* our leading men should refuse light and truth, that door will still *remain open.* The Lord *will raise* up men who will give the people the message for this time. . . .

"Suppose a brother held a view that differed from yours, and he should come to you, proposing that you sit down with him and make an *investigation* of that point in the Scriptures; should you rise up, filled with *prejudice,* and condemn his ideas, while *refusing* to give him a candid hearing? *The only* right way would be to sit down as Christians, and investigate the position presented, in the light of *God's word,* which *will reveal* truth and unmask error. To ridicule his ideas *would not* weaken his position in the least if it were false, or strengthen your position if it were true. If the pillars of our faith *will not* stand the test of investigation, *it is time* that we knew it. There must be no spirit of *Pharisaism* cherished among us."

We deeply regret that we should make public this great neglect on the part of our brethren, and their disinterest in the things of God. As a matter of duty on our part, and love for our brethren, and the church of God, we found no solution whereby to avoid publicity of the things written in this chapter, and yet guard against misunderstanding of our attitude in giving out the book. Not that we wish to shun reproach against ourselves, but for the security of God's church wishing to defend those who may be exposed to the attacks of captious critics. Again we quote from Testimonies to Ministers, page 300:

"Unless those who can help in ——— are aroused to a sense of

their duty, they *will not recognize* the work of God when the loud cry of the third angel shall be heard. When light goes forth to lighten the earth, instead of coming up to the help of the Lord, they *will want to bind* about *His* work to meet *their* narrow ideas. Let me tell you that the *Lord will work* in this last work in a manner very much out of the common order of things, and *in a way* that will be contrary to *any human* planning. There *will be* those among us who will *always* want to *control* the work *of God,* to dictate even what movements shall be made when the work goes forward under the direction of the angel *who joins the third angel* in the message to be given to the world. *God will use* ways and means by which it will be seen that *He is taking the reins* in His own hands. The *workers will* be *surprised* by the *simple* means that He *will use* to bring about and perfect His work of righteousness. Those who are accounted *good workers will need* to draw nigh to God, *they* will need the divine touch."

Seeing the danger approaching as revealed in "The Shepherd's Rod", we have anxiously waited all these months with the fear that we may wait too long, and thereby fail to sound the alarm as well as to go ahead with the sound of the trumpet before we hear from our brethren. While waiting and praying, a certain scripture was revealed to us, found in Micah 6, which we now bring forth to prove that God has spoken to His people by the written word, giving us the instruction to go ahead without delay and give the trumpet that certain sound.

Though the book of this minor prophet was written many centuries ago, it was intended for the church now, at this very time. It was placed in the Bible (scroll) in the days of ancient Israel, written in such a way that they, too, could gain some profit by it the same as other portions of scriptures that were written directly to the ancient nation, and placed in the same scroll for our learning and admonition as expressed in 1 Cor. 10:11, by the great apostle to the Gentiles. But though certain portions of the Scriptures were written as an epistle to ancient Israel, they also would refer to us indirectly, as this advent organization being a duplicate of that ancient movement. However, the book of Micah is written directly to the church at this present time.

Quoting Micah 6:1, "Hear ye now what the Lord saith; Arise, contend thou before the mountains, and let the hills hear thy voice." It is a fact that the prophecy of this chapter has never before been understood at any time, and no one has ever profited much from it, only whatever lesson from a certain passage may have been derived in connection with some other study. The question may be asked, Why has it not been understood? Is it that no one ever tried to study out this part of the Scriptures? Doubtless many godly, earnest students have spent much valuable time without any results as far as revealing the truth of the chapter.

The reason for their failure to unmask the prophecy is because it is in present tense. *"Hear* ye *now* what the Lord *saith; Arise,* contend thou before the mountains, and let the hills *hear* thy voice." From this fact, we know that inspiration never expected that it should be revealed before the time intended, otherwise it would have been grammatically incorrect. In the same manner as Rev. 14:7, "Fear God, and *give* glory to him; for the hour of his judgment *is come."* Had this scripture been in future tense, William Miller would not have made the mistake as to the event that was to transpire in 1844. He who controls the Scriptures evidently did not intend to reveal the truth until after the judgment hour had begun in 1844. The same rule is to be observed in all Bible truths to establish authoritatively a particular prophetic time.

We have previously stated that this truth came through the Sabbath School department in 1929, in the lessons of the first quarter of that year, beginning with Isaiah 54, to the 66th chapter inclusive. The 54th was the first to reveal that these chapters were written directly to the church at this very time as explained on pages 136-40. In Isa. 58:1, we learned that God is to reveal the existing sins in the church, and thereby call for reformation. We quote the verse: "Cry aloud, spare not, lift up thy voice like a trumpet, and shew my people their transgression, and the house of Jacob their sins."

This scripture now has met its fulfillment. After these existing sins were revealed, these studies were put into writing, the document being entitled "The Shepherd's Rod", and placed in the hands of the leading men of this movement. Thus the "Cry" like a "trumpet" is being sounded. The evidence of the existing sins being made known (shown) to God's people and to the house of Jacob, also showing that Laodiceans have neglected the invitations of the True Witness, therefore, the shame of our nakedness has appeared. "I counsel thee to buy of me gold tried in the fire, that thou mayest be rich; and white raiment, that thou mayest be clothed, and *that the shame of thy nakedness do not appear;* and anoint thine eyes with eyesalve, that thou mayest see." Rev. 3:18.

Now we quote Isa. 60:1, "Arise, shine; for thy light is come, and the glory of the Lord is risen upon thee." Note the verb "come" is in present tense. "Light" is truth. This scripture as well met its fulfillment. Think of the wonderful light that has come through those studies as gathered in this publication. Note that it does not contradict the truth the church already has, but it reveals its true magnitude and importance of the message. But this is only a part of the light that has come through those precious chapters. More light will soon follow in another publication.

The call is, "Arise, shine." . . . for "the glory of the Lord is risen upon thee." It is left to the reader to permit this glorious experience to enter first in his own life, and earnestly arise and shine; be ready to meet the opposition from within and without. "God's *displeasure* is upon *his* people, and he *will not* manifest *his power in the midst* of them while *sins exist* among them, and are *fostered* by those *in responsible* positions. *Those* who work in the fear of God to *rid* the church of hindrances, and to *correct* grievous wrongs, that the people of God may see the necessity of *abhorring sin,* and may prosper in purity, and that the name of God may be glorified, *will ever meet with resisting* influences from the *unconsecrated."* Volume 3, pages 270, 271.

Coming back to Micah 6:1, "Hear ye now what the Lord saith." Note the verb "hear" is in present tense, therefore present truth. But what are we to hear? "Arise, contend thou before the mountains, and let the hills hear thy voice." "The mountains" means the same as in Micah 4:1, first part. The only difference between the two is that the latter is singular, but the former is plural. The "mountain" in chapter 4, means God's church (denomination) as explained on page 173, but the "mountains and hills" as in chapter 4:1 (last part) and 6:1, being in plural would mean churches and organizations. In this sense it could not refer to God's church, for He recognizes only one church as His. Also "the hills" being plural would mean sects, or minor movements, etc.

"Let them hear thy voice". The thought that can be derived is this: Our leading men are either taking too long a time, or perhaps never intend to do anything with the new light presented to them in "The Shepherd's Rod", therefore, wait no longer, "Arise *now,* contend before the mountains, and let the hills hear thy voice" (make it public). This being so, we were compelled to publish the book and give it out without delay.

But what are the mountains to hear? What will He contend about? The answer is given in the second verse. "Hear ye, O mountains, the Lord's controversy, and ye strong foundations of the earth: For the Lord hath a *controversy* with his people, and he *will plead* with *Israel."* Note they are to hear that the Lord has a *controversy* with *His* people, and He will plead with Israel (the 144,-000, Israel the true). But how are they to hear? What are the means to carry that voice to the mountains and hills? The answer to this is found in the ninth verse.

"The *Lord's voice* crieth unto the *city,* and the man of wisdom *shall see* thy name: *Hear ye the rod,* and *who* hath appointed it." Micah 6:9. Note it is the *Lord's* voice. The voice is crying in the "city". (City, or Jerusalem are symbols of God's church the same as "mountain", the difference between the symbols being that "mountain" means the entire denomination, but "city" means the leading part of that body.) By what means is the Lord's voice crying in the city (church)? The last part of the verse answers the question: "Hear ye the rod." To hear a rod, it must be the kind that can speak.

The only rod God's people have ever been asked to hear is this "Shepherd's Rod". At the time we gave the name to this book, we knew nothing about the prophecies in the book of Micah, neither did we know this passage was there. We mean to say it is not any of our knowledge of this particular scripture that compelled us to name the book by that title, but we feel it was done by the same divine providence that brought about the entire truth, in order to fulfill the scripture. See also explanation on page 95, under the heading "The Shepherd's Rod".

Again, note "The men of wisdom shall see thy name". The wisdom mentioned is not that which the world can give, but a heavenly one. Douay version reads as follows: "And salvation [wisdom] shall be to *them* that fear [see] thy name: hear, O ye *tribes.*" The same thought is brought over in the seventh chapter, verse 14. "Feed thy people with thy rod, the flock of thine heritage, which dwell solitarily in the wood, in the midst of Carmel: Let them feed in Bashan and Gilead, as in the days of old." "Feed thy people with thy rod": The verb "feed" is to be understood as spiritual food, and that food (truth) is found in the "Rod", therefore we again have the command to give out the book ("Feed thy [God's] people). Carmel, Bashan, and Gilead are used as symbols of good spiritual pasture. These places are where Israel had their victories. Mount Carmel is where Elijah had his experience with the backslidden Israel in the days of Ahab. It was in Carmel where he (Elijah) brought the fire from heaven which consumed the sacrifice upon the altar, after which he slew the prophets of Baal.

We quote verse 15: "According to the days of thy coming out

of the land of Egypt will I shew unto him marvelous things." Note that Micah also, as well as Isaiah, declares that God's people (spiritual Israel) are to experience an experience similar to that of the Exodus movement, as explained in Section 4. Again, note in carrying out the Exodus movement, God said to Moses, "And thou shalt take this rod in thine hand, wherewith thou shalt do signs . . . . and Moses took the *rod* of *God* in his hand." Ex. 4:17, 20. It was by the power in the "rod of God" that Israel came out of Egypt. This advent movement being a duplicate of the one in Egypt, and of the Exodus, we again have "the rod of God".

It is wonderful to note the inspiration of the Scriptures. Perfect they are when their appointed time is come. Only at such an occasion are the Scriptures grammatically correct. We can not take up the entire chapters at this present time, but with the information already given, one can mark out the meaning of every verse with a little studious effort on his part. Read the sixth and seventh chapters and note that past, present, and future tense are in perfect grammatical order when the events are properly understood. Observe the same rule in Micah the fourth chapter as explained on pages 173-81. This is one of the rules to detect present truth. It would be impossible for us to publish in this volume all of the light that has come to us through these studies, but we hope to have them soon in another volume.

THE DUTY—WHO RECEIVES THE TRUTH

IT is evident that the message presented in this publication is not a message to create a new movement, but a message for a change to true godliness. Calling God's people back to His precepts, commandments, and statutes by a strict obedience to His Word to prepare us to meet our God and escape the ruin.

In the days of ancient Israel, God's people departed a number of times from His divine plan, which made it necessary for Him to send messages of warning by His servants, the prophets. These solemn warnings were hardly ever heeded by the ancient nation. Nevertheless those faithful servants of God performed their duty with great care. Though their lives were at stake, their message of love unappreciated, were cruelly abused by the once chosen people. Those faithful servants of God dared not start a movement of their own. Their duty was to deliver the message, and leave the results with Him who is able to handle the situation. Thus it will be now. "There will be a series of events revealing that God is master of the situation." Volume 9, page 96.

Those who receive this message are to arise from their spiritual feebleness to true godly repentance. They are to arise quietly, but openly, to present the truth to their brothers and sisters *in the church,* with zeal and earnestness in the fear of the Lord, doubting nothing, leaving the results with God.

"When I say unto the wicked, O wicked man, thou shalt surely die; if thou doest not speak to warn the wicked from his way, that wicked man shall die in his iniquity; but his blood will I require at thine hand. Nevertheless, if thou warn the wicked of his way to turn from it; if he do not turn from his way, he shall die in his iniquity; but thou hast delivered thy soul. Therefore, O thou son of man, speak unto the house of Israel; Thus ye speak, saying, If our transgressions and our sins be upon us, and we pine away in them, how should we then live?" Eze. 33:8-10.

The Spirit of Prophecy, speaking in view of the events predicted in this publication says, *"Those* who *walk in the light* will *see signs* of the *approaching peril;* but they *are not to sit in quiet, unconcerned* expectancy of the *ruin,* comforting themselves with the belief that God will shelter his people in the day of visitation. Far from it. They should realize that it is *their duty* to labor diligently to save others, looking with *strong* faith to God for help." Volume 5, page 209.

"Cry aloud, spare not, lift up thy voice like a trumpet, and shew *my people* their transgression, and the *house* of *Jacob* their sins." Isa. 58:1.

Objections That May Arise

Since all who had a message of truth had to suffer persecution in ages past, it must be expected now. The enemy of all righteousness, by the human tool in the garb of religion, has opposed God's truth in every step of the way. The death of Abel by the cruel hands of his brother, Cain, was a signal to all followers of truth that persecution was to arise against them by their own brothers in the church. Thus, it has been up to our own day.

The shrewd enemy is too wise to oppose truths and doctrines already accepted to be true, but he will lead men to neglect the principles upon which that truth was established, and step by step supply the lack with human wisdom, thus leading the church into spiritual darkness. Ministers in this state of spiritual condition cannot discern the importance of strict obedience to God's Word. Their congregation is made to feel that their Christian experience is excellent, and the people are lead to trust in human wisdom (accept their decision), instead of searching truth for themselves, with faith in God. "Thus saith the Lord; Cursed be the man that trusteth in man, and maketh flesh his arm, and whose heart departeth from the Lord." Jer. 17:5.

Membership is granted to most all who wish to join the church with but little investigation as to their faith and acceptance of the entire truth. Thus, the unconsecrated of heart creep into the church and by their influence lead others to sin. This continual practice rapidly increases the number of the unfaithful, while the devoted followers of Christ grow fewer and fewer. When light of truth comes, and a call for reformation, the leaders, being blinded with spiritual darkness, rise against the heavenly call. Declaring they have all the truth, and are in need of none, though down in their heart they know it is God's truth, they condemn the message and the messenger like ancient Israel, because it reproves their ungodly deeds. The unconsecrated in heart do not care to investigate for themselves, but accept the decisions of the leaders. The result is that the faithful few are thrown out by a majority vote, while the old devil triumphs with victory. This is especially true in our time, beginning with the Lutheran church, and up the line. William Miller and Miss Harmon were treated in like manner. God allowed this continual practice of robbing God's people of their church properties, and forcing them to start a new movement, but He will not allow it now.

Speaking of the opposition Luther was compelled to encounter, the Spirit of Prophecy says, "In the power of the Holy Spirit he cried out against the existing sins of the leaders of the church; and as he met the storm of opposition from the priests, his courage failed not; for he firmly relied upon the strong arm of God, and confidently trusted in Him for victory." Early Writings, page 223. "As the opposition rises to a fiercer height, the servants of God are again perplexed; for it seems to them that they have brought the crisis. But conscience and the Word of God assure them that their course is right; and although the trials continue, they are strengthened to bear them." Great Controversy, page 610. Said Jesus, "Blessed are ye, when men shall revile you and persecute you, and shall say all manner of evil against you falsely, for My sake. Rejoice, and be exceeding glad: For great is your reward in heaven: for so persecuted they the prophets which were before you." Matt. 5:11, 12. Note:—The prophets were persecuted, and not the priests.

When the truth is told in clear lines it will reveal sin and condemn the guilty conscience of the sinner. Though the messenger, to the exposure of persecution and scoffing, even endangering his life, declares the truth with love to save, the sinner will often arise against a friend of his soul. Said the prophet, "Nevertheless, if thou warn the wicked of his way to turn from it; if he do not turn from his way, he shall die in his iniquity; but thou hast delivered thy soul." Eze. 33:9.

The following accusations may be raised and are expected to be met. Some may say, You are speaking evil, finding fault, and bringing accusations. But the matter of fact is that he who bears a message from heaven to a guilty sinner cannot be charged with any of the above-stated charges. The responsibility is not his who bears the message, but God's, who sends the message. He who speaks evil against the messenger is speaking evil against God to his own hurt.

Some may say, You are not ordained to the ministry, and it is not your business, but He who has a message does not have to be ordained by the hands of men to deliver the message no more than did Amos. He who sends the message is greater than he who is ordained by the hands of men. Amos was only a herdsman, but when God called him, and charged him with a message to deliver to kings and priests of ancient Israel, he declined not but obeyed the voice of God and delivered the message. (Amos 1:1). Is God bound by the strings of men? Jeremiah also was only a child when God called him. Though he thought himself incapable to bear the responsibility, the Lord said, "Say not, I am a child: For thou shalt go to all that I shall send thee, and whatsoever I command thee thou shalt speak." Jer. 1:7.

Men who think their office puts them in the place of Moses and Aaron are making a great mistake. Such men cannot be either one of them. No man can take the place of Moses for he is neither dead nor dumb. The *Bible is* Moses. Jesus said, "Let them hear Moses and the prophets." Aaron is a type of Christ, therefore, he who thinks he is in the place of those two great leaders is throwing aside the authority of the Bible, and Christ the Priest. He who would claim such authority is placing himself in the position of Korah. See Numbers 16; and 26:10. And the end thereof shall be a bitter end.

Dear brethren and sisters:—We beg of you in the name of Christ your Saviour, be true to God as were His great men in the ages past. We call your attention to Daniel, Shadroch, Meshach, and Abednego. Think of how firm these men stood for true religious principle to please God. They risked their lives, but refused to bow to idolatry. As God rewarded them for their faith, He will reward you with life that will measure with the life of God. Refuse to stumble over the stumbling blocks of others. We refer you to the experience of nominal Christians in the early advent movement, as recorded in the writings by the Spirit of Prophecy. We quote from Great Controversy, page 380:

"But the churches generally did not accept the warning. Their ministers, who, as 'watchmen unto the house of Israel,' should have been the first to discern the tokens of Jesus' coming, had failed to learn the truth, either from the testimony of the prophets or from the signs of the times. As worldly hopes and ambitions filled the heart, love for God and faith in His word had grown cold; and when the advent doctrine was presented, it only aroused their prejudice and unbelief. The fact that the message was, to a great extent, preached by laymen, was urged as an argument against it. As of old, the plain testimony of God's word was met with the inquiry, 'Have any of the rulers or of the Pharisees believed?' And finding how difficult a task it was to refute the arguments drawn from the prophetic periods, many discouraged the study of the prophecies, teaching that the prophetic books were sealed, and were not to be understood. Multitudes, trusting implicitly to their pastors, refused to listen to the warning; and others, though convinced of the truth, dared not confess it, lest they should be 'put out of the synagogue.' The message which God had sent for the testing and purification of the church, revealed all too surely how great was the number who had set their affections on this world rather than upon Christ. The ties which bound them to earth were stronger than the attractions heavenward. They chose to listen to the voice of worldly wisdom, and turned away from the heart-searching message of truth."

Said Jesus, "remember Lot's wife". Escape for your life for the elements used on Sodom are to be used in this wicked world at the present time. Compare this message with the Bible and the Testimonies. Do not consent to the decisions of others, but study for yourself. "When a message is presented to God's people, they should not rise up in opposition to it; they should go to the Bible, comparing it with the law and the testimony, and if it does not bear this test, it is not true." Testimonies to Ministers, page 119.

No one should fear or be backward to declare this message right from the Seventh-day Adventist pulpit, for it is pure Seventh-day Adventist doctrine, calling God's people back to the principles upon which this great denomination was established. Some will object and try to put a stop to it while they can not explain the Scriptures in another way. But he who takes the burden to carry the message, must insist and be faithful to conduct his studies.

In the days of Christ His disciples stood firm to their right and declared the risen Saviour in the *temple*. The spiritually-blinded guides ordered them out, but they came back again, and again this was repeated, until the impious Pharisees threw them in jail. By a miracle they were let out and immediately they returned to the temple, and again preached the supposedly strange doctrine in spite of the opposition. Such persistence as this to save their brothers and sisters from the impending doom is called by the enemies of Christ "rebellion", even using Scripture to prove their accusations true. But the matter of fact is, he who is persistent to perform his duty to his God, for the good of his brethren, is not the guilty one. He who would resent the message from heaven is a rebel in the sight of the great God. The office or position of such a one does not clear him any more than it cleared the proud Pharisee in the rabbinical cloak. Though some may point to his own office of authority it will not excuse him, neither will it condemn the messenger of God. Many other excuses and charges will be presented, but he who does the service of the Most High need not be distracted in any way, but go forward in his duty with faith in God to save his brethren from the impending doom. The Spirit of Prophecy, in view of this message says: "Should a case like Aachan's be among us, there are many who would accuse those who might act the part of Joshua in searching out the wrong, of having a wicked, fault-finding spirit." Volume 3, page 270.

In case some one's name should be taken off the church books for carrying on the message, do not be discouraged in any way but press onward as though nothing has happened. Pay your honest tithe and offering to your church, and feel like "IT IS" your Father's house. Continue your work of reform with as many as you can possibly interest. Your membership on the church books is only a church record and the only loss or damage one can suffer from the absence of one's name on such record is that he can not serve as an officer, or have anything to say in matters of church business. Those who are looking for the soon coming of Christ do not wish to serve in office, if their service is not desired by the church. Those who push themselves forward to obtain such a position show their motive to be wrong, and that their heart is not right with God. To retain your name on the church book at the expense of principle would not take you to heaven, neither would the absence of it from such a record bar you from the Holy City.

"How beautiful upon the mountains are the feet of him that bringeth good tidings, that publisheth peace; that bringeth good tidings of good, that publisheth salvation; that saith unto Zion, Thy God *reigneth!*" Isa 52:7.

"Many are tempted in regard to our work, and are calling it in question. Some, in their tempted condition, charge the difficulties and perplexities of the people of God to the testimonies of reproof that we have given them. They think the trouble is with the ones who bear the message of warning, who point out the sins of the people and correct their errors. Many are deceived by the adversary of souls. . . . They think that the people of God are not in need of plain dealing and of reproof, but that God is with them. . . . What disposition will these make of the message of the True Witness to the Laodiceans? There can be no deception here. This message must be borne to a lukewarm church by God's servants. It must arouse his people from their security and dangerous deception in regard to their real standing before God. This testimony, if received, will arouse to action, and lead to self-abasement and confession of sins. . .

"The people of God must see their wrongs, and arouse to zealous repentance, and a putting away of those sins which have brought them into such a deplorable condition of poverty, blindness, wretchedness, and fearful deception. I was shown that the pointed testimony must live in the church. This alone will answer to the message to the Laodiceans. Wrongs must be reproved, sin must be called sin, and iniquity must be met promptly and decidedly, and put away from us as a people." Volume 3, pages 258-260.

> "Arise, shine;
> For thy light has come,
> And the glory of the Lord
> Is risen upon thee."

> Isa. 60:1.

A MOTHER'S APPEAL
By Mrs. E. Hermanson.

"But and if that evil servant shall say in his heart, My Lord delayeth his coming; and shall begin to smite his fellowservants, and to eat and drink with the drunken; the lord of that servant shall come in a day when he looketh not for him, and in an hour that he is not aware of, and shall cut him asunder, and appoint him his portion with the hypocrites." Matt. 24:48-51.

As Adventists, we are taught by the above text that it does not refer only to being drunk with wine, but also with feasting. We can also be made drunk with the cares of this life. See Luke 21:34. This latter text tells us also that we must take heed lest at any time our hearts be overcharged with surfeiting, thereby becoming "that evil servant who shall say in his heart, My Lord delayeth His coming."

As a member of the Seventh-day Adventist denomination, and the mother of three children, it has been my determination to train these children which God has given me in such a way that they might be faithful to God and His truth. It is a great trial to keep them from partaking of the so-called pleasures of the world, and thereby from the spirit of the world, that they might not be misled in their conception of what God desires of us as His faithful children. The task is not an easy one, and the responsibility no less. It is in nowise lessened by taking part with those of the world.

In view of the warning given us in the Scriptures, it doesn't seem consistent that such programmes as the following should be sponsored by the faculty if we are to interest our children and young people in the plain, pointed teachings of our Saviour. Young minds naturally do not grasp the serious side of life, and with the *numerous dates* and *events* which are ever kept before them in this manner, it makes it difficult for them to be interested in *striving* "to enter in at the strait gate." Luke 13:24; Matt. 7:13.

The following are some of the events copied from "Weekly Bulletin" under dates of Nov. 14, and Nov. 21, 1930, and issued by one of our leading institutions in Los Angeles.

ASSOCIATION NEWS

The Interscholastic Faculty-Alumni Swimming Meet: . . . The big feature of the evening was a diving exhibition by Georgia Coleman, women's national diving champion. . . .

November Supper Club: This promises to be another treat. A trio and reader from the Girl's Glee Club of U. S. C. will be a big feature. Bill Hunter, Director of Athletics at U. S. C. will give us a short talk on sportsmanship. Get your tickets early.

COMING EVENTS

Nov. 24: Supper Club.

Nov. 25: Juniors vs. Employees Baseball Game.

Nov. 28: Matched Play Golf Tournament at Montebello Park.

Dec. 2: Faculty vs. Employees Baseball Game.

Dec. 9: Faculty vs. Juniors Baseball Game, 7:00.

    Employees 1st team vs. Employees 2nd team, 5.00.

Dec. 16: Seniors vs. Juniors Baseball Game.

Dec. 21-26: Holiday Cabin Party, Big Bear Lake.

Health Lecture, Y. M. C. A.....................Friday, 8:00 P. M.

Faculty-Interscholastic Matched Play Golf Tournament: Friday morning, November 28. . . .

The faculty-senior baseball game last Tuesday resulted in a score of 3-13. This, however, does not rightly represent the closeness of the contest as compared to previous engagements. A few more games and the faculty will be holding its own provided, however, H——— S——— and W——— do not slug too many home runs. H——— holds the record so far, . . .

The Spirit of Prophecy, commenting on baseball, etc. says, "I was told by my Guide: 'Look ye, and behold the idolatry of My people, to whom I have been speaking, rising up early, and presenting to them their dangers. I looked that they should bring forth fruit.' There were some who were striving for the mastery, each trying to excel the other in the swift running of their bicycles. There was a spirit of strife and contention among them as to which should be the greatest. The spirit was similar to that manifested in the baseball games on the college ground. Said my Guide: 'These things are an offense to God. Both near and afar off souls are perishing for the bread of life and the water of salvation'." Volume 8, page 52.

Why take the young people to the Y. M. C. A. on Friday night to give them a health lecture? Could it not be given in our own buildings? Why this tournament of the Golf Club on *Friday* morning? Are we not told in the Scriptures that Friday is the preparation day for the Sabbath instead of a day of pleasure? As a rule, if one makes the proper preparation, there is not much time to be lost.

There may be no objection to swimming, but what effect will this champion's skill and the athletic director's talk on "Sportsmanship" have on the youth? Will it create a greater desire to serve Christ?

How can we as mothers keep our children apart from the world if the faculty take them to these institutions of the world, where they acquaint them with every element? Are we abiding by the principles upon which this denomination was founded? "For ye are the temple of the living God; as God hath said, I will dwell in them, and walk in them; and I will be their God, and they shall be my people. Wherefore, come out from among them, and be ye separate, saith the Lord." 2 Cor. 6:16, 17.

In view of this onrushing torrent of apostasy headed by misled spiritual guides, in my estimation, the leopard beast of Rev. 13:1-3, has met a most striking fulfillment of symbolical prophecy—"all the world wondered after the beast." The world in general has always been after the beast. For this reason the world is in need of the gospel, but when God makes the statement "ALL the world wondered after the beast", then it must be that those to whom God has given great light have partaken of the spirit of the world, thus fulfilling the prophecy.

Bearing in mind our duty to the world and the third angel's message truly the burden on my heart for the children and young people is a heavy one. I appeal to every loyal Seventh-day Adventist to arise with prayer and fasting against these so-called pleasures of the age, to save our children while the devil is seeking to deceive even the very elect.

Wholesale price of "The Shepherd's Rod," Vol. I, on orders of not less than 5 copies, 50c each. Discounted prices as follows: 10 copies, $4.90; 15 copies, $7.35; 20 copies, $9.80. On orders of 30 or more deduct 3% from regular wholesale price. To foreign countries charging custom duty on religious books the retail price would probably be from 10 to 20% higher than the regular price, 75c per copy. All orders postpaid to any destination.

- -

ORDER BLANK

UNIVERSAL PUBLISHING ASSOCIATION,
5942 So. HOOVER ST., LOS ANGELES, CALIF.

Gentlemen: Send me .... copies of *"The Shepherd's Rod"* in accordance with your offer, carriage paid.

I enclose herewith P. O. Money Order for $..................., full price of my order.

Name ....

Address............................ *City*........................... *State*..................

- -

ORDER BLANK

UNIVERSAL PUBLISHING ASSOCIATION,
5942 So. HOOVER ST., LOS ANGELES, CALIF.

Gentlemen: Send me .... copies of *"The Shepherd's Rod"* in accordance with your offer, carriage paid.

I enclose herewith P. O. Money Order for $..................., full price of my order.

Name ....

Address............................ *City*........................... *State*..................

- -

ORDER BLANK

UNIVERSAL PUBLISHING ASSOCIATION,
5942 So. HOOVER ST., LOS ANGELES, CALIF.

Gentlemen: Send me .... copies of *"The Shepherd's Rod"* in accordance with your offer, carriage paid.

I enclose herewith P. O. Money Order for $..................., full price of my order.

Name ....

Address............................ *City*........................... *State*..................

- -

ORDER BLANK

UNIVERSAL PUBLISHING ASSOCIATION,
5942 So. HOOVER ST., LOS ANGELES, CALIF.

Gentlemen: Send me .... copies of *"The Shepherd's Rod"* in accordance with your offer, carriage paid.

I enclose herewith P. O. Money Order for $..................., full price of my order.

Name ....

Address............................ *City*........................... *State*..................

-Visit Us: www.UniversalPublishing.com

-Email: info@universalpublishing.com

-Contact Us: 1-254-262-8087 (CST)

-Mail: P.O. Box 24027, Waco, Texas 76702

www.ingramcontent.com/pod-product-compliance
Lightning Source LLC
Chambersburg PA
CBHW021617120626
46545CB00001B/266